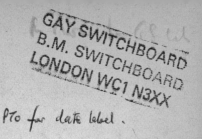

Pro for date label.

Anna Coote was born in Dorset in 1947. She joined her first women's liberation group in 1971, helping to found the Women's Report Collective, and, in 1972, the women's rights group of the National Council for Civil Liberties. A journalist, she worked for the *Observer* from 1968 to 1971 and as a freelance writer and broadcaster until 1978. She is now deputy editor of the *New Statesman*. She is co-author of the first edition of *Civil Liberty: The NCCL Guide* and three editions of *Women's Rights: A Practical Guide* (both guides published by Penguin), as well as several pamphlets, including *Hear This Brother: Women Workers and Union Power* (New Statesman, 1981), *Family in the Firing Line* (NCCL/CPAG, 1981) and *Positive Action: The Next Step* (NCCL, 1981).

Beatrix Campbell was born in Cumbria in 1947. She joined her first women's liberation group in 1970 in East London. In 1972 she helped launch the socialist–feminist magazine *Red Rag*. She was a reporter for the *Morning Star* from 1967 to 1976 and a member of the news staff at *Time Out* from 1979 until 1981 when, after a long industrial dispute, she joined with forty other ex-*Time Out* staff to start the new magazine *City Limits*. She has contributed to *Conditions of Illusion: Papers from the Women's Movement* (Feminist Books, 1975), *The Popular and the Political* (Routledge, 1981) and *No Turning Back* (Women's Press, 1981).

I want a women's revolution like a lover,
I lust for it, I want so much this freedom,
this end to struggle and fear and lies
we all exhale, that I could die just
with the passionate uttering of that desire.
Just once in this my only lifetime to dance
all alone and bare on a high cliff under cypress trees
with no fear of where I place my feet . . .

taken from *Monster* by Robin Morgan

Anna Coote and Beatrix Campbell

Illustrations by Christine Roche

Sweet Freedom

The struggle for women's liberation

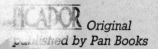 *Original*
published by Pan Books

For our Sisters
especially Judy, Belinda and Tina

First published 1982 by Pan Books Ltd,
Cavaye Place, London SW10 9PG
in association with Basil Blackwell Publisher Ltd
© Anna Coote and Beatrix Campbell 1982
© Illustrations – Christine Roche 1982
ISBN 0 330 26511 3
Printed in Great Britain by
Richard Clay (The Chaucer Press) Ltd, Bungay, Suffolk

Contents

1 New beginnings 9
2 Work 48
3 Family 81
4 Legislation 103
5 Unions 143
6 Learning 171
7 Culture 189
8 Sex 211
9 The future 235
  Index 249

Acknowledgements

Love and thanks to Melissa Benn for her excellent, painstaking research; to Carol Fisher who scrutinized every chapter and gave such sterling advice; to Dale Spender for her invaluable help and support; to Angela Lloyd and Jessica Sacret for their care and attention; to Neil Myers for Kung Fu; to Margaret Bluman for everything; to Rosalind Coward for her rigorous criticism and timely intervention; to *Red Rag* and the NCCL women's group, with whom some of the ideas in this book originated; and to Christine Jackson, Fran Bennett, Patricia Hewitt and Tess Gill for giving us their time, and such useful comments on the manuscript.

1 *New beginnings*

If *all Men are born free*, how is it that all Women are born slaves? As they must be if the being subjected to the *inconstant, uncertain, unknown, arbitrary will* of Men, be the perfect Condition of Slavery?

Mary Astell, 1700

Consider ... whether, when men contend for their freedom ... it be not inconsistent and unjust to subjugate women, even though you firmly believe that you are acting in the manner best calculated to promote their happiness? Who made man the exclusive judge, if woman partake with him the gift of reason?

Mary Wollstonecraft, 1792

The great social injustices are the subjection of labour and the subjection of women. They are co-equal manifestations of the spirit of tyranny.... It is the characteristic of sex rule as much as of class rule that those in power dictate the activities as well as withold the rights of the rest.

Christabel Pankhurst, 1902

At regular intervals throughout history, women rediscover themselves – their strengths, their capabilities, their political will. In short, there is a women's uprising. But they have never yet secured the means of communicating their endeavours truthfully beyond the boundaries of their own movements. And since men have not found it in their interests to convey an accurate picture, the ideas and activities of these rebellious women have largely been omitted from the records. Their writings have been left to gather dust in corners. Children are not taught about them in schools – except as curiosities which seem to have no root or reason.

Men are often heard to lament their children's innocence of war. No less lamentable are the generations of girls who have grown up in ignorance of their grandmothers' politics. Only when they reinvent rebellion for themselves do they begin to disinter the buried remains of that knowledge. Each time, they

9

find that although the setting is new, the battle they are fighting is essentially the same.

This book is about our time. Our women's liberation movement. We are not writing from nostalgia, bidding a fond farewell to the struggle that began in the 1960s. We are aware that there is a danger, in the bitter climate of the 1980s, of being forced into retreat. It has happened before. Shall we late-twentieth-century feminists be reduced to fragments of political archaeology before we are even in our graves? This time, we want to be sure that history doesn't repeat itself.

Let's begin by drawing a link between the Burning Pillar-Box and the Burning Bra. The first is real, a part of women's history; the second is unreal, a part of male mythology.

In 1905, a young woman called Jessie Stephen was employed as a domestic servant in Glasgow. A member of the Women's Social and Political Union, she took part in the militant campaign which began, she explains, 'because the politicians treated the movement with contempt, as being run by eccentrics – which only goes to show how stupid politicians can be sometimes!' Throughout Britain, there was a series of highly organized raids on property ('the thing authority regards as more sacred than human life'). Castles were burned, plate-glass windows were smashed and, in particular, Jessie Stephen remembers the occasion when every pillar-box in Glasgow was set on fire, without a single arrest:

Scores of us were involved and the timing meticulously set for every section. I know I walked from my place of service in my uniform and dropped the acid container in the pillar-box and made my way without interruption by anyone. A few minutes later the contents were aflame. . . .

A maid fire-bombed a pillar-box in Glasgow. One incident among many thousands, it was part of a major political development, a women's uprising. Sixty-four years later, Jessie Stephen's own account of it appeared in one of the first publications of the new women's movement – the magazine of Bristol Women's Liberation, *Enough!*[1] But what had happened to the information in the meantime? Most people had read about the suffragettes, but few (if any) had learned enough to appreciate what they actually did, or what they really stood for. From the meagre information that was readily available, it seemed that women had campaigned for the vote in the early part of the century . . . that some of them were a bit 'extreme', chaining

10

themselves to railings and throwing themselves under horses ... and that after the war the vote was won, and that was the end of that.

Newcomers to feminism in the 1960s began to refer back to the suffragette era and to re-examine it. It has taken some time for the meanings to sink in. Women in the early 1900s were not fighting for the vote alone, but for liberation (although they used a different vocabulary). They saw the vote as one step on the way to getting what they wanted. Feminists at that time were no less vigorous or resourceful than we have been, and it was a women's movement every bit as large and strong as ours: complex and multifaceted, combining those for whom hope lay in constitutional reform with others who believed in the necessity of revolution. It did not die simply because the vote was won. It lost momentum as social and economic conditions changed and women had not developed a firm strategy for the future. Moreover they lacked the means to transmit their politics to a new generation and so to consolidate their gains. We are now beginning to understand these facts, *in spite* of their being consistently misrepresented by those who have power to construct our sense of history.

And what has all that got to do with the Burning Bra? In 1968, the Miss America pageant in Atlantic City, USA, was the scene of the first public manifestation of a new wave of feminism. For about two years before that, small numbers of American women had begun to meet and talk to each other, to organize and to develop their own political theory. They took the view that the Miss America pageant degraded *all* women, contestants and viewers alike; its fake standards of beauty forced women to push and pull their bodies into alien, uncomfortable shapes, merely for the pleasure of men. They decided to stage a protest – and to illustrate their point they dumped bras and girdles into a 'freedom trash bucket'. Imaginary flames were added later by a news agency reporter, and the idea caught on in a big way. The media loved it. Sexy and absurd, it neatly disposed of a phenomenon which would otherwise have proved rather awkward to explain.

'Bra-burning' became an international by-word for women's liberation. Well into the 1970s, on both sides of the Atlantic, this remained the image which was most widely associated with feminism. So farcical did it seem that it put paid to any serious questions being asked (outside the movement) about *why* women wore bras, or why some women now chose to stop

11

wearing them. Even the original connection with the Miss America protest was forgotten.

Just as the scale and coherence of suffragette militancy had been hidden from view, so the smokescreen of the 'burning bra' helped to obscure the real nature of the women's liberation movement. It wasn't a result of a deliberate conspiracy; it was simply an example of what happened as the dominant sex went about its daily business of managing information and opinion.

A 'strange stirring'

If the new wave of feminism was not just an outbreak of underwear arson, what was it? And why did it happen at that time?

In one respect, it was a reaction to the fetishized femininity of the previous decade. After the Second World War, accepted notions about what women should be and what they should do changed quite rapidly. Their work in the home as wives and mothers was emphasized, as men came back from the war to reclaim their jobs. As the shops filled up with food and clothes and domestic appliances, women were designated a key role, as shoppers-in-chief, in the new consumer economy. They weren't altogether unwilling participants – it made a change from the austerity of the 1940s – but in the process they developed a new, restricting sense of what femaleness entailed. 'The fifties was an era of elaborate hairdos, and constraining clothes and Dr Spock,' records the feminist historian Sheila Rowbotham. 'The child psychologists stressed breast-feeding. Women with husbands who had been in the war went through paroxysms of guilt at the thought of leaving their small children. The bogey of mother deprivation was let loose. The nurseries closed. . . . In England the young Queen and her family reinforced the idyll of love and marriage.' [2]

At the same time, women had more potential choice and freedom than ever before. The Pill had arrived: an imperfect drug, which brought with it a range of unpleasant side effects, it nevertheless enabled women to choose with some certainty when to have children. There were more jobs for women than ever before – assembly-line jobs in new manufacturing industries, cleaning and catering jobs in fast-growing service industries, professional and para-professional jobs in Britain's developing welfare state, and a constantly expanding supply of office jobs.

There was bound to be a conflict between these new opportunities and the powerful propaganda of post-war 'femininity'. Women were not expected to combine employment and motherhood. Some did, out of preference or necessity, yet this was never recognized as something that 'real' women did; the two had to be combined almost covertly, and at the individual's own peril. Many others stayed at home – sensing, perhaps, that there was more to life than that, but unable to articulate their discontent. Isolated within their increasingly privatized families, and knowing they were doing what 'real' women were supposed to do, housewives could only conclude that if they felt unhappy with their lot, then they had only themselves to blame. This was what American social scientist Betty Friedan described, in her book *The Feminine Mystique*, published in 1963, as 'the problem without a name':

It was a strange stirring, a sense of dissatisfaction, a yearning that women suffered in the middle of the twentieth century in the United States. Each suburban wife struggled with it alone. As she made the beds, shopped for groceries, matched slip cover material, ate peanut butter sandwiches, chauffered Cub Scouts and Brownies, lay beside her husband at night, she was afraid to ask even of herself the silent question: 'Is this all?' [3]

Betty Friedan exposed the fraud of the fifties and provided the beginnings of a vocabulary for women's liberation. In 1966 she founded the National Organization for Women (NOW), to campaign for equal rights and opportunities. It was a middle-class initiative, with a programme which many feminists today would describe as 'reformist' – but at the time, and when combined with the newly felt anger of radical women emerging from the civil rights and anti-war protests, its implications were revolutionary.

Radical politics in the 1960s provided an excellent breeding ground for feminism. Men led the marches and made the speeches and expected their female comrades to lick envelopes and listen. Women who were participating in the struggles to liberate blacks and Vietnamese began to recognize that they themselves needed liberating – and they needed it now, not 'after the revolution'. Black leader Stokely Carmichael was heard to say that in the SNCC (Student Non-Violent Coordinating Committee) the only place for a woman was 'prone'. Here was the front-line hero of the radical left, who seemed to favour not simply the *deferment* of liberation for women, but their continued subordination. Judging by the number of times that remark has been quoted since, it did as much to fuel the fire for a women's movement as the publication of *The Feminine Mystique*.

The personal is political

Small groups of women began to get together. They began to talk to each other in a way they had not done before. They discussed their day-to-day experiences, and their feelings about themselves, their jobs, their husbands, their lovers, their children and their parents. Of course, women had been doing this since language was invented – but what was new was that they were now drawing political conclusions from their personal experiences. They began to see that it was both necessary and possible to change their lives, and they realized that this would require a fundamental shift in the social order. It was not *they* who were at fault after all, but the men who organized and controlled their lives. They began to value each other and to be proud of being women. As one of them later recalled, 'It was like that old cliché of the light bulb going on over my head.' None of it was organized or orchestrated, but the news got around – by word of mouth, through the bush telegraph, it seemed to spread like pollen in the wind, to towns and cities throughout the United States.

New phrases were coined to account for new concepts. 'Consciousness-raising' was what happened when women translated their personal feelings into political awareness. 'Sisterhood is powerful' expressed their new sense of solidarity. They adapted the terminology of black liberation and anti-imperialism. 'Racism' became 'racism with roses' and then 'sexism'. And 'chauvinism', a term applied to US aggression in South-East Asia, became a useful way to describe men's efforts to subjugate half the world's population.

The new feminists began to publish their ideas – in scores of pamphlets, journals and manifestos. 'We are engaged in a power struggle with mon...' declared the New York Radical Feminists in 1969. 'For while we realize that the liberation of women will ultimately mean the liberation of men from their destructive role as oppressor, we have no illusion that men will welcome this liberation without a struggle.' The most influential document was the first manifesto of women's liberation, drawn

14

up by the Redstockings of New York; it deserves to be quoted here at length:

Women are an oppressed class... We are exploited as sex objects, breeders, domestic servants and cheap labour... Our prescribed behaviour is enforced by threat of physical violence.

Because we have lived so intimately with our oppressors, in isolation from each other, we have been kept from seeing our personal suffering as a political condition. This creates the illusion that a woman's relationship with her man is a matter of interplay between two unique personalities, and can be worked out individually. In reality, every such relationship is a *class* relationship, and the conflicts between individual men and women are political conflicts that can only be solved collectively. We regard our personal experience, and our feelings about that experience, as the basis for an analysis of our common situation. We cannot rely on existing ideologies as they are all products of a male supremacist culture. We question every generalization and accept none that is not confirmed by our experience. We identify with all women. We define our best interest as that of the poorest, most brutally exploited woman. In fighting for our liberation we will always take the side of women against their oppressors. We will not ask what is 'revolutionary' or 'reformist', only what is good for women.

By 1969, a few women's groups had appeared in Britain – and they emerged with a similar spontaneity. Many of the thoughts and feelings had been there all along; now there began a process of naming the discontent – and because it was about women's own existence, rather than about society 'out there', there also began a process of self-transformation.

Contrary to popular belief, the new feminists were not footloose and fancy-free; most were married and freshly acquainted with motherhood. 'I had been at home for about a year after the birth of my first son,' Valerie Charlton recalls. 'I found it impossible to adapt. I had the baby when I was twenty-seven, and in one year I had gone from feeling confident and in charge of myself, earning a living, to being completely collapsed and lonely.'

Many were members of the left-wing intelligentsia – a staunchly masculine society in which women were active and committed, yet felt themselves confined to the periphery. Catherine Hall experienced the political turbulence of 1968 not chiefly as an activist, but as a university wife:

I was pregnant during the occupation of the university, and I was distanced from it both by being pregnant and by being a woman. The only women who were involved in it were the ones who were having

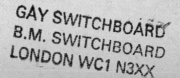

15

relationships with the men. If you couldn't be part of the university culture you were completely marginalized.

It was this knowledge of radical politics, combined with a sense of exclusion from it, which led many women to feminism – just as it had in the United States. Rosalind Delmar went to her first women's meeting in 1968, at the Revolutionary Students' Federation, which had been set up after another student occupation at the London School of Economics:

A male trade unionist came in and started telling us what to do. We told him to go away, no one was going to listen to him. There had always been a tendency on the student left to defer to industrial workers because they were felt to be more strategically important than anyone else – certainly more than women. I was very impressed with what we had done.

Once the news was abroad, it travelled at extraordinary speed, and soon reached well beyond the campuses. In Peckham Rye, south London, a group of predominantly working-class women found each other at a 'One O'Clock Club', laid on by the local council, for mothers with small children. They formed themselves into one of the first women's liberation groups in the country. 'I used to push my kids round and round the duck pond, wishing I could push them in it,' Jan Williams remembers:

Instead, I went straight to the group. It was really good. We talked about the same things again and again – about children, about sex, about being used. I had started a part-time job and my husband had said he would look after the kids, but he didn't. I began to feel that there was something wrong with the unfairness and inequality of it. If you're at home all day and you keep everything together, you feel completely buffeted. Then you're expected to make love and it's just another imposition, another chore.

In 1969, Audrey Battersby had just had two of the most difficult years of her life:

My marriage broke up in 1967, leaving me with three small children, one of them brain-damaged by whooping cough vaccine, to bring up alone. The feelings of despair, failure, anxiety about the children (how could I cope?) were almost overwhelming.

Predictably, I leaned heavily on a few women friends and we spent many, often happy enough, hours looking after each other's children and belly-aching about men, clothes and menstruation, and wondering where it all went wrong... but we never made the links between politics and our individual feelings of disillusionment and discontent.[4]

That summer, she and a friend attended a short course at the 'Anti University', which had been organized by radical academics as part of the student protest movement. Run by Juliet Mitchell, the course was entitled 'The Role of Women in Society'; it led her to read *The Feminine Mystique* and other new feminist writings. . .

Then the bells rang and the connections were made and there was that feeling of militancy that I'd never experienced before despite involvement in various left-wing groups. I was no longer alone, but part of a movement which was primarily political but could be personal to me.[5]

Out of socialism

While women's liberation in Britain drew some considerable inspiration from the United States, it had its own, independent beginnings, too. This is not to make a patriotic point, but to help demonstrate that a women's uprising is bound to be deeply rooted in the cultural and economic life of the country where it takes place: it cannot simply be imported. The first major exponent of socialist feminism was the English academic, Juliet Mitchell, whose essay 'The Longest Revolution', published in *New Left Review* in 1966, began the heavy work of hauling the 'woman question' back into the consciousness of the radical left. 'The problem of the subordination of women and the need for their liberation was recognized by all the great socialist thinkers in the nineteenth century,' she wrote. 'It is part of the classical heritage of the revolutionary movement. Yet today, the problem has become a subsidiary, if not an invisible element in the preoccupations of socialists. Perhaps no other major issue has been so forgotten.'[6] Continuing the theme, Sheila Rowbotham's brilliant pamphlet *Women's Liberation and the New Politics*, published in 1969, had a profound influence on the development of feminism. Linking housework with unequal rights at work, and placing both in the context of cultural traditions which objectify and silence women, she insisted that such an analysis was crucial to socialist theory:

Unless the internal process of subjugation is understood, unless the language of silence is experienced from inside and translated into the language of the oppressed communicating themselves, male hegemony will remain. Without such a translation, Marxism will not be really meaningful. . .[7]

17

This explosion on the left was paralleled by a new mood of militancy within the labour movement, and with an unprecedented wages offensive at the end of the decade. Women trade unionists had launched an equal pay campaign during the 1950s, but it was not until 1968 that they made any real impact on the trade union movement. Women sewing machinists at the Ford motor factory in Dagenham, Essex, came out on strike – shortly followed by their sisters at the Halewood plant in Liverpool. These women wanted to be hoisted from an unskilled grade to the equivalent of semi-skilled production workers (who were predominantly male). Amid national clamour, with the women being entertained to tea by Employment Secretary Barbara Castle, the first equal pay strike to enter the political stage was politely settled. The women were conceded 95 per cent of the men's rate – but only within their old 'unskilled' grade. To this day, the sewing machinists at Ford have not secured regrading. But in the tradition of triumphalism, the strike was hailed by the labour movement as a great success. And certainly it was a source of inspiration for other women workers.

Soon a group of trade unionists formed themselves into the National Joint Action Campaign for Women's Equal Rights (NJACWER). They adopted a five-point charter which included a call on the TUC to lead a campaign for equal pay and opportunity; and in May 1969, they held a rally in Trafalgar Square. Not unnaturally, these events had a formative influence on the newly emerging women's liberation movement. Ellen Malos of Bristol remembers trying to organize a coach to take women to London for the Trafalgar Square rally. They didn't make it to the rally, but as a result a small group began to meet on a regular basis – and Bristol Women's Liberation was born.

The factory dispute and the physical discovery

We have asked a large number of women what they remember as being most influential in leading them to feminism in that early stage of the movement. We were struck by how many mentioned in almost the same breath the Ford strike and a paper written by an American, Anne Koedt, which had begun to circulate on ill-typed roneoed sheets among British women in 1969. Entitled 'The Myth of the Vaginal Orgasm',[8] it pointed out that the clitoris, not the vagina, was the centre for sexual pleasure for women, and it drew attention to the manner in which this potent little fact had been suppressed.

The startling disparity between the two catalysts – the factory dispute and the physical discovery – is more apparent than real. Women clearly sensed that the two were part of the same problem, although few would have consciously spelt out the connection at the time. In a sense they symbolize the link between 'the personal and the political' which has been the essence of women's liberation. Not only do they express the range and complexity of female oppression, but they also measure the breadth of the stage on which women were beginning to create a political movement of their own.

Anne Koedt cited research by the sexologists Kinsey, and Masters and Johnson, who had established that the clitoris was the throne of women's sexual sensitivity (with no other function than pleasure, which often rippled throughout the pelvic region) while the vagina was largely devoid of feeling. 'Today, with anatomy, and Kinsey, and Masters and Johnson, to mention but a few sources, there is no ignorance on the subject,' she wrote. 'There are, however, social reasons why this knowledge has not been accepted.' She observed that men failed to see women as total, separate human beings, defining them only in terms of how they benefited themselves; for men, penetration was the most effective way of reaching orgasm; and they feared that they could become sexually expendable if the word got around that the penis was not, after all, the key to female ecstacy.

The position of the penis inside the vagina, while perfect for repro-duction, does not usually stimulate orgasm in women... women must therefore rely on indirect stimulation in 'normal' positions.

Many have described the impact of Koedt's paper as 'revo-lutionary'. It didn't tally with every woman's experience, nor did it lead to wholescale abandonment of heterosexuality. But it did enable women to talk about their sexuality in their own terms, to escape from male definitions of 'normality' and 'frigi-dity', to feel they had a right to make demands, and to perceive what had previously seemed to be their own individual 'prob-lems' as part of a pattern which was essentially political.

It was a necessary antidote to the 'permissive society' of the 1960s which, far from permitting women to do anything, had kidnapped them and carried them off as trophies, in the name of sexual freedom. In the era of flower-power and love-ins, of doing-your-own-thing and not being hung up (especially about sex), 'girls' were expected to *do it*, and impose no conditions. The more they did it, the more 'liberated' they were deemed to be. It is true that the sixties' counter-culture challenged a lot of old ideas and allowed new ones to blossom; thus far, it nourished the roots of emergent feminism. But at the same time it added a new dimension to the oppression of women – setting them up, in their mini-skirts and mascara, alongside the whole-foods and hippy beads and hallucinogens, in a gallery of new toys with which men were now free to play.

Germaine Greer's *The Female Eunuch*, published in 1970, gave a perspective on patriarchy from within that culture. She poured scorn on many of the new feminist writers, including Anne Koedt, and wagged a finger at faint-hearted women, whom she saw as partly to blame for their own subordination:

> It would be a genuine revolution if women would suddenly stop loving the victors in violent encounters. Why do they admire the image of the brutal man? . . .[9]

Women had to pull themselves together, give up their bad habits, reassert their potency and, above all, have a good time: 'The chief means of liberating women is by replacing compulsiveness and compulsion by the pleasure principle. . .' (We examine her views on sexuality in more detail later on, p. 222.)

Greer sought neither to blame nor to diminish men; nor did she meddle in economics. But *The Female Eunuch* was powerfully written and often wise; it was widely publicized and wildly popular. It dug a channel through to the women's movement from the Love Generation, and introduced many thousands of women to a new sense of themselves.

The Ruskin conference

In February 1970 the first National Women's Liberation Conference was held at Ruskin College, Oxford. Like so many events at that stage of the movement, it happened almost by accident, taking everyone by surprise. A handful of women had attended one of the Ruskin history workshops, organized by the college to bring worker historians and academics together. As usual, it was entirely dominated by men and the work proceeded as though the female sex had no part in history at all. But this time, the women historians would not stand for it. They held a separate meeting to discuss the problem. At first, they resolved that the next history workshop should be about women, but as they went on talking they grew bolder and decided that it would be not just a history workshop, but a national women's liberation conference. 'I remember the Saturday morning it began, sitting in the pub and getting rather pissed, amazed it was actually happening,' says Sally Alexander, one of the organizers. They expected three hundred, but nearer six hundred came. Most were from the new women's liberation groups which had sprung up in London and a few other cities and campuses. Some were from NJACWER, some from political groups on the Maoist and Trotskyist left. There were even a few from organizations which dated back to the suffragette era – like veteran resistance fighters who'd heard the good news and come down out of the hills. There was a crèche for children and it was run by men – a revolution which was to set the pattern for future women's conferences.

There were bound to be passionate disagreements at such a diverse gathering. But there was also a great sense of exhilaration. The women knew they were in at the start of something big. They discussed proposals to lobby for a Sex Discrimination Act; to research into women's history; to campaign for free contraception and abortion on demand; and to study alternatives to the nuclear family and conventional ways of bringing up children. Sally Alexander recalls a speech by a woman from the shopworkers' union, USDAW, whose name was Audrey Wise:

She said: 'When we run out of toilet paper in our house, *either* my husband *or* I go out and buy some more. We both work, we both bring up the children and we both share the shopping and the cooking and the cleaning.' I sat there open-mouthed – I'm sure many others did too. She spoke intensely about being a socialist and a feminist and a working-class woman.

In 1970, it was an entirely novel experience to hear someone talk in those terms. But then, everything about the conference seemed new. It was the first time most of them had seen a woman chairing a political discussion and – more important – the first time they had been together in such numbers. As Sally Alexander puts it: 'All those women! Women I've become very close friends with since. . . we just spent a lot of time talking, talking about our kids and laughing. And walking round Oxford in gangs of women. It was wonderful!'

For the average Ruskin student, it was a traumatic occasion, especially on the Sunday, waking to find slogans daubed all over the walls. ('Sisterhood is powerful!') Two of the conference organizers spent a couple of fraught hours in the morning, scrubbing the walls to spare the college cleaners – only to find later that the town was full of slogans too.

Ellen Malos, who was there, was struck by the way in which the women's discontent, once articulated, swept inevitably towards radical conclusions. In the face of a feminist critique, it seemed that no part of the patriarchal house-of-cards could remain standing.

The most strongly expressed wish was for a total transformation of society from the bottom up, not only a change in economic and political organization, but in the organization of the family and personal relationships.

She remembers there was also a 'deep disillusionment with traditional forms of political activity'. The conference challenged the orthodoxy of left-wing groups, whose passionate commitment to the struggle against capitalism and imperialism had never been examined from this perspective. 'I'm absolutely bored with hearing these series of accounts of the war in Vietnam,' complained one woman. Someone else retorted that it was 'anti-liberating' to go on talking about housework because such discussions emphasized 'the negative reasons for fighting'. 'Our main task is to overthrow capitalism,' another speaker said helpfully, but that was missing the point. The women were not less committed than others to the class struggle and the liberation of Vietnam, but they were determined to assert their own political place.

It was a terrible test for women who had been brought up on a theoretical diet which specified one absolutely determining contradiction in society – that between classes. There was nothing in the history of revolutionary socialism which allowed even the possibility of the sexual contradiction being instrumental to the organization of human society. The same history was charged with disdain for so-called 'bourgeois feminism'. So it was not lightly that a speaker from the London women's liberation workshop declared: 'We want women to be in charge of their own lives, therefore we must be in control of our own movement directly.' And the words of one of the conference organizers, who pointed out that 'the relation of men to women is the missing gap in the discussion', were momentous at that time.

The first formal act of the conference, the setting-up of a

National Women's Coordinating Committee, celebrated variety, not vanguards. They adopted a structure of small autonomous groups based on localities or special interests, each with equal status, loosely coordinated through national meetings, to which each group could send two delegates.

From this beginning, women's liberation developed into an autonomous political movement. It was self-starting, self-regulating and self-directing, owing no allegiance to any other organization or set of beliefs. Women recognized that the form and practice of their politics were crucially important. In the magazine *Shrew*, which the new women's liberation groups took turns to produce, the Tufnell Park (North London) group explained in October 1969 why they emphasized the need for 'small group discussions':

Our first priority isn't to get over information, but to know what everyone in the room thinks. We believe in getting people to interact, not to listen to experts. We want them to *themselves* make an analysis of their situation, which will lead them to action...

There would be no hierarchies, no lines of authority, no leaders, no stars – and by implication, there would be no purgings or palace *coups*.

Miss World and the first march

Nine months after the Ruskin conference, in November 1970, came the first experiment with civil disobedience. In a carefully organized operation, about one hundred feminists infiltrated and then disrupted the Miss World competition, put on by Mecca at the Albert Hall and compèred by American comedian Bob Hope.

We were all dressed up to the nines and terrified. When the rattle went, that was the signal, we rushed down the aisles, throwing out leaflets and mice. Why on earth did we have *mice*? At the planning meeting people had talked about letting off white mice and somehow that got transformed into plastic mice. We were charged with riotous behaviour and throwing dangerous weapons – you know, leaflets and mice...

Smoke bombs, bags of flour and stink bombs were hurled towards the stage as well. It wasn't a protest against the contestants, but against the contest. 'We've been in the Miss World contest all our lives ... judging ourselves as the judges judge us,' they wrote later in a pamphlet assessing the event. In protesting against women's 'narrow destiny', they were striking a blow against the passivity of both the contestants and themselves. Later, at their trial, most of them insisted on conducting their own defence and having their friends around to consult while they were in the dock. Their action also expressed the movement's desperation to communicate with other women. Having no means of access to the media, they chose 'propaganda by deed' and found themselves suddenly on the screen before millions. But their fears that the media would distort their message were soon justified – especially as they had no experience of handling reporters and there seemed no alternative but to race back into seclusion. The protest attracted a lot of publicity; much of it was hostile. It nevertheless helped put the movement on the map.

The first women's marches took place in London and Liverpool on International Women's Day, March 1971. The Women's National Coordinating Committee had worked out four basic demands, to be carried on banners: equal pay now, equal education and job opportunities; free contraception and abortion on demand; and free 24-hour nurseries. The first three speak for themselves, but the latter has been widely misunderstood as the expression of some heartless desire to dump children in institutions and leave them there around the clock. Clumsily worded, perhaps, it was the most sophisticated of all the demands and focussed on the importance of high-quality, flexible child care available to all families. As one of the originators later explained: 'The emphasis was on the child and the child's needs. I remember thinking it was the only demand which was really worth having. You had to combine the idea that there should be proper child care with the idea that women worked, and that many of them worked unsocial hours. It was all argued through. Women with children were the main protagonists.'

The four demands were not intended to represent the politics of women's liberation; they were designed simply to unite as many women as possible around the new campaigns. If anything, it was the atmosphere of the first women's march which best summed up the movement. It was an optimistic, iconoclastic piece of theatre. There were plenty of kids and a fair smattering of men. One women's group brought along a wind-up gramophone on a set of wheels and danced through the snow (yes, snow) to the refrain of Eddie Cantor's 'Keep Young and Beautiful'. A group of child care campaigners brought a twelve-foot-high Old Woman's Shoe, with the nursery rhyme suitably rephrased and written out in giant letters. Others rigged up an irreverent simulation of child-birth, on a float bedecked with strings of cardboard cut-out babies and sanitary towels. There was a caged woman displayed as 'Misrepresented' and banners appropriating the admen's appropriation of the movement. One carried an ad showing three women striding across the desert, clad only in bras and corsetry, under the slogan 'Freedom'. 'We want freedom not corsets,' said the feminist banner. Names were collected of women who wanted to meet again, and in London alone more than fifty new groups were formed after the march.

There is a remarkable similarity in the descriptions women give of the moment of recognition, the sudden, excited discovery of . . . of what exactly? Of themselves, of the value of women and the pure pleasure of their company, of a new sense of identification and a new intimation of power. Nan Fromer recalls her first encounter with a women's group: 'Fifteen minutes after my arrival I was aware I would not miss another of these meetings if I could help it. So many of the women in that small sitting-room, despite their surface differences, seemed to share what for so long I believed to be my own, idiosyncratic suffering.' And in another city at about the same time, the same sort of thing happened to Catherine Hall: 'It was like a Christian conversion, suddenly we found these friendships. They completely changed my life.'

The elation of sisterhood did not mitigate the pain, however, of coming confrontation. This could be uncomfortable and frightening – whether it meant starting an argument at home about who did the housework, or finding things suddenly intolerable at work and having to strike out in a new direction, or ending an affair or marriage which could not be transformed. Mary Barnes, a young married woman, remembers being lent a copy of Anne Koedt's paper, 'The Myth of the Vaginal Orgasm':

I don't know why I felt so upset by it, but I do remember just flinging it across the room in an incoherent rage. Maybe it was because it showed me that I didn't know my body, but beginning to find out about my body was too dangerous, it was like I knew what it would mean – I would have to take steps to change a relationship in which *I* had always been seen as the problem. Somehow staying that way was less dangerous than showing my husband that *he* was the problem. I wouldn't have known where to start.

The meeting and talking continued. And since there were no set texts, nor any 'line' to follow, different groups set about producing their own analyses of what was wrong, and what needed to be done. A paper prepared by the Bristol Group in 1971 [10] gives a picture of how these early discussions were conducted:

We went around the room trying to establish when each of us first discovered that it was a disadvantage to be a woman, and in what context. It was quite clear that in important ways all the things which seemed disadvantageous related to the family set-up. . .

The Bristol women identified the family as the area which 'defines the oppression of *women as a group different from other groups*'; they recognized that 'although the oppression of women is related to class oppression, it is not the same thing'; and they understood the importance of ideology:

In order to change the economic structure of society *and* to liberate women it is going to be necessary to change our ideas, and changing the ideas of women towards consciousness of the need for their own liberation . . . will begin a process by which they see the need to change society. So we need to pay attention to consciousness and to *all* the aspects of the oppression of women. To concentrate entirely on the economic basis of oppression, to talk only of class questions is too schematic. We need to work out more carefully the relationship between the oppression of women and class oppression *for our own time and place.*

The paper was presented to the second National Women's Liberation Conference, held at Skegness in 1971, where it met with broad agreement. The ideas and strategies of the movement were gradually devised and accumulated in this manner, as the years passed.

Later, three further demands were added to the original four: in 1975, 'financial and legal independence', and 'an end to all discrimination against lesbians and a woman's right to define her own sexuality', and in 1978, at the last national conference of the decade, 'freedom from intimidation by threat or use of violence or sexual coercion, regardless of marital status; and an end to all laws, assumptions and institutions which perpetuate male dominance and men's aggression towards women'.

Radical feminism
The 1978 conference, like most others before it, was dominated by a split between what appeared to be two divergent schools

of thought. Since the early 1970s, many feminists within the women's liberation movement have identified themselves as 'radical feminists' or as 'socialist feminists' and the gap between the two has seemed increasingly wide and unbridgeable. Both sides have highly complex political analyses which are still being developed. From an early stage, each has had different preoccupations, different analytical approaches and different strategic priorities. Between their further fringes, there is very little in common. However, when it comes to their understanding of the forces which perpetuate female subordination, the majorities on both sides hold strikingly similar positions.

As we have seen, the original radical feminist groups of New York City were responsible for the first policy statements of the women's liberation movement. Their most important contributions to feminist thinking, and the foundation stones of their own politics, have been their designation of women as an oppressed *class* and their formulation of the 'pro-woman line'.

The sex-class analysis was expressed (in a rudimentary form) in the Redstockings' manifesto of 1969. It was a bold initiative, aimed at constructing a theory of a dynamic of power, rather than of an unequal relationship arising out of a fixed distinction. It was spelt out in more detail by Shulamith Firestone, a founder-member of the Redstockings, in her highly contentious and influential book, *The Dialectic of Sex*, published in the UK in 1971. In this, she inverts the analytical methods of Marx and Engels in order to identify the primary cause of conflict between women and men – which she locates in the relations of reproduction. She argues that pregnancy and the dependence of small children upon their mothers put women at a disadvantage from the start of human society and make it possible for men to wield power over them. Since then, she says, those first causes of inequality have been overcome. We have learnt to regulate pregnancy, and we have created an environment (in parts of the world at least) where survival does not depend on physical strength and where children are routinely sheltered from most natural hazards. Yet men have maintained their supremacy by developing ideas and customs which enhance the dependence of children upon adults as well as that of women upon men. She points to the fact that 'childhood' as we know it scarcely existed two centuries ago; it has since been constructed – by treating children not as young adults, but as an almost separate species, with special pastimes, playthings, clothes and language. Similarly, the economics of family life

27

and the notions and trappings of 'femininity' and romantic love have served to keep women financially and psychologically in the thrall of men.

For women to free themselves, Firestone argues, they will have to seize control of reproduction, just as the working classes must seize control of production to free themselves from economic oppression. She quotes approvingly Simone de Beauvoir's observation that 'human society ... does not passively submit to the presence of nature but rather takes over the control of nature on its own behalf'.

She is at her most controversial, however, when she comes to recommending a course of action. For although she notes that the biological basis of male power has been undermined (by the regulation of pregnancy, etc.) and that men have adopted cultural and socio-economic strategies to defend their supremacy, she nevertheless recommends that women fight back *at a biological level*. She advocates 'not just the elimination of male privilege, but of the sex *distinction* itself'. And finally she proposes the development of artificial means of reproduction, together with a form of communism described as 'cybernetic', in which human labour is replaced by machine labour, so that women and children can be fully integrated as equal social beings.[11]

But Firestone's thesis cannot be taken as entirely representative. Her views on cybernetics would be dismissed by most radical feminists as an extravagant footnote. Many disagree with her biological formula for 'seizing control of reproduction', while agreeing – broadly – with her sex-class analysis. They propose other measures for controlling reproduction – by women gaining power to determine for themselves when to have children, with whom and in what context, and being able to give birth and raise their young in conditions which are neither economically dependent on men nor socially subordinate to them.

Since *The Dialectic of Sex* was published, a range of philosophical and strategic ideas have devloped out of the 'radical feminist' current. Some take the view that it is not the biological base of male power that needs to be destroyed, so much as the social, cultural and economic structures which have developed out of the biological difference between women and men, and which constitute the patriarchal system that now holds women in subordination. (This comes close to the socialist-feminist position on patriarchy, which we examine later on.)

A precept which unites all radical feminists is that the fight for women's liberation is primarily *against men*: they see it as overriding all other struggles and are deeply suspicious of any attempt to link it to a wider political strategy. The question then is whether one is fighting in order to destroy *masculinity* as a social construct, and so transform men as human beings, with a view to developing a harmonious relationship in which they wield no power over women; or whether one seeks to end the necessity of the biological distinction by establishing ways of living and reproducing which are entirely independent of men. There are radical feminists who take the former position, and others who take Firestone's biological determinism to its logical conclusion, insisting that women must live separately from men, repudiating not only heterosexual intercourse, but boy children as well. For others, a degree of separatism is necessary, but as a strategy – in order to make the fight for women's liberation more effective – rather than as an end in itself.

The first major statement by British radical feminists was a paper presented to the National Women's Liberation Conference in November 1972. They pointed out that a change in the political system would not necessarily change the way men behaved 'in pubs, in the home, in the bedroom, in the office, or on a darkened street at night'. They insisted that women's personal and political autonomy could be safeguarded only if women's relationships with men were severely curtailed: 'As long as women's sights are fixed on closeness to men, the ideology of male supremacy is safe.' As for sex, they concluded that 'liberation for women is not possible as long as vaginal sex is accepted as the norm rather than as a possible variation'. Separatism for them seemed to be a strategic necessity rather than a political goal. 'We hope to show,' they said, 'that we are not anti-man but pro-woman.'

This was a reference to the founding principle of the Redstockings. In formulating it, the New York feminists were influenced by the politics of American blacks, who had developed out of the Civil Rights movement a new sense of the validity and significance of black experience. ('Black is beautiful' was a slogan which tried to express it; the Black Consciousness movement which emerged in South Africa in the late 1970s is based on the same concept.)

The pro-woman line was a way of recognizing and affirming female experience, as well as the strategies women adopt to cope with their subordination and their manoeuvres within it.

In an interview published in the British feminist magazine *Spare Rib* in 1979, two of the founding Redstockings, Kathie Sarachild and Collette Price, explained what it meant to them:

Women were OK, we weren't damaged, we weren't inferior; if we were honest and paid attention to our feelings, we could come to a correct evaluation of our situation... It gave a certain authenticity to what we were feeling and going through, and it prompted a certain kind of honesty...

The pro-woman line was essentially against the 'it's-all-in-your-head' analysis of women's oppression... [it said] that oppression was real, our behaviour was based on real options or lack of options, and changing our head was not going to free us... You have to find out what the truth is when you're fed lies, you have to study things that *men* weren't studying about oppression...[12]

It didn't necessarily mean that everything women did was always in their best interests:

The pro-woman line was that everything women do is an *effort* to be in their interests. It has a rational basis. It doesn't mean you can't make mistakes.[13]

So thoroughly had women in the 1960s been programmed to undervalue, despise or psychoanalyse-away their experience that the importance of the pro-woman line as a starting point for female liberation cannot be underestimated.

Later expressions of radical feminism were more determinedly separatist than the Redstockings' manifesto or the 1972 statement of UK radical feminists. In a paper entitled *The Need for Revolutionary Feminism*, which began to circulate in Britain in 1977, Sheila Jeffreys set out to translate the political theory of radical feminism into a revolutionary strategy. This would involve, she said,

the determination to wrest power from the ruling group and to end their domination. It requires the identification of the ruling group, its power base, its methods of control, its interests, its historical development, its weaknesses and the best methods to destroy its power...

She and other women who identified themselves as 'revolutionary feminists' were in no doubt that men were the 'ruling group' and, accordingly, women who lived with men, had sex with men or worked alongside men politically were regarded as being in danger of collaborating with the enemy. In a 1979 statement, the Leeds Revolutionary Feminist Group declared: 'We do think that all feminists can and should be political lesbians.' (We examine feminist debates on sexuality in more detail in a later chapter, p. 211.) This position seems at odds with the pro-woman line and has been criticized by many who identify as radical feminists, as well as by those who call themselves socialist feminists.

It is a common misconception that the radical-socialist divide reflects a split between lesbians and heterosexuals. This is not so. As we will reiterate in Chapter 8 the women's liberation movement has encouraged love between women, it has celebrated active female sexuality, and it has enabled women to discover how their bodies work and what gives them pleasure. This has led no small number of women into bed with each other; for some it was a brief adventure; for others it has become a continuing option; and for some it has coincided with a permanent change in their sexual relations. However, lesbians do not all think that men are the enemy, any more than heterosexual women all think men are ideal comrades and life partners. A considerable number of heterosexuals have espoused the radical feminist cause, while many lesbians are committed socialist feminists.

Socialist feminism

The development of socialist feminism as a distinct political current within women's liberation began as a response to the challenge of radical feminism. For the most part, it was made up of women who were determined not to abandon their association with left-wing politics. They belonged, variously, to the Labour Party, the Communist Party, the International Socialists (later the Socialist Workers' Party) and the International Marxist Group; and the majority were non-aligned feminists.

One characteristic which has distinguished the British from the American women's movement is the strength of the organized left. In Britain there has been a mass-based Labour Party in government and a trade union movement which constitutes the biggest working-class assembly in the country. British feminism has always been more socialist than its American counterpart.

Socialist feminists saw their feminism as the human face of socialism; it was a critique of the male chauvinism of the left, which would transform much of its conduct and many of its priorities. They knew they would have a job on their hands to make male socialists recognize the importance of feminism, but

31

they did not see it as being essentially a fight against men, or precluding alliances with them.

They were convinced of the importance of understanding economic forces and of Marx's analysis of class conflict. For the committed Marxists especially, the radical feminists' sex-class analysis, with its inversion of Marx's analytical methods and rejection of Marx's own prognosis, was unacceptable. In their view, the pro-woman line raised awkward questions about the role of women who reaped the privileges of capital and strove to uphold its power. They rejected separatism both as a strategy and as an end in itself, for a range of reasons – from a commitment to class unity and a common struggle with men, to alienation from a political creed which cited husbands, lovers, fathers, sons, brothers, comrades and friends as 'the enemy'.

There was also the consideration of building popular support. They wanted to draw as many women as possible, especially working-class women, into the women's liberation movement, and to enlist male support – in the trade union movement and elsewhere – for feminist demands. They guessed, not unreasonably, that radical feminism, with its strong tendency towards separatism, would alienate a great many women and almost all men. It was therefore necessary to make the distinction clear.

Socialist feminists have not (yet) issued any manifestos. Having begun with a rejection of some aspects of radical feminism and an expression of commitment to the politics of the left, they have developed in the late 1970s and early 1980s an increasingly detailed and sophisticated analysis of the construction of male power and female subordination. This process is still under way. Their ideas can be found in countless magazine articles, conference papers and books, many of which we have drawn on for this book.

They have been concerned with understanding the historical development of patriarchy (a term with many interpretations, but which can be taken – broadly – to mean the combination of social, economic and cultural systems which ensures male supremacy), and with unearthing the patriarchal character of economic class relations. They have drawn on psychoanalysis to examine the specifically sexual dynamic between women and men (which is not necessarily reducible to economic determination), and the construction of masculine and feminine psychologies which again cannot be accounted for in Marxist theory of class exploitation. They do not conclude that biology is the root of the evil: in their view men oppress women not by virtue of their biological maleness but by virtue of their social and economic relations with women. It is these relations which need to be transformed. The fight to end women's subordination is, in the socialist feminist analysis, inextricably bound up with the class struggle and cannot be lifted above it – because capitalism itself is not only grounded in patriarchy, but has changed the shape of it. From this perspective, socialist feminists have begun to develop an exacting critique of theories of class exploitation. They insist on the centrality of ideological struggle, which has been all too glibly nudged to the periphery of politics by much of the left. Reproduction and family relations are placed at the heart of social and economic theory and strategy.

It is at this point that the gap between radical feminism (in its non-biological-determinist form) and socialist feminism is at its narrowest. What distinguishes the two is that socialist feminists' politics entail neither a rejection of men nor a withdrawl from them, but an urgent necessity to fight *both in and against* male-dominated power relations; for them, the women's liberation movement is not a sanctuary from male supremacy, but a means of combative engagement with it. They want to transform the struggle for socialism, not supercede it.

Inevitably, there are differences among socialist feminists. Some are more sceptical than others about the commitment of male socialists to feminist objectives and the degree to which men will allow women to make gains that conflict with their own interests. The experience of the last decade has tended to swell the ranks of the sceptics.

Arguments between socialist and radical feminists have shaken the women's liberation movement at times. Yet feminists on both sides have seen eye-to-eye and campaigned together on a number of specific issues, and for most of the decade, the movement managed to remain as one – a singularly heterogeneous body, in which radical and socialist feminism cohabited.

The problem with men

The debate underpinned another controversy which loomed large within the UK movement in the early 1970s. This concerned the participation of men in the politics of women's liberation. It was not clear in the early days that the movement was to be for women alone, and a number of groups included men – as did the first two national conferences. A few women (notably two small groups of Maoists) insisted that it was politically correct to include men in what was, after all, a mere colony in the empire of class struggle. Most didn't care, or definitely didn't want them there because their presence disrupted discourse between women. It seemed impossible to create the conditions in which men could cooperate. 'We met with the husbands at first,' says Hazel Galbraith of the Peckham Rye group, 'but they took over, so we had to stop.' Invariably, women found that the presence of men altered the *quality* of their conversation and diluted its potency, absorbing their attention and stilling their imagination. Either too little was said – or too much. Jean Hart remembers what happened when her group in North London decided to admit men, after some of the husbands had asked to come along:

The women whose husbands came were very deferential at first, trying desperately to negotiate the two worlds. They wanted the women to be seen as jolly decent people. But people were goaded into honesty by the group. One couple ended in a slanging match, with the man shouting thinks like 'I can't look after the kids because I go to work' (as if the roles were made in heaven!). One woman confessed that she didn't have orgasms with her husband. He yelled back, obviously pushed to extremity, 'You don't because you're frigid!' My husband didn't come to the meeting. I didn't want him to. I was fighting a gentle battle at home, I was cautious about expressing my worries. In the group I was fiery and opinionated, and I couldn't bring these two selves together...

Women's experience of getting together on their own, and the political imagination generated by their mutual understanding and sense of solidarity, were too precious to forfeit.

At the second national conference at Skegness in 1971, a small but symbolic incident put an end to the permissive line on men's attendance. Conference proceedings have not always been 'ladylike' in the traditional sense of the word. At a certain point on that occasion two women became involved in a wrangle over the microphones, and the husband of one of them rushed to her aid. At the sight of a man intervening in a physical confrontation, row upon row of women surged forward, plugs were pulled – and men were barred from all but the post-conference discothèque. But at the next conference, in Manchester, there was another punch-up between a man and a woman at the disco, and henceforth these, too, were an all-female affair.

There was a long argument among London feminists in 1973 over whether or not men should be admitted to any part of the new women's liberation workshop, about to be opened in Covent Garden. Affiliated groups sent delegates to a series of meetings that autumn, and on 17 November they voted for exclusion by 117 votes to 30, with 20 abstentions. Most socialist feminists voted for exclusion along with the radical feminists – if only on the ground that it was better for the cause of female solidarity to keep men out if some women objected to their presence. However, since the dispute was no longer over whether men should attend meetings, but whether they should be allowed across the threshold of a women's centre, it raised questions about just how separatist the character of the movement should be. It seemed to many that the radical feminists had seized the strategic initiative. The wrangling was bitter and it demoralized many of the stalwarts of the movement, who began voting with their feet. For the argument about men seemed to have become an argument against categories of women. In truth, the majority of feminists didn't much care about the exclusion of men, but were appalled by the prospect of women feeling excluded by their relation to men. What they wanted above all was *autonomy*. They wanted their movement not to reject men so much as to be independent from them.

It was this same determination to preserve the movement's independence which led to the dissolution of the Women's National Coordinating Committee in 1971. Although the committee had been devised initially to avoid any take-over, its meetings had become a sectarian battleground, with the Maoists, in particular, trying to capture it. What the Maoists could do today, the Trotskyists, or liberal reformists, or any other group could no doubt do tomorrow – and so it was decided at the Skegness conference that it was best to have no committee at all. (The disgruntled Maoist at the conference door, handing out boycott leaflets, was to become a familiar sight: 'SHAM SOCIALISTS HELP BRITISH IMPERIALISM DIVERT THE WOMEN'S MOVEMENT. . .')

Most women were confident that the movement would hang together without a coordinating committee – and it has remained a loose federation of small groups, linked chiefly by a sense of involvement and a common cause. That it has survived for more than a decade is a measure of the strength of the *idea* that has held it together. It is also due to the fact that the movement's lack of formal structure has been a positive, not a

35

negative feature, and one to which feminists have given careful and critical consideration. A paper entitled 'The Tyranny of Structurelessness' [14] began to circulate among women's groups in the early 1970s and became one of the key documents of the movement. The author, American feminist Jo Freeman ('Joreen'), describes how an absence of leadership and organization can encourage informal élites with vested interests, allow 'stars' to emerge, and lead to undemocratic decision-making and political impotence. She sets out principles for democratic structuring, stressing the importance of such things as wide distribution of authority, accountability, rotation of tasks, and equal access to information and resources. 'The group of people in positions of authority will be diffuse, flexible, open and temporary,' she explains. 'They will not be in such an easy position to institutionalize their power, because ultimate decisions will be made by the group at large. The group will have the power to determine who shall exercise authority within it.'

Most of these ideas have been tried out in various ways and some have become standard practice. Efforts to be genuinely democratic have absorbed a lot of energy and they have often caused anger and frustration, especially when there has seemed a need for swift, effective action. But the process has been a creative one, which has played a vital part in the development of feminism and has even determined the nature of women's demands. (To give just one example, it is likely that a feminist campaign to set up a nursery would include a demand that it be organized along democratic lines, with parents and workers being involved in decision-making.)

Campaigning

While women's liberation can't be understood without appreciating the quest for analysis and democratic forms, nor can the movement be understood without its campaigns. One of the first arose in the early 1970s, when the Conservative government under Edward Heath was planning to abolish family allowances and replace them with a tax rebate (or 'credit') for the family breadwinner: in most families this would have meant transferring resources for child support from the mother to the father. The same government intended to introduce a new pension scheme which offered women inferior benefits. And meanwhile the Society for the Protection of the Unborn Child had begun its attack on the liberal 1967 Abortion Act. Defensive

36

campaigns on these fronts, combined with a new offensive for a law against sex discrimination, were major items on the agenda. The first edition of the feminist newsletter *Women's Report*, launched in the winter of 1972–3, tells us that a group in Southampton was organizing a petition to retain family allowances, while one in Watford was organizing a petition in favour of the (then) Anti-Discrimination Bill, and another in Hemel Hempstead was carrying out a survey on women's reaction to the government's tax credit scheme. At the same time, the Women's Abortion and Contraception Campaign was working towards 'free contraception and abortion on the National Health Service as every woman's right, and an end to forced sterilization', while a group called 'Mothers in Action' were campaigning for paid maternity leave.

Alongside operations such as these were others focussed more directly on the workplace. For example, a major campaign of the early 1970s was one which aimed to persuade office cleaners to join a union. Office cleaning was – and still is – a job done mainly by women and at night. May Hobbs, the outspoken East Londoner who set the campaign going, pointed out that women do night work because their family responsibilities make it impossible for them to work during the day, and they need money 'for little luxuries like food, rent and clothes for their kids'. It's tough, dirty work. 'And because these women need the money so desperately they will bow to anything, and that is the reason why you have to get this industry organized.'[15] Her aim was to get the cleaners to join the Transport and General Workers' Union as a first step towards negotiating better pay and conditions. She drew support from London women's liberation groups, who turned out in considerable numbers to leaflet office buildings as the night cleaners came into work. Further north, a women's liberation group in Rochdale, Yorkshire, exposed the scandal of young Filipino women working in a local mill, held in near slavery on low wages and in dismal, overcrowded conditions.[16]

Campaigns to achieve equal rights at work increasingly brought the women's liberation movement into contact with the trade unions. On 16 February 1974, shortly before the fall of the Heath government, the feminist Women's Rights Unit of the National Council for Civil Liberties held a women's rights conference at the headquarters of the TUC, to which delegates were invited from the unions and from women's groups. Five hundred and fifty attended. It was the first time that feminists and trade unionists had met together in any substantial numbers, and the first occasion on which representatives of the two movements explicitly recognized each other's strategic importance. Proceedings were opened by Betty Harrison, veteran organizer of the tobacco workers' union:

This Conference is a real breakthrough. Here we have industrial workers, professional workers, women from the new women's liberation movement, who are to discuss and decide what we must do in the future to fight for equality... I have the highest respect for the women's liberation movement. The propaganda they've done has raised the cause of women's rights in a way that it hasn't been raised for a generation...[17]

The following month, the London Trades Council launched a ten-point charter for working women, which was drawn up by feminists in the Communist Party. It called for eighteen weeks' maternity leave on full pay, free contraception and abortion on demand, free day nurseries, a big increase in family allowances and a national minimum wage – as well as for equal pay and opportunity and an end to discrimination in tax and social security. It led to the development of a large campaign, with a network of Working Women's Charter groups around the country. The campaign made contact with the unions mainly through unofficial channels and tended to be viewed with suspicion in higher quarters. It helped raise awareness among female members and eventually nudged the TUC into publishing a similar list of demands (see p. 145).

Child care

Child care has been a major preoccupation of the women's liberation movement. From the early 1970s, groups formed all over the country to try to organize nurseries and playgroups. Some operated on a self-help basis; some tried to get funds from their local councils. Others negotiated for workplace nurseries with funding from employers.

Valerie Charlton remembers her initial approach when she first became involved in a women's liberation group: 'We thought the problem was women at home, kids; the key issue is to get into nurseries. We thought that was all you had to do.' After almost two years' campaigning, she and half a dozen others persuaded the council to give them a small grant and a short-life property in Dartmouth Park hill, where they set up the

Children's Community Centre – a full-time, free, parent-controlled, non-sexist nursery for children aged 2½ to five. Some half-dozen London feminist groups set up nurseries during the same period.

The Birmingham women's liberation group tried to raise money from the council to start a nursery but failed, and so started a women's liberation playgroup, which aimed 'to counter positively the conditioning of children into restricting sex roles, and to encourage the formation of strong friendships among the children, and between the children and adults other than their own parents'. In 1977, a group of women employed at the TUC headquarters in London, together with other women at nearby workplaces, set up the Kingsway Children's Centre, with up to thirty places: two-thirds of the cost of each place was to be met by employers, one-third by parents.

Interwoven with the planning and negotiation that went into setting up and running child care facilities were some difficult problems of principle. Feminists who launched such campaigns were predominantly middle-class but were keen to provide places for working-class children, and to involve all parents in running the facilities. However, working-class mothers were usually out at work all day, and did not have time to get involved; sometimes, too, they were put off by the intellectual language of the middle-class women, and stayed away from meetings, leaving the rest to carry responsibility.

If sufficient funds to pay nursery staff were not forthcoming from outside sources, women could either organize voluntary rotas or plan to employ staff on lower wages; yet they firmly believed in paying decent wages, and in not using unpaid labour to undercut the jobs of those (largely working-class) women who were qualified nursery nurses. If employers could be persuaded to pay for workplace nurseries, there was a danger that they would have undue control over their female employees: women who had nowhere else to leave their kids might be forced to put up with rotten pay and conditions. If parents themselves were to bear the full costs of a nursery, they might expect to have full control over it; but without any subsidy, costs would be very high indeed, and that would contradict the objective of child care being available to all, regardless of income.

By the mid-1970s, it was becoming harder than ever to raise money for nurseries. There seemed to be a choice between self-help, or no nurseries at all. Did feminist-inspired child care have to be an *alternative* to the welfare state? Feminists were not content to slot meekly into the 'voluntary sector'. They wanted to make claims on the state *and* to change it, as well as to maintain the integrity of their own ventures. (We return to this in Chapter 3.) Assessing four years' experience of the Camden Children's Community Centre, Valerie Charlton commented in 1975 that women now knew what kind of nurseries they wanted, but these were still a long way off:

We know a great deal about the needs of women and children. We know what changes we want in the working conditions of nursery workers and we know that men must take up their responsibility in the care and education of their own and all children. We talk of the millions of working mothers for whom lack of nurseries is a problem; but the millions of working fathers also have to see this as their problem, which it most certainly is. But the missing component as yet is the organized power to force the government and local councils to provide what we want and need.[18]

By the end of the decade, the importance of comprehensive child care for all under-fives was recognized (on paper, at least) by the TUC, by many individual unions, by the Labour Party and by the Equal Opportunities Commission. Yet nurseries were being closed down at an alarming rate, under pressure of public expenditure cuts. In July 1980, groups from all over the country got together to form the National Child Care Campaign. The work continues.

Women's Aid

It is interesting to compare this with the relative success of the Women's Aid Federation. In 1972 Erin Pizzey set up the first refuge for battered women, in Chiswick, West London. A skilled publicist, she succeeded in attracting considerable attention from the media – even a spot on the *Jimmy Young Show*. Hitherto, the fact that men regularly beat up women in the privacy of their homes had been unmentioned and unmentionable. Suddenly it was news – and the public had to face the fact that domestic violence was widespread and often severe. (It has taken longer to dispel the myth that it is a purely working-class phenomenon. In 1974 a judge remarked on the case of a 'gentleman' who was found guilty of beating his wife: 'If he had been a miner in South Wales I might have overlooked it. . . There are some sections of the community where beatings of one's wife are not the same as others.')[19]

Unlike the child care campaign, Women's Aid attracted funds from government, from charitable trusts and from individual donors. People (usually men) who had money at their disposal were evidently unmoved at the thought of mothers and children needing nurseries. But wife-battering was different. Perhaps it pricked their consciences, or perhaps it genuinely shocked them. It was certainly more sensational. And refuges were a lot cheaper than nurseries. *Women's Report* commented: 'Too bad women have to be beaten senseless by their husbands before the rest of society will take their cause seriously.'[20]

In towns and cities throughout the country women began to form groups with a view to setting up local refuges. In 1974, twenty-seven groups from as far afield as Dublin and the north of Scotland gathered at a national conference organized by Chiswick Women's Aid. Pizzey herself eventually alienated many of the others, who felt that she was monopolizing the publicity, keeping too much of the money for her own refuge and wanting too much personal control. At a second national conferences in 1975 (attended by twenty-eight groups who had already set up refuges and eighty-three more who were working at it), Pizzey stormed out after a row and has gone her own way ever since. She has continued to be identified as a leading authority on domestic violence, but her own views diverge sharply from those of other Women's Aid groups. She sees wife-battering essentially as a psychological problem and claims that certain kinds of women are 'violence prone' and invite assault. To feminists, this is dangerous nonsense: they see domestic violence as an expression of the power that men wield over women, in a society where female dependence is built into the structure of everyday life. From their own extensive experience of working in refuges they conclude that wife-battering is not the practice of a deviant few, but something which can emerge in the 'normal' course of marital relations.

Since 1975, the growth of the Women's Aid movement – to a total of ninety-nine groups and two hundred refuges in 1980 – has largely been the work of feminists, although in some towns refuges were initially opened by social workers and other professional people who did not associate themselves with women's liberation. The Women's Aid Federation, to which almost all groups who run refuges belong, operates quite separately from Erin Pizzey's Chiswick outfit. It has its own headquarters, its own non-hierarchical structure and explicitly

41

feminist objectives. Its aims include the demands of the women's liberation movement, as well as an insistence that each group within the Federation be autonomous; that refuges maintain an 'open-door' policy so that no woman is turned away; and that women in each refuge have a right to 'self-determination'.

The campaign bore fruit in Parliament too when the Domestic Violence Act was passed in 1976. Introduced as a Private Member's Bill by Labour MP Jo Richardson, it aimed to simplify and strengthen the procedure whereby a woman could obtain a court injunction to restrain a violent husband or cohabitee. The law remains a clumsy and ineffective means of dealing with the problem, but at least this new Act represented a shift in official thinking. Hitherto, it had generally been assumed that wife-battering was a private affair in which the forces of law and order should not intervene. In many ways, Women's Aid has been the most productive of all campaigns within the women's liberation movement. Only the National Abortion Campaign can compare with it in terms of scale, organizational strength and effectiveness.

National Abortion Campaign

NAC was launched in the spring of 1975, with the single aim of defending the 1967 Abortion Act. Opposition to the Act had by that time built up formidably, headed by the Society for the Protection of the Unborn Child and a similar body called Life. Both were supported by the Catholic Church (as well as by numerous individual Anglican clergy) who provided money and facilities, and helped to organize demonstrations and letter-writing campaigns to MPs. They sought not only to make it more difficult for women to get legal consent for abortion, but also to make safe, legal abortion much harder to obtain, by undermining the charitable abortion agencies.

A number of groups were working to defend the Act and these were linked by the umbrella organization Co-ord (Co-ordinating Committee in Defence of the 1967 Abortion Act). Among them, NAC was chiefly responsible for providing a radical impetus for the campaign, and mass support for a woman's right to choose. It was a specifically feminist initiative, with a non-hierarchical, federated structure linking NAC groups in most major towns and cities. Together with Co-ord and a remarkably determined group of women MPs, NAC succeeded in defeating a series of Private Members' Bills which embodied some of the aims of SPUC and Life. But its greatest achievement was to spur the trade unions and the TUC into taking action in defence of the 1967 Act. (More of this later, p. 147.)

Women against violence

Male violence was the focus of much feminist activity in the later 1970s. In March 1976 a group of women opened Britain's first Rape Crisis Centre in North London, with a short-life property from the Department of the Environment and funds from two charitable trusts. Working as a collective, with two paid employees and a large number of volunteers, they aimed to provide practical advice, counselling and a sympathetic environment, to help women cope with the experience of rape. Evidently, they answered a need. Five years later, there were sixteen similar centres in cities throughout Britain. At the time the first one opened, many women were outraged at the way rape trials were conducted, with the victim herself effectively put 'on trial' as defence lawyers attempted to prove that she had 'asked for it'. Largely as a result of feminist lobbying, another Private Member's Bill was passed in 1976, the Sexual Offences (Amendment) Act, which provided better safeguards for the privacy of the victim during the trial. However, as with the Women's Aid movement, the chief aim of the Rape Crisis Centres has been to provide a woman-centred framework of support, rather than just to win legal concessions from the state. Women set out to help each other, knowing that the cause of the problem was deeply embedded in the social fabric, and could not be solved by piecemeal reforms.

This same knowledge erupted into open protest with the first of the 'Reclaim the Night' demonstrations on 12 November 1977. *Spare Rib* recorded that on that night, 130 women joined hands and sung protest songs in a huge circle in City Square, Leeds; 400 took to the streets in Manchester; 100 marched with torches through Newcastle; 80 sang and danced their way around York. In London, several hundred women invaded Soho, chanting, singing and slapping stickers on windows, greatly discomfiting the male clientele of massage parlours, porn shops and strip joints. A banner proclaimed: 'We are walking for *all* women – all women should be free to walk down any street, night or day, without fear.' [21] At the end of the decade this developed into a large and more explicitly political campaign, 'Women

Against Violence Against Women', which we describe in Chapter 7.

Component parts of a revolution

Parallel with these action-based campaigns ran a multitude of other activities. Women's health groups learned the art of self-examination. A group called 'She Can Do It' operated as a work-exchange for women doing traditionally male craft jobs, and later Women in Manual Trades emerged as a pressure group to encourage women to train as plumbers, electricians, carpenters, bricklayers and mechanics. 'Women in Media' campaigned for better jobs for women in the press and broadcasting, and against sexist bias in the content of the media. Women in rural areas set up their own support network. Film-makers organized a women and film collective; artists a women's art alliance; writers a feminist writers' workshop.

In the early 1970s there was a move into theory – reading groups were started where women read together the work of Marx, the Italian revolutionary Gramsci, the French philosopher Althusser, and the work of feminist theorists like Juliet Mitchell and Simone de Beauvoir. There was a feminist history workshop, a literature collective, a women and psychology group, and several groups concerned with education. Women at colleges and universities set up women's studies courses and a group of teachers and academics set up the Women's Research and Resources Centre.

Information about the women's liberation movement was pooled and dispersed by a collective known as WIRES, who produced a regular newsletter. The magazine *Spare Rib*, launched in July 1972 to compete with traditional glossies such as *Honey* and *19*, has been produced by a feminist collective since late 1973, and has held its own in the market. The first feminist publishing imprint, Virago, was launched in 1975 and has flourished since, producing more than three hundred titles. By the end of the decade there were three more feminist publishers, the Women's Press, Women Only Press and Sheba. (All four survived when the economic recession sent the book trade into a nosedive in the early 1980s.) There have been socialist feminist conferences and radical feminist conferences and lesbian conferences . . . all these and countless other activities, which we cannot do justice to here, have comprised the women's liberation movement.

These are the component parts of the revolution which seeks (as Ellen Malos said in 1970) 'a total transformation of society from the bottom up'. They are the core of a broad alliance of women, who do not all necessarily identify with 'women's liberation', but who support feminist demands and participate in the struggle to achieve them. Some are based in trade unions, in political parties and in conventional women's organizations; some are individuals who don't belong to anything at all. Their numbers have grown at a phenomenal rate since the early 1970s.

'Women's liberation' cannot be understood as a vanguard leading the masses – that approach would be quite alien to its politics in any case. The boundaries between the wider women's movement and women's liberation are not fixed in any way and are impossible to distinguish. You *can* look up 'Women's Liberation' in the London phone book and find a whole series of addresses and numbers belonging to various enterprises. But it is more than a federation of small groups. It is a collective experience accumulated over more than a decade, and it continues to grow and change. It is reformist and revolutionary. It is a source of political energy, a developing body of theory, a battleground, a sisterhood.

In the following chapters we explore the main areas where the women's liberation movement has been politically engaged. We try to assess how much progress has been made towards feminist objectives, to examine the nature of the struggle and the character of the opposition. It is not a matter of simply finding out how close women have come to achieving specific demands. The struggle for women's liberation is taking place on several different levels. It involves women changing themselves as well as the external world.

On one level, women are demanding justice and equality. They are saying to men: you have closed the door on us, let us in; you have kept us on short rations, give us more. And since they can't rely on men being decent enough to say yes, they are trying, on another level, to stop men having the power to say no – the power to oppress them. To this end, they are fighting to change the cultural, social and economic systems which express and maintain male supremacy.

However, women are not simply held in place by the force of male oppression. They are subordinate, as men are dominant, and their subordination goes under their skin, below the threshold of consciousness. This is not to say that women's

46

oppression is 'all in the head', but that women need to recognize and then struggle to transform the social construction of feminine psychology – as well as men's constructed sense of masculinity – as a crucial part of their fight against oppression. In a way, this is the key to women's liberation.

Notes to Chapter 1

 1 *Enough!*, no.1, Bristol Women's Liberation, 1969.
 2 Rowbotham, S. *Women's Consciousness, Man's World*, Penguin, 1973.
 3 Friedan, B. *The Feminine Mystique*, Penguin 1976.
 4 Quoted in 'Nine Years Together', a history of a women's liberation group, in *Spare Rib* 9, April 1978.
 5 Ibid.
 6 Mitchell, J. 'The Longest Revolution' in *New Left Review*, November–December 1966.
 7 Rowbotham, S. *Women's Liberation and the New Politics*, Spokesman pamphlet, no. 17, 1969.
 8 Koedt, A. 'The Myth of the Vaginal Orgasm' in *Notes from the Second Year*, 1970.
 9 Greer, G. *The Female Eunuch*, Paladin, 1971.
10 *The Oppression of Women in the 1970s*, Bristol Group, 1971.
11 Firestone, S. *The Dialectic of Sex*, Paladin, 1971.
12 *Spare Rib*, no. 79.
13 Ibid.
14 Freeman, J. (Joreen) 'The Tyranny of Structurelessness' in *The Second Wave*, vol. 2, no. 1.
15 Hobbs, M. *Born to Struggle*, Quartet, 1973.
16 *Women's Report*, vol. 1, no. 3, 1973.
17 Hewitt, P. (ed.) *Danger! Women at Work*, National Council for Civil Liberties, 1974.
18 Charlton, V. 'A Lesson in Day Care', in *Women in the Community*, ed. Marjorie Mayo, Routledge & Kegan Paul, 1977.
19 Quoted in *Red Tape*, 1974; reprinted in Gill, T. and Coote, A. *Battered Women and the Law*, Inter-Action & NCCL, 1977.
20 *Women's Report*, vol. 2, no. 1, 1974.
21 *Spare Rib*, January 1978.

2 Work

In December 1980, the Equal Opportunities Commission issued an attractive new booklet, entitled *Breakthrough*. To commemorate the enactment of Britain's new law against sex discrimination and the proud moment of the Commission's own birth, it was a 'record of five years' progress towards sex equality'. It was not a large booklet. In words and pictures (big pictures, few words) on glossy pages, it told the stories of thirty-nine individual women who had 'broken through'. There was a blacksmith, a docker, a motor mechanic, a metal broker, a bricklayer, a pilot and many more, all doing jobs that are normally done by men.[1]

This had become a familiar theme by the end of the 1970s. Newspapers regularly celebrated female pioneers: the first 'girl' on a building site, the plucky young thing in the stock exchange, the 'lady' in the lorry cab ... all living, breathing proof that women were winning equality at work. But the pioneers can be numbered in their hundreds. For the remaining ten million women workers, the story has been different altogether. Far from making progress towards equality, they have found it slipping away from them.

Neither the ten-year campaign by the women's liberation movement nor the Sex Discrimination Act has hindered the steady process by which women have been eased out of skilled jobs throughout this century. Between 1911 and 1971, women's share of skilled (higher-paid) manual work dropped by nearly *half*, from 24 to 13.5 per cent. Over the same span of years, their share of unskilled manual jobs more than *doubled* – from 15.5 to 37.2 per cent. This astonishing trend, which amounts to a 'breakthrough' of men into a near-monopoly of skilled work, continued during the 1970s.

Nor has the trade unions' pledge to fight for equal pay, or the Equal Pay Act itself, achieved any real 'breakthrough' for women. Female pay has been held down with such remarkable tenacity that by the end of the 1970s, women workers were still taking home 36 per cent less money than men. In 1979, for every £1 in the average man's pay pocket, there was only 63.6 pence in the average woman's. That gap has been narrowed by less than ten pence in ten years.

Nothing has happened to disturb the patterns of paid and unpaid work that have prevailed for more than a century – in which women have been designated a particular function in the home (as unpaid child-minder, housekeeper, cook, nurse and cleaner) and a corresponding function in the labour market. If we consider the call for 'equal opportunity' in this light, it has a hollow ring about it. 'Opportunity' implies 'choice', yet there has never been any real choice for women. Their position as low-paid, part-time, intermittent, secondary wage earners has determined their role in the home since the beginning of the industrial revolution. Correspondingly, their role in the home has determined their position in the labour market. Both were set in train by the efforts of male workers to defend themselves against a new breed of employers in the early stages of capitalism; they endure as strongly as ever today.

It is true that in more recent years there has been a dramatic influx of women into the labour market. The numbers of 'economically active' females increased by 45 per cent between 1931 and 1970. In the same period, the number of married women going out to work increased fourfold. The number of male workers, meanwhile, remained stable; in 1980, there were approximately 10.4 million women and 15.6 million men in the labour force. This represents a significant change for women: gone are the days when marriage, or the arrival of the first child, was expected to lift them out of the labour market and deposit them at home for good. But when women have entered the workforce, they have not done so freely or at random. They have been drawn in, and then confined to a handful of industries and occupations.

As Catherine Hakim has demonstrated in her research for the Department of Employment,[2] these have not been male dominated occupations, but 'slowly-expanding female-dominated occupations for which the supply of single women became inadequate'. Women have worked separately from men, apartheid-style, in low-paid jobs which hold out little hope of advancement. And they have entered the waged labour force on the strict but unspoken condition that this will not interfere with the unwaged work they perform in their homes.

The efforts of women to win equality at work have foundered

because their strategies have been designed to attack the symptoms, not the causes of the problem. Since the early 1970s we have begun to understand more fully how inequality is constructed, and to see it as part of a system in which men have power and women do not.

Moreover, women's demands were formulated at a time when the economy was relatively healthy. In 1970, there were just over 800,000 registered unemployed and the figure dropped to 556,200 in 1973. Industry was fairly buoyant, the welfare state was burgeoning; it was easier to believe that new jobs could be opened up for women in the higher-paid, skilled areas. While Labour was in government and the social services were still expanding, the prospect of child care and other facilities being provided on a community basis and financed by the state did not seem all that remote. It was possible to imagine women going out to work on the same terms as men, with only minimal disruption to the lives of men themselves. But, it was a vision which was unlikely to be realized even in continuing prosperity, and it has inhibited the development of more useful strategies.

Since the first years of the women's liberation movement, the economic and political weather has changed dramatically – from the promise of spring to the bitterness of winter (summer never came). Unemployment has rocketed and by the early 1980s Britain's industrial life and its welfare state have been brought to the point of collapse. There is no immediate prospect of improvement and it is clear that, even with a new Labour government, recovery from the economic recession will be a long, slow, painful business. There will be little or no economic growth and there can be no hope of any prosperous overlay of new 'opportunities' for women.

In the following pages we consider some of the main components of women's subordination as waged workers. How far are women kept in separate jobs from men, and why has this *segregation* developed? How has the notion of *skill* been constructed, and to whose advantage? How has the idea arisen that there should be one main breadwinner for each family – the ideology of the *family wage* – and what are the implications for women? How far do female and male workers have different relationships to *time*, bearing on their different roles at home, and what effect does this have on their relative positions in the labour market? What are the characteristics of female and male *pay*? What has been the impact of *new technology* and *unemployment*? By examining these issues we hope to show why

50

women have made so little progress towards equality at work, and why we need to develop new approaches to the problem.

Men's jobs and women's jobs

In 1979, the Department of Employment published its first thorough survey of job segregation.[3] When these findings (by Catherine Hakim) are combined with other data collected in the late 1970s,[4] we can see the full extent of occupational apartheid.

First, women are concentrated overwhelmingly in the service industries. (These are industries which do not produce goods – such as banking, hairdressing, cleaning and public administration.) Between 1961 and 1980, more than two million women have joined the service industries and more than half a million women have left the production industries. As a result, by the early 1980s more than three-quarters of all female workers are in the non-productive sector.

Women are confined to specific industries within each sector. For example, half of all women in the productive sector are in only four of the nineteen industrial groups: food and drink, clothing and footwear, textiles and electrical engineering. And they are in a very narrow range of occupations. More than half of all women workers are either caterers, cleaners or hairdressers, or are performing 'other personal services', which include nursing and secretarial work.

Catherine Hakim highlights the concentration of women in lower paid jobs and shows how this has increased dramatically since the beginning of the century. We have seen that men have monopolized skilled manual work. Among non-manual workers women have increased their share of managerial and administrative jobs by a tiny margin – from 19.8 to 21.6 per cent – in the course of seventy years; but in the same period they have more than tripled their share of clerical work – from 21.4 to 73.2 per cent. Jobs which at the beginning of the century had a balance of male and female workers typical of the economy as a whole were transformed by the 1970s into 'typically feminine' jobs. Ninety-nine per cent of all typists, shorthand writers and secretaries are women, but only 14 per cent of office managers. In other occupational groups, there are deep divisions too. Among electrical and electronic workers, 84 per cent of assembly-line workers are female, but only 1.4 per cent of 'linesmen and cable-jointers'.

51

There is a staggering degree of total segregation – that is, women and men doing jobs where there are *no* members of the opposite sex doing the same thing at the same workplace. A 1980 study has revealed that 45 per cent of women and about 75 per cent of men work in totally segregated jobs.[5] The likelihood of men doing work which is all-male or nearly all-male has increased considerably in the course of the century.

This trend towards greater segregation has been occasioned partly by changes in the structure of the labour market. Old jobs have disappeared, new ones have been created. With the expansion of the public sector after the Second World War, and the rapid growth of administrative work and retail distribution, traditional sources did not yield enough labour – and so new ones had to be tapped. For the first time in peace time, mature women were employed who had hitherto been confined to the home, either because of formal 'marriage bars' against their employment or because of a general consensus that motherhood was a full-time occupation.

But this alone cannot explain why the idea has developed that there are 'men's jobs' and 'women's jobs', rigidly divided from each other; or why men's jobs are more skilled and higher-paid, while women's are less skilled and lower-paid; or why both are part of a system in which women work unpaid at home and men are regarded as the main family breadwinners.

It cannot be explained away as a 'natural' consequence of women's unique capacity to bear and breastfeed children. Why should this dictate the way children are looked after when they are not being breastfed, or how domestic work is done? Why should the bearers of children do unskilled, low-paid jobs? We know from contemporary experience that women/mothers are as capable as men/fathers of doing skilled work, yet only exceptionally do they do it. Caring for children is no more a 'naturally female' pursuit than cleaning kitchen floors or typing letters; nor is it more 'natural' than it is for a man to operate a lathe, or manage a bank or go to the pub on Friday night. These are social roles, social habits, which have developed over time and which are the product of political struggles.

Skilled workers of the world unite
It has been common, even among socialist theoreticians, to accept women's domestic role as *given*, to take it for granted, and to view women's role in the labour market from that basis.

Feminist historians and economists have begun to delve deeper into the structure of inequality. One significant part of this is the relationship between sex, skill and control.

In the nineteenth century, as production became factory-based, the social and economic order was transformed, and the struggle between labour and capital began in earnest. The only established means of resistance for workers were craft-based organizations. These were self-regulating, determining for themselves who should acquire skills and who should gain entry to them. They had their roots in pre-capitalist society, which was patriarchal; women were generally excluded from them. They set a precedent for the development of trade union-ism in the later years of the century. Access to skill was as-sociated with access to working-class political organization and self-defence; and together they afforded some measure of con-trol over income. To be outside this axis of skill and organization was to be relatively poor and powerless. Since women were excluded from trade unionism, their bargaining position was weak, and the pay they could command was consequently low. In turn, this meant that they could be accused by men of un-dercutting them.

Skill was about control over production as well as over in-come. In some of the staple industries of the new capitalist system, skilled craftsmen contracted work from the factory owner and engaged other workers as sub-contractors, among whom income was unevenly distributed and whose access to new skills was blocked. Soon, employers sought to reduce their dependence on well-organized, higher-paid male workers. Apart from wanting to reduce the cost of labour, they needed to weaken the control which skilled craftsmen exercised over the production process. One strategy was to break down the work of skilled individuals into a series of simplified, routine tasks, to be carried out by cheaper labourers, whose produc-tivity could more easily be measured and controlled; another was to invest in machinery which simplified or replaced human labour. As a result, more and more jobs were created which were neither highly skilled nor heavy, and which could be done as easily by women as by men.

Skilled workers tried to defend their control over production and to stop earning power being undermined by unskilled workers, male and female. As part of their defence, they sought to preserve the patriarchal relations that had prevailed in pre-capitalist society, in which men had authority and control over women and children, based in the family home. Capitalism in its early stages had disrupted family life, forcing women, children and men out of their traditional communities and into towns and factories, where human labour was required, regardless of sex or age. Patriarchal relations were consequently under some threat. In a bid to reassert control in the new economic order, men developed a role for themselves as chief family wage-earner – leaving the rest of the work in the home to be performed, unwaged, by women. Thus the attrition between capital and early craft unionism helped to ensure the survival of patriarchy and served the interests of capital by arranging for labour to continue to be reproduced and sustained without paying the people who were doing the necessary work.

This is not to suggest that women were helpless victims of a male conspiracy. We know that many of them fought for the right to waged work and the right to organize. But they were relatively powerless. Moreover, for many of them it may not have seemed an intolerable arrangement to perform a role which approximated – however tenuously – to that of their mothers and grandmothers before industrialization. The appeal of tradition helped to mould familiar relations in the early days of capitalism, and staved off the resistance of women when there was otherwise a strong possibility of change.

This was the arena in which the character of contemporary wage bargaining was formed. It has been concerned with preserving differentials; it has been shaped by the balance of power between different groups of workers; and it has produced hierarchies within the working class with skilled men at the top and women at the bottom.

As new manufacturing processes were developed in the later part of the nineteenth century, male workers followed the pattern set by craftsmen (whether or not they themselves had originally been trained in craft skills) – carving out areas of work, which were designated skilled or semi-skilled, and defending them against intrusion by the lower-paid. As new trade unions were formed, women were usually excluded from these too, as part of men's defence against the danger of having their wages undercut.

William Lazonick and others have pointed out in their study of the textile industry that when the mechanized mule was introduced, it could have been operated by either sex. Instead, men operated the bigger mules and defended their control over the production process:

... the persistence of the internal sub-contract system, with its hierarchical divisions of labour, meant that the job of mule-spinner ... [came to involve] a supervisory as well as an operative function.[6]

The men's union opposed the employment of women as mule-spinners. This had a cumulative effect. By securing the job for themselves and retaining control of skilled and supervisory functions, the men built a basis for stronger trade union organization. And so they were better equipped to fend off threats from female labour, which continued to be low-paid because of women's weak bargaining position. There were similar developments in most manufacturing industries.

The notion of skill in many areas of work eventually had less to do with the content of a job and more to do with the gender and bargaining power of whoever was doing the work, as the history of the English clothing industry illustrates. Throughout the twentieth century, machining in this industry has been done by women and by men. Where it is done by women it is semi-skilled and where it is done by men it is skilled. The two sexes have seldom worked side by side. They have used different machines, usually in separate workshops. However, their respective machining work has not been sufficiently disparate to justify the separate 'skilled' and 'semi-skilled' labels.

The men who worked in the clothing industry at the beginning of this century were engaged in a struggle to preserve dignity, status and control. These attributes relied heavily upon their authority as heads-of-family. The men were forced to take on machine work which was usually done by women and defined as semi-skilled, but they redefined their own machining as skilled labour:

For them, craft status was identified with manhood, and the struggle to maintain their position in the upper level of the labour hierarchy was fuelled by a determination to maintain the traditional balance of power in families where men had always acted as primary breadwinners.[7]

At the present day, women are employed in both the paper-box and cardboard carton industries. They use hand-fed machines to make paper boxes, but the carton-making process is more automated and so requires less concentration. However, in the paper-box industry, the work is considered unskilled, while in carton making it is considered semi-skilled. As Ann Phillips and Barbara Taylor observe in their paper on 'Sex and Skill':

It is hard to escape the conclusion that it is because of the similarities between the work of men and women in the carton industry that women in carton production are considered more skilled than box workers. Men and women work in a similar process; men are recognized as semi-skilled rather than unskilled workers; therefore carton production must be semi-skilled. The women producing paper boxes are simply women producing paper boxes, and however much the work itself might seem to qualify for upgrading, it remains unskilled because it is done by typically unskilled workers – women.[8]

When women were drawn into office work in their thousands at the beginning of this century, they acquired a number of skills – typewriting, shorthand, telephoning, office administration. But they were carefully distinguished from male workers, often in segregated offices with separate entrances. Male clerks – the 'black-coated workers' of the nineteenth century – disappeared from office life and re-emerged in new guises, as managers and trainee managers, accountants and trainee accountants, executives and junior executives. In offices, as in the textile factories, men defended their status by retaining control over key jobs which ensured them a degree of power. The jobs of female office workers were designated *less* skilled than those of men, simply because they were performed by women. And their low status was further confirmed as the work itself became 'feminized'. The female secretary looked after her boss as only a woman could. She brought him cups of tea, dusted his desk, dialled his telephone calls, took his suits to the cleaners, bought presents for his relatives ... became, in short, the office wife. Typists and clerks were regarded (because of their sex) as junior secretaries rather than as junior managers or as a separate category of skilled manual workers – and they, too, found themselves performing wifely duties for the men in the office. Thus, patriarchal relations were re-created in the workplace, guaranteeing the superior status of the male.

Something similar happened in the area of health work. Women were, of course, the original health workers (witches, wise women, midwives)[9], but were supplanted by men, who tried to turn the whole business into an exact science and a closed shop. In the nineteenth century, women re-established themselves in the field by creating their own profession –

largely due to the efforts of Florence Nightingale – to ensure that they were *paid* workers, not voluntary aides (an important gain). To do this, they had to win recognition from the male establishment and the price was to reassure doctors that the female interlopers would pose no threat to their supremacy. The nurse, in Nightingale's words, was to be 'the skilled servant of medicine' who operated 'in strict obedience to the physician's or surgeon's power'. The need to distinguish men's work (diagnosis–prescription) from women's work (treatment–observation) determined the assessment of their respective skills and the very character of health work. And all was justified by defining the woman's role in the workplace in the same terms as her role in the home – as though it were her 'natural' destiny. 'The best nurse is that woman whose maternal instincts are well developed... The connection between mothering and nursing is very close,' decreed *Hospital* journal in 1897; and in 1902: 'A good nurse must first be a good housemaid.'[10]

Will the real breadwinner please stand up?

As men guarded 'skilled' work and organization as exclusive male territory, so the working class remained divided, with a gun at the heads of the strongest sector in the form of a weak, cheap and abundant source of alternative (female) labour. The idea which lay behind this development, and which also served as a defence of male pre-eminence, gathered strength towards the end of the nineteenth century: this was the idea that the man was the main breadwinner for the family. The woman's main role is at home, looking after husband and children. In theory, she does not need paid employment because her husband supports her.

In practice, this support has rarely been forthcoming in most families. Working-class women, however demanding their domestic responsibilities, have always had to turn their hand to a bit of cleaning, child minding, sewing or suchlike for somebody else, to eke out the man's wage. But where this has been the case, the woman's employment has been afforded a different status from the man's work, on the ground that it is only a secondary activity, carried on in addition to her real occupation; her wages and her job are regarded as 'extras' – not of primary importance.

In the early nineteenth century, the idea of an individual male breadwinner earning enough to keep a wife and children was

not at all familiar, and when factory production began to separate the home from the workplace, initially whole families
would go out to work. In agriculture, farmers favoured employing married men, because their wives and children would be
available for seasonal work.

Within the middle class, as commercial and professional
activities increasingly took place outside the home, married
women were transformed, in Ray Strachey's words, 'from partners to parasites' – symbols, in their apparent idleness, of their
husbands' prosperity. Hilary Land explains in her paper, *The
Family Wage*:

Some historians of this period have argued that the working-class man
believed that by restricting the hours women and children could work
in the factory, his hours and conditions would also have to be improved. So too would his pay, for women and children would have
less opportunity to undercut his wages, or indeed to replace him. If
women and children could be removed altogether, then the labour
supply, which throughout much of the nineteenth century was in ex-
cess, would be restricted, and at the same time men could argue more
forcefully and from increased bargaining strength that they needed
wages high enough to support a family, i.e. *a family wage.*[11]

The idea became firmly embedded in trade union philosophy
and has continued to exert a robust influence throughout the
twentieth century. Clearly, women's increased participation in
the labour market has distorted its function in that market. The
family wage is dead – but long live the family wage. It lives on
in the rules which govern supplementary benefits, it lives on in
the minds of men, it lives on as the concept of a 'living wage',
and it underpins the determination of male and female pay.

In her essay 'Class Struggle and the Working-Class Family',
Jane Humphries quotes a labourer's appeal in the *Trades Newspaper*, 16 October 1825:

I recommend my fellow labourers, in preference to every other means
of limiting the number of those who work for wages, to prevent their
wives and children from competing with them in the market...[12]

Humphries argues that women's labour was one of the few
sources of working-class control over labour supply, and it was
one which enjoyed the support of bourgeois ideology. As we
shall see, the failure of working-class men to defend women's
right to waged work is today supported by the most conservative of ideologies.

Almost a century and a half later in 1966, at the annual conference of the Civil Service Clerical Association, a male delegate declared: 'What we want is to give breadwinners throughout the country enough pay to keep their wives at home.'

The National Board for Prices and Incomes (set up by a Labour government with the approval of the TUC) reported in 1971 on the pay and conditions of workers in the contract cleaning industry. This industry had expanded massively since the war, employing some 90,000 general cleaners by the early 1970s; and it was very profitable. Yet, it paid an average hourly rate of 43p, which was 15p less than the median rate for manual workers at that time. The Board maintained that contract cleaning could 'not be seen as a low-paid trade as a whole'. It based its bizarre observation on the fact that it 'set female part-time earnings in the context of their families' income' and, since women's contribution was 'not a major part of the family income', women were therefore 'not in general low paid'.[13]

The Board processed and policed wages and prices; low pay was one of its major targets. It was evident in the early 1970s – as it is now – that the problem with low pay was women's pay and the problem with women's pay was low pay. But the Board managed to camouflage this connection and in doing so it determined the official approach to women's wages which prevails to this day. It defined women's pay as being a separate problem from that of low pay – one which might be dealt with by the new Equal Pay Act (passed in 1970 but not enforced until 1975), but which was not to be dealt with on the same terms as men's low pay. The Board was being not a little disingenuous in assuming the Equal Pay Act would solve the problem for women.

When the Board reported on the pay of health service auxiliary workers in 1971, it noted that a third were men, who were 'among the lowest-paid men in the country'. Their full-time women colleagues grossed only two-thirds of the men's average earnings, but they were 'not low-paid by comparison with women in general'. In its next report, on *General Problems of Low Pay*, the Board remarked that it was

necessary to consider the position of men and women separately; otherwise the problem of low pay could be practically synonymous with that of low pay among women, and this could ignore the social significance of the fact that men's earnings are normally the main source of family income...[14]

This, then, was the triple formula for by-passing the problem of women's pay. First, women's income was not 'a major part of the family income', and although this was *because* they were low-paid, it was also deemed to be the reason why they could not be regarded as low-paid. Secondly, it was recognized that women were often paid less than men, but this aspect of the problem was discarded as something that would magically disappear under the Equal Pay Act. Thirdly, if all else failed, the problem of unequal pay could be overcome by comparing women's pay not with men's pay but with that of women in general.

At the end of the decade, the concept of the family wage was still occupying an important place in wage determination. The term itself has passed out of use in trade union circles, but negotiators – especially those in the lower-paid, blue-collar sectors – will argue that, in order to maintain living standards, it is essential that their members' wages should not fall below supplementary benefit rates for a 'typical family unit'. For example, in 1979, when the unions organizing local authority manual workers submitted their claim to the Clegg Commission on pay comparability, they pointed out that 'in 1978 about half of all full-time workers in local authority services were earning less in terms of their net earnings than a typical family would obtain through social security'.

More than three-quarters of the members for whom these unions were negotiating were female. Not only did this line of argument bear no relation to the real lives of women (wives were not entitled to claim any supplementary benefit at all), but also, as we shall see (p. 151), it did nothing to help the majority of female workers improve their earnings in relation to those of men.

From about 1978 onwards, feminists have begun to challenge the concept of the family wage. They have pointed out that half of all married women go out to work; and it is absurd to suggest that families are not dependent on female earnings, since it has been estimated that the number of families in poverty would *quadruple* if wives did not take paid jobs. In addition, there are some 920,000 one-parent families, bringing up more than 1.5 million children. According to the 1978 General Household Survey, out of the entire 'economically active' population, *only five per cent* can be described as representative of the supposedly typical family unit (i.e. the breadwinning man with a wife and two children to support). The idea that one person's wage

61

should be sufficient to support a family takes no account of the number of children; hence, large families are penalized while childless couples live in clover. What families really need is a substantial increase in child benefit, so that children can be adequately supported regardless of whether one or both parents work, or how much they earn. However, the problem of ensuring a proper income for all families is not a simple one, and is still being argued among feminists – and among trade unionists – at the time of writing. There is a danger in families becoming too dependent on state support, since it is clear from experience of the Thatcher government that benefits and services can swiftly be undermined. Why should not employers be obliged to pay all workers enough to support their dependent relatives?

On the other hand, in pay bargaining, the 'family wage' proposition can be turned against workers: employers can survey the workforce and use the same formulation to justify maintaining differentials between women and men: 'Wives don't need so much money because they don't have families to support.' It is not necessarily safer for families to rely on wages than on the state. After all, what good is the idea of the 'family wage' to the unemployed?

The crux of the feminist case is that the ideology of the 'family wage' has played a vital part in shaping the labour market and in setting women apart from men in lower-paid jobs. It bears a little relation to family needs in the 1980s, yet it still has considerable force, perpetuating inequality between women and men. We take up the question of a new approach to incomes and wage bargaining later, p. 242.

The time factor

Female workers, as we have seen, have been confined to certain kinds of jobs which are regarded as less skilled and which attract lower pay. Linked with this has been the appropriation by men of the role of chief family breadwinner, and the designation of women as unpaid domestic labourers. Men's superior bargaining strength has left women no choice about this: they have continued to do paid work but, because of their domestic role, they have developed a very different relationship to working time. And this has intensified their unequal position in the labour market.

Women need to work to earn money, but they are busy: they

have to look after their homes, husbands and children. They cannot work long hours of overtime, or awkward shifts which interfere with cooking family meals or dispatching children to school. There are periods of their lives when they need to work short hours; and there are times when they cannot work at all.

By makeshift means and from necessity, they have reduced their hours of paid employment to what might, in any other time and place, be considered a model schedule for a working week. It has never been viewed as such, and has never been given organized political muscle. For reducing the working week, women have been financially penalized, and made to suffer contractual and professional disadvantage. Men's relationship to working time expresses their absenteeism from domestic responsibility. The fiction of a full-time working week depends on long hours being worked by people who are in turn dependent on others to do their domestic work for them. The time-and-motion constraints on motherhood (fatherhood being the passive mode of parenthood) are nowhere more manifest than in the pattern of the waged working time.

Two out of five female employees work less than 30 hours a week, compared with one in twenty men. About one in four women work less than 16 hours. Ninety per cent of women who work less than 30 hours are married and two-thirds have dependent children. Men work longer basic hours: among full timers, 40 per cent of women and only 27 per cent of men work a basic week of 35–39 hours, while 48 per cent of women and 65 per cent of men work 44–48 basic hours a week. Almost twice as many men as women work overtime.

Women's working lifetime has a different pattern from men's. Before the Second World War, women most commonly worked in their late teens and early twenties before they got married, and then left the labour market altogether. By 1971, the pattern had changed entirely: most women now work until their mid-twenties and then return to employment after a period of child-rearing, in their late thirties and forties. If they work in between, it tends to be on a casual, intermittent basis.

According to a major survey published in *Woman's Own* in February 1979, 27 per cent of mothers with children under five and 20 per cent of mothers with children aged 5–16 were not employed, but wanted to be. Families with growing children need more money than young, childless couples, or middle-aged couples whose children have left home. But the *Woman's Own* survey showed that four out of five mothers would still want to go out to work, at least some of the time, 'even in an ideal world where all financial pressures were removed'. The same survey identified a 'lack of suitable child care facilities' as a major stumbling block. Nearly one in five mothers with children under eleven had given up their employment because they couldn't make adequate arrangements for their children.

The uneven distribution of working time between women and men has a bearing on the kind of work that women are obliged to do, and on the degree of protection they enjoy from exploitative rates of pay and from redundancy. As they have defined themselves as the main wage earners for their families, men have negotiated with employers (explicitly or implicitly) to reach a definition of a *proper* job, and to agree an appropriate life-style for a *real* worker. A 'proper' job begins after school or college and continues without a break until retirement age. It lasts for at least eight hours a day; it might spill over into evenings and weekends; and its most demanding phase tends to be the first twenty years, as training is acquired and vital steps are taken towards a higher earning capacity. This coincides with the period when children are young and most in need of parental time. However, a 'real' worker does not have distracting family commitments, and is available for overtime and night work if necessary. A 'real' worker is able to move from one part of the country to another if that is what the employer requires.

Jobs that are normally done by men have developed along these lines. In some instances, the work itself demands that jobs are organized in a certain way – for instance in industries which rely on continuous processes, or in hospitals, where the work cannot cease. But more often than not, the gender of the worker plays a large part in determining the structure of the job, just as it helps to determine how far the job is regarded as 'skilled'.

Women are not considered 'real workers' because they cannot normally fulfil the necessary conditions (and even if they can it is assumed that they can't). Many of the jobs they do are arranged to fit in more easily with their prior commitments at home; but these are not seen as 'proper' jobs. They are casual and peripheral; they have no place in any career structure. Young women are often passed over for training and promotion because they intend (or are expected) to have a break from employment while their children are young. When they return to the labour market they are thought to have missed (rather than gained) valuable experience; only the lower-paid jobs are available to them.

Laws were passed in the nineteenth century which prohibited female factory workers from working long hours of overtime or at night. Few women actively desire to do so, unless they have no other way of earning a living; nor for that matter do many men. To repeal the laws at this stage (as the CBI and the Equal Opportunities Commission propose) would no doubt only increase the exploitation of female workers since they could be forced to work long, unsocial hours if no other paid jobs were available, while continuing to do a second, unpaid job at home. Nevertheless these 'protective laws' are an expression of men's status as wage earners with only minimal commitments at home. In the past they have helped to exclude women from a range of better-paid manual jobs and to confirm their domestic role.

Some women take work into their own homes where, for a degree of control over their time, they pay a heavy price. It has been estimated that there are between 100,000 and 150,000 'homeworkers'. They sew, knit, pack, assemble and paint goods. Isolated from their fellow workers, they are almost entirely unorganized. They may choose their own hours and pace of work, but they are otherwise powerless and can neither bargain for their pay nor secure a steady supply of employment. Less than one per cent of homeworkers are male.[15]

A homeworker has no legal protection – against sacking, redundancy or the hazards of her work – unless she fights to be recognized as an employee (rather than a self-employed person) before an industrial tribunal. A handful have fought and won, but the great majority neither know that the opportunity is open to them, nor dare to risk their livelihood by taking action against their employer.

Women who work short hours are penalized in a similar way. Like homeworkers, they are not considered 'real' workers and do not get the same legal protection as full-timers. A person who works less than sixteen hours a week has no legal protection from unfair dismissal or redundancy unless she has been in the same workplace for at least five years – and then only if she works more than eight hours a week.[16]

Only certain kinds of work are available to people who cannot work more than thirty-odd hours a week. The labour market has been designed in such a way that women whose time is taken up with domestic responsibilities have no choice but to do different jobs from men – jobs which carry lower status, fewer benefits and less pay. The very description 'part-time worker' carries a kind of stigma. Yet why should less than thirty hours (or less than twenty for that matter) be considered only 'part-time'? Only in a labour market regulated by men could such a term be accepted.

So well established are these patterns that it makes little difference whether or not individual women actually *have* family responsibilities, or whether they are suited to 'women's work'. They are edged into it by a combination of their own education, which prepares them for 'women's work', the expectations of employers, who usually judge them according to their gender rather than their individual aptitudes, and the reluctance of men in general to envisage any other way of arranging paid employment and domestic labour. (A study published jointly by the National Union of Teachers and the Equal Opportunities Commission in 1980,[17] showed that although women were concentrated in the lower-paid teaching jobs, this could not be explained by their family responsibilities. Many had none, but it did not seem to help their careers. There was a large element of straight discrimination, camouflaged by a general supposition that teachers were mothers of young children.)

Pay and the patriarchal bonus

As we have seen, women and men are often segregated by employers in order that women can be paid less. Men have monopolized work which is defined as 'skilled', commanding higher pay, and they have appropriated the role of family breadwinner. Women have always been more poorly organized than men. And where they are restricted by their domestic responsibilities to certain jobs (which men don't do) employers are able to exploit them with greater ease. These are the main factors which have determined the relative strengths of male and female pay.

Homeworkers, who are at the bottom of the pile, earn a pittance. A 1979 survey found that nearly two-thirds of homeworkers earned under 60 pence an hour (less than a third of the national average hourly earnings); and as many as a third of homeworkers earned 20 pence an hour – a *tenth* of the national average.[18]

Part-time workers usually earn well below what is considered 'low pay' (£60 a week in 1979) because of their restricted hours.

In addition, they earn less per hour than full-timers. In 1979, for example, 79.5 per cent of part-time women workers (i.e. nearly two and three-quarter million) were earning less than £1.50 an hour, compared with 47.8 per cent of full-time women and 12.5 per cent of full-time men.[19]

Most women who work full-time are excluded from higher-paid jobs because they cannot spend as much time in paid employment as men can, and because they are ill-prepared to compete on equal terms with men. As the tables on p. 78 show, in 1970, women's average gross earnings were £16.20 a week, which amounted to 5.5 per cent of the male average of £29.70 a week. By 1979, they had risen to £63 a week, but were still no more than 63.6 per cent of the male average £99. Their hourly earnings caught up a little faster, but not much – from 63 per cent of the male average in 1970 to 73 per cent in 1979.[20] (The reasons for this discrepancy between weekly and hourly earnings will soon become clear.)

Women are still concentrated in lower-paid jobs in all areas of employment. They have also remained concentrated in the lower-paid industries, where unionization is weak, and where the only safeguards against exploitation are the myopic, toothless watchdogs of the Wages Councils. These were set up at the beginning of this century to mitigate the poverty of the 'sweated trades'. They include representatives of workers and employers, and they establish statutory minimum rates, below which they are supposed to ensure wages do not fall. These rates are very low. For example, in January 1980, the minimum was £40 a week for toy makers, £36 for employees in hairdressing and £43.50 for boot and shoe repairers. They do nothing to cushion women from the effects of unequal pay. In April 1979, when the average Wages Council minimum was £39 a week, the average earnings of men in the Wages Council industries was £79.30, while the female average was only £49.75. It is left to 150 investigators employed by the Wages Inspectorate to make sure there are no illegal underpayments. In 1978, the Inspectorate visited less than ten per cent of all workplaces covered by Wages Councils – and even then it managed to find an underpayment rate of 26.5 per cent.[21] Clearly, the Wages Councils, like the Equal Opportunities Commission (which we examine in another chapter, p. 123) serve only to *contain* the problem they were allegedly set up to solve.

Not only are women located in lower-paid jobs and in lower-paid industries, but their pay is structured differently from men's. A range of extra payments has been organized by men to accompany the 'proper' jobs that 'real' workers do. A 1980 Department of Employment survey looked at the incomes of women and men who were doing the same work for the same employer. The researchers found that although both sexes were getting paid the same basic rates and were usually working the same basic hours, there was still a big difference in their take-home pay:

Men work more overtime, do more shiftwork, have been employed for longer to qualify for length of service awards and hold a disproportionate number of merit or responsibility positions.[22]

This confirms the results of the 1978 New Earnings Survey, which found that 41 per cent of male workers received overtime payments, compared with only 12 per cent of women; and that 16 per cent of men and only 9 per cent of women received shift premia.

The fact that most women's working lives are divided into two phases has a devastating effect on their pay. It prevents them earning long-service increments and – even more damagingly – it closes off promotion to higher-paid jobs. As the NUT survey has shown, this affects even women whose careers are not broken by family responsibilities.[23]

Productivity payments are another important source of extra money for men. The 1978 New Earnings Survey found that 29 per cent of men and only 13 per cent of women received additional 'payment by results'. Women are concentrated in service jobs which are often unsuited to productivity agreements. (How do you organize an incentive scheme for nurses, home helps or secretaries?) And women tend to have a different approach to their jobs – perhaps because they carry over into paid employment their attitudes to the work they do for their families. In November 1980 we visited a weekend women's school of the public employees' union, NUPE. The women were invited to consider a list of six bargaining issues (pay, child care, bonuses, etc.) and to list them in order of priority. Most of them put pay near the top of the list, but they all put bonuses right at the bottom. Later, when they discussed what they had done, there was great hilarity as they discovered their mutual hatred for the productivity bonus. They all felt it would taint their commitment to their work, and, moreover, in most of their jobs, productivity could not be measured.

The left in the labour movement has consistently opposed

productivity deals on the grou...
arbitrary privileges to some wor...
threaten safety in some industries...

What all these factors add up to is ...
of men's earnings – something appro...
pay packet – accrues to them as a res...
tionship *as men* to domestic life and to p...
massive patriarchal bonus has proved to ...
the campaign for equal pay by the unions...
movement, and to the limp intervention of the ...

During the 1970s, the character of the labou... ...egan
to change dramatically, and in ways which ha... ...iminished
rather than enhanced any prospect of improvement for women.
One source of change has been the spread of micro-technology; another has been the steady rise in unemployment,
brought about by the economic recession and the government's
new infatuation with monetarist policies.

A chip off the old block

The silicon chip has been associated with the female sex ever
since it made its first major appearances in public. It was
photographed on the tip of a model's nose, and as a tiny speck
on a pretty woman's front tooth. What a delightful, amusing little
thing it was! When we learned of its immense powers, it was
just like science fiction – and we were lulled by the sense of
fantasy. It was exciting to imagine machines doing all that work
for us, and impressive to know that the human race was capable
of inventing such a marvel. We were told it would improve the
quality of our lives, give us more leisure, make our jobs more
streamlined, cleaner and more pleasant, make Britain prosper
again. By the time we began to fear that it would take control
of our lives and destroy our jobs (another science fiction fantasy, difficult to grasp as something that was really happening),
it was too late. For there it was already – the word processor
on the desk top, the robot on the factory floor, the calculator in
our pockets, the space-age gadgets in our homes. It was 'progress' and therefore (surely?) inevitable and A Good Thing.
Who wanted to be branded as a Luddite?

The trade unions were in a dilemma. How could they defend
their members' jobs *and* embrace the new technology? They
tried to sustain a rosy image of Britain's micro-chip future. In
1979, the Trades Union Congress passed a composite motion

as the harbinger of a new (perhaps even presented, said the motion, a

unparalleled opportunity for Britain to improve its economic performance and also its competitiveness in world markets whilst improving living standards, affording more leisure to employees, eliminating dreary work and improving communications between people and nations.

That same year a delegation (all male, all white) from the TUC Economic Committee visited the famous Silicon Valley in the United States, and reported on its return that 'to be a significant industrial nation, the UK has to put a major effort both into chip manufacture and its applications'. When the government decided to put money into Inmos, a new enterprise to mass produce the latest type of integrated circuit, this was welcomed by the left. Such criticisms as there were concerned the relatively low level of British investment, compared with similar ventures in the US and Japan. The main thing was that Britain should not be left behind in the international race. Only passing attention was paid to one of the main reasons why foreign manufacturers were such formidable competitors – and that was their exploitation of cheap, unorganized female labour, especially in the Third World.

Rachael Grossman worked for ten weeks in the microelectronics factories of Southeast Asia and published a report in the *Southeast Asia Chronicle* in 1979. The women in the factories mounted and tested chips under microscopes, for starvation wages, and in hazardous conditions, often resorting to prostitution when their usefulness on the assembly line had come to an end.

After three or four years of peering through a microscope, a worker's vision begins to blur so she can no longer meet the production quota. Workers who must dip components in acids and rub them with solvents frequently experience burns, dizziness, nausea, sometimes even losing their fingers in accidents. It will be ten or fifteen years before the carcinogenic effects begin to show up in the women who work with them now.[24]

Most computer hardware includes components produced by such women. It remains to be seen how far the nature of the work, pay and conditions at Inmos will resemble those offered in the factories of Southeast Asia. And what will the wondrous new generation of chips do for workers in other industries who are still lucky enough to have jobs?

Estimates of the numbers of jobs that will be lost through the introduction of new technology have varied enormously. However, no one has disputed the fact that micro-technology is ideally suited to replace many of the unskilled and semi-skilled jobs that are normally done by women. Nor does anyone doubt that employers find it a great deal easier to introduce new machinery where they do not have to reckon with strong trade unions. (In Fleet Street, trade union resistance has delayed the introduction of new printing technology for more than a decade.) Among the most vulnerable areas of women's work are assembly-line jobs in manufacturing, stock control in retailing, telephone operating, banking and – above all – secretarial and clerical work.

Emma Bird, an employee of a computer consultancy firm who produced a report for the Equal Opportunities Commission in 1980, predicted that 64,000 word processors would be installed in British offices by 1985; one in three would replace one worker, causing 21,000 job losses in the secretarial and clerical fields.[25] APEX, the office workers' union, was less sanguine, predicting that one job would be lost for each new machine.[26] But a more useful perspective is provided by the following reports of changes that have already taken place:

- Bradford Council reduced its staff in one section from 44 to 22 with the introduction of nine word processors, resulting in an increased productivity of 19 per cent and an estimated annual saving of £59,000.

- The British Standards Institute created a centralized specialist work processing department when it installed ten IBM word processors. The Institute handles a large quantity of long technical documents that go through several drafting and correction stages. The number of secretaries and typists employed fell by a third.

- The Provident Financial Group installed three IBM memory typewriters into a central typing pool. They reduced their full-time typing staff from twenty-seven to seventeen, their part-time staff from thirteen to three, and increased the workload. (Jobs were cut through natural wastage.)

- The Halifax Building Society progressed from automatic typewriters which they had used for ten years to a system of sixteen IBM word processors. The workforce was not reduced, but the workload almost trebled. The typists are at the new machines all day apart from two fifteen-minute breaks and a lunch break.

- The Central Electricity Generating Board has reduced the number of 'girls' employed at its typing centre in Bristol from over fifty to twenty-six. The advantage of the new machines, the supervisor reports, is that 'a less experienced typist is able to produce the same quality of work as a really skilled girl and almost as quickly'.[27]

Manufacturers of word processing machinery have stressed the inefficiency of conventional office working arrangements. And well they might. Most secretarial workers spend very little time actually *producing*, since their main function is to service male workers – or, at any rate, to be available in case servicing is required. Few people care to contest the claim of one management consultancy firm that the typical secretary spends only two per cent of her time typing, the rest being occupied with a range of tasks and diversions, including talk, fetching-and-carrying, making coffee and waiting for work. It may be a luxury the employer can no longer afford, as this 1980 advertisement in the *Guardian* suggests:

The Olivetti 401 word processor can do well over a month's work in a week, and the lease works out at only £26 per week. About the same as it costs to employ a secretary for a day...

Clerical and administrative workers make up 30 per cent of all workers in manufacturing industries, and 45 per cent of the total UK workforce. In the harsh economic climate of the late 1970s and early 1980s, it seems increasingly likely that in this single instance the interests of capital will override the interests of patriarchy. The 'office wife' will be put out of business, at all levels except the very top, where senior executives will no doubt retain them as symbols of their superior power. The rest of the men will have machines instead. These are becoming more and more sophisticated, threatening to take over not only shorthand and re-typing of draft documents, but filing and posting as well, by transmitting the written word electronically from one 'business centre' to another and filing copies automatically.

Not that patriarchy will be threatened in any serious way. For there is no question of this 'micro-chip revolution' improving the lot of female office workers. If women are not put out of work altogether, they may perhaps be retrained to operate the new machines. Their old skills are redundant, but their new function requires hardly any skill at all. Neither speed nor accuracy is necessary to be a competent keyboard operator, since typing errors can swiftly be erased and the machines print automatically and very fast. A worker loses the chance of expressing her individuality – for example, by devising her own filing system or by establishing a personal rapport with her boss. Her work can be closely monitored and measured. In short, she loses what little control she previously had over her job. Jane Barker and Hazel Downing have described the 'culture of resistance' which is peculiar to the female office worker:

She can sit on work and pretend to be too busy to have a chat, she can find any number of excuses for the lateness of a particular document ('I ran out of paper and had to go to stationery'; 'the ribbon got stuck'). Control also over her space and movements; going off to the loo for a chat and a cigarette, to touch up make-up or to read a book; going to visit someone on the next floor on the pretext of collecting a document. Those extra little jobs which women are expected to perform just because they are women, such as making the tea, watering the plants, organizing leaving present collections, going out to the shops to collect something for the boss, while on the one hand reinforcing ideologically their role as 'office wife', can be used to create *space* and time away from the routine of typing.[28]

Office automation changes all that. Plugged into a set of earphones, connected to a centralized dictating system, the keyboard operator just types. The machine monitors the speed at which she works and banks up new work, to be fed to her as soon as she is free. She is an assembly-line worker, with no means of resisting her employer's control. This unofficial report on the introduction of office automation to Bradford Council offices gives a taste of things to come.

The machines are in constant operation, and are programmed by the rate material comes in. The workers have one ten-minute break in the morning and afternoon, and otherwise have no contact with other workers during office time. All the new work comes in through a special anti-static glass box, and no non-section workers enter the room. The operator has almost no contact with the finished product. . . the existing tenuous relationship between a typist and her work is finally broken altogether. There is no sense any longer in which it is *her* work.[29]

Some may argue that the transformation of the 'office wife' into a semi-skilled manual labourer has its advantages. By breaking the (misconceived) bond of loyalty between the worker and her boss, it may encourage her to become involved in trade union activity, and so to replace one means of resistance with another – this time one that doesn't depend on her sexual subordination. Both forms of employment are grossly exploitative, for different reasons; but the crucial factor is how much control women can exercise over their work.

Unemployment: the largest female ghetto

Secretarial work has been the last of the female work ghettos to offer a relatively abundant supply of jobs. By the end of the 1970s, that was changing fast. Where human labour has not been replaced by machinery, it is in danger of being dispensed with anyway, and this trend has intensified as the recession has deepened.

Throughout the country, jobs have been disappearing at a phenomenal rate. As tables 4 and 5 (pp. 78–9) show, in all but two years of the decade, a larger proportion of women than men have joined the dole queues; and in industries where they are concentrated, the *proportion* of women out of work has risen steadily. The great post-war boom in female employment has been abruptly halted and thrown into reverse. In particular the public services, a chief source of new jobs for women, have been cut back savagely. According to official figures, there were 737,200 women unemployed in September 1981.

The figures reflect only the numbers who register as unemployed. More women began to do this after May 1977, when newly married women ceased to be able to opt out of paying full National Insurance contributions. (Women who before 1977 took up this 'married women's option' to pay reduced insurance and who have retained it since, aren't eligible for the dole. Even when they are unemployed, they often don't bother with the registration process, which is a precondition of claiming the dole, but is of no benefit to them.) Nevertheless, there are still vast numbers of women who would work if they were able to find jobs, but who do not register. Some have children and other responsibilities at home; they want paid employment and would find ways of combining it with their domestic work, but in the meantime they are kept busy at home and don't identify themselves among 'the unemployed'. Many others are part-timers who have lost their jobs and consider themselves unemployed, but are barred from registering because they are not available for full-time work. And then there are the thousands of mothers who are unwillingly out of a job, because they cannot make arrangements for their children: technically they are not available for work and so cannot register, yet they too are unemployed and keen to get jobs. Men are not constrained in these ways. The official figures present a far less comprehensive picture of female than male unemployment.

A survey conducted in January and February 1981 by Market and Opinion Research International (MORI) showed that one million people, the great majority of them women, were without jobs, available for work and yet did not show up in the official unemployment statistics. When this missing million was added to the government's figure, then 2.5 million out of work, the number of unemployed women almost matched the number of unemployed men. Yet the official figures showed jobless men outnumbering jobless women by 2½ to one. Although there is a great deal of talk on the left about the need to reduce unemployment, and indeed to create 'full employment', the prospect of this happening in the 1980s is very remote. Peter Kellner has pointed out that, in order to reduce the level of *registered* unemployment by 2½ million, four million new jobs would have to be created; at the same time, the number of people of working age is expected to increase by almost 800,000 before 1987.[30] One problem is, of course, that 'full employment' means different things to women and to men, because of their different relationship to working time.

It is apparent that women still represent a 'reserve army of labour', to be called up and disbanded again, according to the vagaries of the economic and political climate. This can be seen most clearly in relation to 'part-time' women in manufacturing. Irene Breughel has analysed fluctuations in the workforce to show that in 1973–4, when the economy expanded briefly, the employment of part-time women in manufacturing rose by 15 per cent; but in 1974–5, when the 'mini-boom' was over, it fell by 10 per cent, and by another 8 per cent the following year.[31]

The pattern is not always so straightforward. Some employers try to reduce their core workforce of relatively expensive full-time men, and draw upon the cheaper, casual labour of homeworkers or part-time women, as demand ebbs and flows. On balance, however, part-timers and homeworkers fare a lot worse than full-timers. It is easier to get rid of them because they are less well-organized and they don't have the same legal protection. Moreover, the very work they do is often seen as peripheral, and therefore more dispensable as far as the employer is concerned.

As jobs for men have grown scarcer, so the idea has gathered strength that they, not women, should have the first claim on whatever paid work is available. In a national survey conducted in 1980, male and female workers were asked if they agreed with the statement: 'Where jobs are scarce, married women should be discouraged from working.' Of the men, 38 per cent agreed; of the women, 28 per cent. Among blue-collar workers, 42 per cent of men and 27 per cent of women agreed.[32] Women's domestic role marks them out as a separate category from men. Men are designated 'real' workers. Women are not. Not only is their 'right' to work illusory, but their foothold in the labour market is far more tenuous than they have supposed.

There has nevertheless been a profound change in women's consciousness and a new consensus about what it is *possible* for women to do. This has emerged out of the women's liberation movement, and has been reinforced by the new 'equality' laws, whose propaganda effect has certainly exceeded their practical impact on working life. No one is outraged to hear from the Equal Opportunities Commission that a woman has become an engineer or a trade union organizer, and increasing numbers of women want to do these things: an important step in the right direction.

There has also been a mass entry of women into trade union membership – which expresses a new determination to organize, even if they have been frustrated to find they are still excluded from power. Valuable lessons have been learned from the ten-year fight for 'equal opportunity' which have led women to reshape their demands and call for 'positive action' in favour of women, instead of just an end to discrimination against them.

We review women's experience of the 1970s legal reforms, and their efforts to establish a footing in the unions, in Chapters 4 and 5. But first we look at the political developments of the later 1970s, which have altered the context in which the struggle for women's liberation continues.

Table 1
Women workers in major occupation groups, 1911–1971

Female workers as a percentage of all workers in each of the
major occupation groups identified by Bain and Price*

Occupational groups	1911	1921	1931	1951	1961	1971
Employers and proprietors	18.8	20.5	19.8	20.0	20.4	24.9
White collar workers	29.8	37.6	35.8	42.3	44.5	47.9
(a) managers and administrators	19.8	17.0	13.0	15.2	15.5	21.6
(b) higher professionals	6.0	5.1	7.5	8.3	9.7	9.9
(c) lower professionals and technicians	62.9	59.4	58.8	53.5	50.8	52.1
(d) foremen and inspectors	4.2	6.5	8.7	13.4	10.3	13.1
(e) clerks	21.4	44.6	46.0	60.2	65.2	73.2
(f) salesmen and shop assistants	35.2	43.6	37.2	51.6	54.9	59.8
All manual workers	30.5	27.9	28.8	26.1	26.0	29.4
(a) skilled	24.0	21.0	21.3	15.7	13.8	13.5
(b) semi-skilled	40.4	40.3	42.9	38.1	39.3	46.5
(c) unskilled	15.5	16.8	15.0	20.3	22.4	37.2
Total occupied population	29.6	29.5	29.8	30.8	32.4	36.5

Source: Table 3 in G. S. Bain and R. Price, 'Union growth and employment
trends in the United Kingdom 1964–1970', *British Journal of Industrial
Relations*, 10, November 1972, pp. 366–381. The authors' analysis of
census data 1911–1961 was repeated with 1971 census data for Great
Britain to update their time series, with the following modifications of their
method:

(a) 1971 census separately identified/self-employed with or without
employees. The self-employed with employees were classified in the
'Employers and proprietors' group and the self-employed without
employees were added to their respective occupational group.
(b) Lists of occupational groups in each order as given in G. S. Bain,
The Growth of White Collar Unionism, Clarendon Press, Oxford, 1970,
pp. 189–190 were adhered to except when an overlap in definitions
required 1971 figures to be split proportionately to the 1961 census
distribution.

Quoted in Hakim, C. *Occupational Segregation*, Department of Employment,
1979.

Table 2
Average gross hourly earnings excluding the effect of overtime, employees aged 18 and over, 1970–1979

						Pence per hour	
	1970	1974	1975	1976	1977	1978	1979
Men	67.4	104.8	136.3	162.9	177.4	200.3	226.9
Women	42.5	70.6	98.3	122.4	133.9	148.0	165.7
Differential	24.9	34.2	38.0	39.5	43.5	52.3	61.2
Women's earnings as a % of men's	63.1	67.4	72.1	75.1	75.5	73.9	73.0

Source: New Earnings Survey 1970–79, Part A. Tables 10 and 11.

Table 3
Average gross weekly earnings, including the effects of overtime, employees aged 18 and over, 1970–1979

						£ per week	
	1970	1974	1975	1976	1977	1978	1979
Men	29.7	47.7	60.8	71.8	78.6	87.1	99.0
Women	16.2	26.9	37.4	46.2	51.0	56.4	63.0
Differential	13.5	20.8	23.4	25.6	27.6	30.7	36.0
Women's earnings as a % of men's	54.5	56.4	61.5	64.3	64.9	64.8	63.6

Source: New Earnings Survey 1970–79, Part A. Tables 10 and 11.

Table 4
Rate of increase each year of male and female unemployment 1971–80 (UK)

Year	Male Increase in 000s	% increase	Female Increase in 000s	% increase
1971–2	+ 11.3	+ 1.6	+ 12.1	+ 8.6
1972–3	−248.3	−35.0	− 57.9	− 37.9
1973–4	+ 70.3	+15.2	+ 23.2	+ 24.6
1974–5	+351.3	+66.0	+144.5	+122.0
1975–6	+176.5	+20.0	+133.7	+ 51.0
1976–7	+ 64.5	+ 6.1	+ 88.9	+ 22.5
1977–8	− 83.2	− 7.4	− 8.2	− 1.7
1978–9	−105.0	−10.1	− 18.2	− 3.8
1979–80	+442.7	+47.3	+202.3	+ 44.1

Table 5
Women as % of unemployed by industry 1975–1980

	1975	1976	1977	1978	1979	1980
Clothing & Footwear	66.5	68.5	71.9	75.1	76.9	75.0
Professional & Scientific Services	43.6	49.3	53.0	55.2	58.1	59.3
Miscellaneous Services	30.3	35.2	38.0	39.6	41.0	40
Distributive Trades	32.6	37.7	40.3	42.8	45.0	44.8
Insurance, Banking, Finance & Business Services	26.5	33.0	35.9	37.7	39.8	41.3
Leather, Leather Goods & Fur	24.6	28.7	33.1	31.9	35.8	37.1
Textiles	29.8	34.3	35.8	40.1	40.3	39.4
Public administration & Defence	16.7	21.2	24.3	25.3	29.5	29.6
Food, Drink & Tobacco	25.4	29.6	31.6	33.7	36.0	36.7

Source: Department of Employment Gazette, 1975–1980.

Notes to Chapter 2

1 *Breakthrough*, EOC, Manchester, 1980.
2 Hakim, C. *Occupational Segregation*, Department of Employment Research Paper no. 9, November 1979.
3 Ibid.
4 Coote, A. and Kellner, P. 'Women Workers and Union Power' in *Hear This, Brother*, New Statesman, 1980; and IFF Research Ltd, 'Inquiry into the Employment of Women', *Department of Employment Gazette*, November 1980.
5 IFF Research Ltd (see 4, above).
6 Lazonick, W. *et al.* 'Division of Labour in the Textile Industry', *Cambridge Journal of Economics*, no. 3, 1979.
7 Phillips, A. and Taylor, B. 'Sex and Skill: Notes towards a Feminist Economics', *Feminist Review*, no. 6, 1980.
8 Ibid.
9 See Chamberlain, M. *Old Wives Tales*, Virago, 1981.
10 Gamarnikow, E. 'Sexual Division of Labour: The Case of Nursing', in Kuhn, A. and Wolpe, A. *Feminism and Materialism*, Routledge & Kegan Paul, 1978.
11 Land, H. *The Family Wage*, Eleanor Rathbone Memorial Lecture, 1979.
12 Humphries, J. 'Class Struggle and the Working-Class Family', in Lamsden, A. H. (ed.) *The Economics of Women and Work*, Penguin, 1980.
13 NBPI Report no. 165, *Prices, Profits and Costs in Food Distribution*, Cmnd. 4645, HMSO, London 1971.
14 NBPI Report no. 169, *General Problems of Low Pay*, Cmnd. 4648, HMSO, London 1971.

15 Crine, S. *The Hidden Army*, Low Pay Unit, London 1979.
16 Sedley, A. *Part-Time Workers Need Full-Time Rights*, NCCL, London 1980.
17 *Promotion and the Woman Teacher*, EOC, Manchester 1980.
18 Crine, S. op. cit.
19 Hurstfield, J. 'Part-time Pittance', *Low Pay Review*, Low Pay Unit, June 1980.
20 Equal Opportunities Commission, *Fourth Annual Report*, EOC, Manchester 1980, pp. 79–80.
21 Low Pay Unit, *Minimum Wages for Women*, EOC, Manchester 1980.
22 IFF Research Ltd, op. cit.
23 *Promotion and the Woman Teacher*, op. cit.
24 Grossman, R. 'Changing Role of S.E. Asian Women', *Southeast Asian Chronicle*, Pacific Research, SRC no. 66/PSC, vol. 9(5).
25 Bird, E. *Information Technology in the Office: the Impact on Women's Jobs*, EOC, Manchester 1980.
26 Association of Professional, Executive, Clerical and Computer Staffs (APEX), *Office Technology, The Trade Union Response*, London 1979.
27 Counter Information Service, *The New Technology*, CIS Anti-Report, no. 23.
28 Barker, J. and Downing, H. *Office Automation, Word Processing and the Transformation of Patriarchal Relations*, January 1979.
29 Ibid.
30 Kellner, P. 'Maggie's Missing Million', *New Statesman*, 27 March 1981; and 'But what exactly is Labour's alternative?', *New Statesman*, 3 July 1981.
31 Breughel, I. 'Women as a Reserve Army of Labour', *Feminist Review*, no. 3, 1979.
32 Coote, A. and Kellner, P. op. cit.

3 Family

The idea of women as a reserve army of labour is double-sided, in a sense. Women are a spare resource for employers in times of expansion; they are also a spare resource for politicians to call upon in times of recession. When it ceases to be convenient to spend money on public services, responsibility is handed back to those two euphemisms for unpaid female labour, 'the community' and 'the family'. The family is the basic unit of the community and the vast increase in numbers of women going out to work has made little difference to the division of labour in the family home.

Women still do the lion's share of the work and – no less important – still carry the responsibility for getting it done. Women take care of planning meals, shopping, cooking, cleaning, washing, ironing, mending, equipping and ordering the household, clothing and caring for children . . . and much more besides. Women remember to pay the milkman; they listen, soothe, praise and comfort their menfolk and their children; they anticipate needs, watch for signs of ill-health or distress, remember where things are, keep spare light bulbs, telephone relatives, and pop in to see the old lady round the corner . . . this is not a sentimental catalogue of How Wonderful Mum Is, but a job description. It is the work women do while men put in a few more hours of overtime to increase their pay, or stay late at the office to put themselves in line for promotion, or go to union meetings to improve their bargaining power, or go to the pub or a football match to maintain a sense of male solidarity, or keep pigeons or play snooker to amuse themselves, or tinker with the car or potter in the garden (work of a kind, but not *essential* work), or read the newspaper or watch the television or rest after a hard day, or (perhaps a bit more than in the past) *help* around the house. This is the way family work is arranged in most British households, whether or not both parents are engaged in paid employment. It is seldom measured scientifically, but the evidence is all around us. Oc-

casionally figures emerge in the course of more general research – like these from the Gallup Poll on child care conducted for *Woman's Own*:

One in six husbands has never looked after his child on his own. One-quarter have never put their children to bed. One in three has never even read to their own children. Younger wives get slight help but, generally, wives are still left to shoulder the overwhelming majority of work involved in being a parent. Even in families where the mother works full-time, three-quarters of fathers never take time off work if their children are ill, and never collect them from school.

(17 February 1979)

In this chapter, we look at the politicians' campaign to promote 'the family' as an alternative to the welfare state, which has amounted to a concerted attack on the rights and status of women. We examine the implications of spending cuts in the public sector, and the reasons why traditional relations within the family have remained so intransigent.

Women's 'right' to work for wages has been open to doubt, but their 'right' to work for nothing – as wives, mothers and general servants in their own homes – has been considered absolute. In the early 1970s, it seemed possible that the effect might be mitigated: the trend was towards more, not fewer, social services to relieve the burden of women's domestic labour. But by the end of the decade the trend had been reversed – first by a Labour government under James Callaghan and Chancellor Denis Healey and then, to a fanatical degree, by a Conservative government under Margaret Thatcher and Chancellor Sir Geoffrey Howe.

The decision to cut back public services was first presented as an economic necessity. Britain was spending more than it was earning and therefore, we were told, the spending would have to be cut. There were alternatives, of course: to increase taxes, cut the defence budget, reduce the prison population or withdraw from the Common Market. But they were not politically expedient. 'Regrettably', therefore, less money would be available for health, welfare and education. These services were often passionately defended at a local level, but anger, on the whole, was muted.

A change had taken place in public opinion since the 1960s, aided by Tory propaganda and abetted by right-wing Labour leaders. By the late 1970s, there was a general recognition that Britain was a nation in decline, accompanied by a growing sense that somehow this was *our* fault; we therefore no longer deserved the welfare state (which somehow belonged to 'Them', not us) as we had done before. Its institutions frequently came under attack, and not without some justification. Schools were said to be too large and unruly ... hospital waiting lists were too long ... social workers left children to be battered to death ... there were too many bureaucrats ... too much red tape ... too many 'scroungers'. Feminists criticized the machinery of the welfare state for its methods of policing women within the family, and its premise of women's financial dependence on the men with whom they slept. By the time the Conservatives launched their all-out attack on the welfare state in the run-up to the 1979 general election, the ground had been well prepared for them – by Labour's own cuts, by the signs of a general loss of faith, and by the failings of the services themselves, diligently noted in the Tory press.

The family takes a bow

The Tories seized the initiative in reconstructing the family in popular ideology. On 12 October 1977, Conservative social services spokesman Patrick Jenkin reminded the Conservative annual conference that the family was 'an enduring institution':

It had been the foundation for virtually every free society known to history. It possesses strength and resilience, not least in adversity. Loyalty to the family ranks highest of all, higher even than loyalty to the state. It is no accident ... that dictatorships whether of the Left or the Right seek first to devalue and then to destroy the family...

This 'enduring institution' was under pressure, Mr Jenkin went on. What were the signs?

The rising tide of juvenile crime, the growth of truancy, the break-up of marriages, family violence, the loneliness of the aged, the growing dependence on the social services, the steadily mounting numbers of children in care – these are the toll exacted by the strains on family life.

And what were the causes? A 'profound change', he said, had been 'occasioned by the number of married women who now take a job outside the home':

I am told there is now a word for 'latchkey kid' in every European language ... in more and more families mothers are combining earning with home-making... There is now an elaborate machinery to ensure her equal opportunity, equal pay and equal rights; but I think we ought to stop and ask: where does this leave the family?

More to the point, where did this leave women? The Conservative spokesman was in no doubt: 'The pressure on young wives to go out to work devalues motherhood itself. . . Parenthood is a very skilled task indeed and it must be our aim to restore it to the place of honour it deserves.' Once women were restored to their 'place of honour' in the home, they could, he implied, take a lot of expensive work out of the hands of the social services:

We hear today a great deal about social work . . . perhaps the most important social work of all is motherhood. . .

And the second most important social work, it seemed, was caring for the elderly at home: 'The family must be the front-line defence when Gran needs help.'

This was to be the theme of all Conservative electioneering around the welfare state. On 17 June 1978, at a National Children's Centre conference, Patrick Jenkin (who continued as chief propagandist) attacked the new TUC *Charter for the Under-Fives*. The Charter called for care and education to be made available to all children under five whose parents wanted it. Mr Jenkin was 'dismayed'; he could not 'conceive of any change which would do more to turn a highly personal individual service into yet another arm of the bureaucracy'. Instead, he wanted more pre-school playgroups. Young mothers, he said, were 'often isolated and depressed' (though why they should be in the bosom of such a splendid institution as the family he did not explain); and when 'the only alternative may be increasing isolation and a course of Valium', what could be better than a voluntary stint at the local playgroup?

This new campaign by the Conservatives, who claimed to be 'the party of the family', soon had the Labour leadership engaging in the sincerest form of flattery. At the National Conference of Labour Women in May 1978, Prime Minister Callaghan made the same connection as the Tory spokesman between 'the impact on the family . . . [of] more mothers going out to work', the 'growth of vandalism and hooliganism' and the need to preserve 'the beneficial influence of the family as a whole . . . in this changing situation'. And he too linked the idea of strengthening the family with caring for the old and the sick:

The nature and strength of the family and our attitude towards it will include our attitude to care for the old and weaker members of our society.

But this put Labour in a bit of a dilemma. Think of all the wonderful things the party had done to help women *go out* to work! Equal pay and opportunity laws ... statutory maternity leave ... protection from unfair dismissal during pregnancy ... a special new pension scheme... If they all went off to be plumbers and computer analysts who'd be left to 'preserve the beneficial influence of the family'? For, as Callaghan noted in the same speech, 'the woman usually is the centre of the family'. Well, she would just have to do both – and that would evidently require shorter and more flexible hours, and more peripheral jobs. As Callaghan put it:

We have to pay much more attention than we have done in the past as to how industry organizes woman's *role* at work, so that her influence as the centre of the family ... is not weakened. [Our italics].

A month later, on the same day as Jenkin's Valium speech, Callaghan took another tack, announcing in the Market Hall, Brecon, that 'change' must be harnessed 'to our principles and to our values'. Among these he named not only 'care and compassion for those in need' and 'the unique bonds of family life', but also 'the qualities found in the home', which included 'service before self'. Labour, said Callaghan, had done a lot 'to open up new opportunities for women who go out to work' and that was all very well.

But equally – and here I want to make a very important point, one which I think is not made often enough – those women who choose their families as their lifework, devote their energies to their homes, their husbands and their children are equally valuable members of society and fulfil themselves.

This new focus on the family represented a greater ideological leap for Labour than for the Conservatives; it expressed confusion at the level of policy and a degree of conflict within the Labour Party. Public spending on the caring services had increased massively under the Wilson governments of the late 1960s and early 1970s. This directly affected women's workload – both by providing paid employment, and by taking into the social sphere responsibilities which had previously been left to mothers, daughters and neighbours. However, this particular effect of the expanding welfare state was never celebrated as a benefit for women. It did not seem to be a conscious part of Labour's thinking, and it was never a priority. Indeed, the one

86

service which could have revolutionized women's lives – child care provision – expanded very little, from a capacity for 22,000 children in 1966 to 26,000 in 1974. The official Labour view on the role of women remained ambiguous, open to variable interpretation. Moreover, since the publication of the Seebohm Report and the 1974 reorganization of the health and social services, there had been a new emphasis upon reducing institutional care and speedily returning the sick, the geriatric and the disabled to the care of the 'community'. Professionals in the field were already favourably inclined towards reasserting the role of the family, the basic unit of the community.

The politicians' battle over the family grew more baroque as the general election approached. Callaghan floated the idea of a Ministry for Marriage. Patrick Jenkin proposed that government ministers should be asked 'to accompany any new policy proposals with an assessment of their impact on the family, a Family Impact Statement, if you like'. Margaret Thatcher apparently did not like. No more was heard about 'family impact statements' after the Conservatives won the election. It was soon hard to disguise the fact that Tory policies were very bad indeed for the family. But as the new government set about dismantling the welfare state, the ideology had to be sustained.

In July 1980, Patrick Jenkin addressed the Church of England Children's Society on the problem of handicapped children. 'Every child deserves a proper family life,' the Secretary of State for Social Services declared. The aim must be to keep the family together, with the child at home; that might be difficult and the family would need support, advice and encouragement; but *professional* help could 'actually undermine the confidence and competence of ordinary parents'. In its place should come support 'from people operating on a self-help basis and making use of resources within the community'. And in case anyone doubted who these 'people' were, Mr Jenkin was already on record with the following statement, delivered during a *Man Alive* programme the previous year:

If the good Lord had intended us all having equal rights to go out to work and to behave equally, you know he really wouldn't have created man and woman.

Cuts take their toll

It is hard to judge how far members of the public were seduced by such propaganda. Certainly it expressed the 'social policy' of the right-wing populism of the Thatcher regime. The shift in consensus was towards the anti-social and the individualistic as spending cuts took their toll on services and jobs. There was an inexorable logic to it: not only would women have to compensate for work no longer done by public employees, but the great majority of jobs that were being cut were women's jobs and many of the services were those which enabled women to take paid employment in the first place. If the government's policies were not resisted and overturned, it would soon become both necessary and normal for women to stay at home. A Conservative minister would then have no need to invoke the 'good Lord' to legitimize his argument; he could simply point to the evidence around him and declare with all the heartfelt conviction of a fully employed male politician that it *must* be right for women to stay at home. For, look, that was what most of them were doing anyway – and more and more were doing it all the time! Where would the nation be without them? The rest would soon be confirmed as 'deviant'.

The effect of the Conservatives' spending cuts was drastic enough to disturb some of the apathy which had prevailed at the time of their election. However, Thatcher and her team managed to deflect opposition to the cuts away from themselves by making local authorities do the cutting. Local authorities had become the big spenders of the state sector. Between 1951 and 1975, their share of the gross national product almost doubled, from 9.8 per cent to 18.6 per cent; and their share of all government spending rose from a quarter to a third. Yet only ten per cent of their revenue came from rates. As the scale of their operations increased, so did their political significance and their power, but at the same time their financial dependence on central government grew. Ultimately, the Conservatives broke their political autonomy by insisting on strict cash limits.

The Thatcher government ordered local authorities to cut spending by 3 per cent in 1979 and by a further 5.6 per cent in 1980. Some Labour-controlled councils were unwilling to cut services, but found they were damned if they did and damned if they didn't. If they did, they incurred the wrath of their Labour supporters, who accused them of reneging on election promises; and if they didn't, they had to raise the rates, which incurred the wrath of ratepayers, many of whom were also Labour voters. They had no hope of being bailed out if they failed to stick to the limits. On the contrary, the government resolved to 'fine' recalcitrant authorities by taking an extra cut out of their next grant.

Many councils tackled the problem by deciding on an order of priorities and making deeper cuts in some areas, so that others would suffer less. Nursery care and education were often the first to go. East Sussex, for example, planned in 1980 to close all nursery schools and classes by 1982, shedding forty-five jobs and saving £233,600; at the same time its social services department named the day nursery services among its 'lowest priority items'. In Nottingham, more than two hundred nursery nurses were sacked. Oxfordshire announced it would close all its nursery schools rather than pare down the service all round. These patterns were repeated throughout the country. Nursery nurses and nursery teachers – almost all women – lost their livelihood. Working mothers who had previously relied on the services now had to choose between leaving their jobs and allowing their children to become (in Patrick Jenkin's favourite phrase) 'latchkey kids'.

School meals were another early target. Some authorities hiked up prices, greatly reducing the numbers of children who ate the meals. Others cut the quality. Bromley Council in Kent replaced hot dinners with cold snacks and issued redundancy notices to four hundred staff; two local independent nutrition experts were able to show that on every score (protein, energy, fibre, Vitamin C content) the new snacks would have a detrimental effect on the children's health. Dorset County Council rid itself of 950 school meals staff and in September 1980 abolished all school meals for children under twelve. A survey carried out by the National Union of Public Employees in November 1980 found that throughout the country some twenty thousand school meals staff (almost all female) had lost their jobs. And where jobs were not cut altogether, hours were cut – reducing women's earning power as well as the quality of their work, as meals suddenly had to be prepared in two hours rather than three. Mothers were left with the responsibility of providing alternative midday meals, or extra nutrition in the evenings, or of coping with the adverse effects on their children's health.

Homes for children, old people and the disabled were closed down relentlessly. Some councils seized upon Mr Jenkin's familiar theme. Tory-controlled East Sussex, for one, declared proudly that its aim was 'to provide the help and support that families and the community need to look after these frail members of society', and stressed that 'voluntary organizations are vital in strengthening community life'. Other councils were forced to take similar measures, however unwillingly, or else defy the government. Labour-controlled Sheffield let it be known that if the 1980 cuts of 5 per cent were implemented across the board, certain results were unavoidable:

Reduction in preventive and remedial work with children of £80,000.
25 children removed from foster care.
3 adult homes closed, 2 of them old people's homes – 100 places lost.
2 day centres closed, 150 people affected.
Drivers and administrative and support staff jobs lost – around 50.
Home help and warden services withdrawn from 400 people, with job loss of 50.
80 to 100 meals on wheels lost.
300 families or individuals would lose social work support.
25 fewer aids and adaptations requests dealt with each month – 300 each year.
Grants to voluntary organizations reduced.
2 community workers withdrawn.
50 telephones for the housebound withdrawn.[1]

Most local authorities followed their instructions to cut spending, but a few Labour councils stood firm and, by mid-1981, were shaping up for a major confrontation with the government. Lothian regional council, the second largest local authority in Scotland, which covers Edinburgh and the surrounding area, was ordered to cut its budget by £53 million, which would have meant reducing its spending for the rest of the financial year by *25 per cent*. The council was already committed to increasing its expenditure per head of population by 23 per cent over four years. Explaining why, it pointed out that its transport policy had enabled 100,000 elderly and disabled people to travel free on buses; that it had one of the best teacher-pupil ratios in the country; and that its social work policy, by adding the equivalent of nearly one thousand full-time jobs since 1978, was playing a vital role in establishing a 'caring community'. Yet there was still a shortage of special accommodation for the elderly, adult training centre places, hostel places for the mentally handicapped and residential units for the physically handicapped.

To break Lothian's intransigence, George Younger, Secretary of State for Scotland, threatened to withdraw £47 million from its rate support grant. There was a danger of individual councillors being surcharged, and early in August, the council agreed to a £15 million package of spending cuts.

The Thatcher administration's antipathy to local government as a big spender, and to local government autonomy, was spelt out during the summer of 1981 when it was faced with a municipal rebellion. The Minister for Local Government explained that if voluntary cuts could not be secured, legislative powers would be taken in 1982 to curtail municipalities' current expenditure. 'The end of local government as we know it is a risk – a very great risk – in the present situation,' he told the annual conference in Bournemouth of the Chartered Institute of Public Finance and Accounting on 14 June 1981.

Cuts in the health service had already been set in train by Labour. Capital spending on NHS hospitals and community health services declined from £586 million to £359 million between 1971 and 1977 (at 1977 prices). Between January 1976 and June 1978, 143 hospitals in England and Wales were closed down or otherwise 'rationalized'. In an attempt to redistribute resources more fairly between the regions, some districts lost out badly. For instance, between 1977 and 1979, London's health budget rose by only 2 per cent, compared with 5.8 per cent in the North-West. A report published by NUPE estimated that London would lose 31 per cent of its hospital beds between 1975 and 1986, with a total loss of 24,548 health service jobs.[2]

As young people moved out of central London, so the average age of the population increased, putting ever greater strains on services for the elderly. NUPE reported in 1978:

Many geriatrics are already occupying beds in acute wards; and demand will also increase for these facilities due to lack of earlier treatment. Patients are being transferred to inadequate local authority social services, or *returned to friends or relatives*. [Our italics.][3]

Many health districts tried to cut costs by sending hospital patients home earlier than before. In the London health district of Brent, hospital beds were reduced by 25 per cent in four years, without any increase in waiting lists. According to an official report from the Area Health Authority:

This has been done by discharging patients earlier (five days earlier, for example, in General Medicine) and by drastically cutting the time between one patient going out of hospital and another one coming into the bed. This has all happened *without any extra community staffing*. [Our italics.][4]

The Conservatives did not step up health service cuts, but

91

instead boosted the private sector – which was geared far more to the needs of middle-class employed men than to the needs of any women (except where abortion was concerned). National Health abortion services were hard hit, and increasingly this became something women could not obtain unless they could afford to pay. The proportion of health service abortions fell from 41.3 per cent in the period of June to September 1978, to 37.6 per cent in the same period just a year later.

The idea of taking needy people out of hospitals and other institutions and returning them to the 'community' was known to be unsatisfactory in many quarters well before the Conservatives came to power. A Birmingham study revealed in 1977 that the cost of supporting elderly bedridden people at home was about £41 per week. This compared to a cost of £45 per week for care in a geriatric hospital; and about one-third of the patients at home were receiving support considered by district nurses to be inadequate.[5]

Problems such as these intensified from 1979 onwards, as local authorities made drastic reductions in all the services designed to support 'community care': home helps, meals on wheels, day centres, holidays for the elderly and the disabled, social work teams and so forth. Here again, the vast majority of work had been done by women (paid), and would be replaced as far as possible by the work of women (unpaid). The social services department in Tory-controlled Kent came up with the idea of paying 'neighbours' a nominal fee to look after housebound old people in need of residential care. Nicholas Stacey, director of social services, explained: 'By paying neighbours fairly little we get quite excellent, loyal and devoted service. You pay a neighbour £15 a week and get £50 service.' Not one of the newly helpful neighbours was a man, and that was quite appropriate in Stacey's view:

When you've got male unemployment, how much better that women, who more naturally incline to a community-based life, do this sort of thing.[6]

What a perfect solution! For in addition to all the nursery nurses and nursery teachers who were losing their jobs; in addition to all the school dinner ladies, nurses, nursing auxiliaries, hospital cleaners, and all the staff of children's homes, old people's homes and homes for the disabled; and in addition to all those who worked in day centres, and as social workers, home helps and meals on wheels staff ... there were many,

many more women who were being put out of work. They could *all* be good neighbours for a pittance. There were part-time teachers in primary and secondary schools, and some full-time teachers too. There were school cleaners and school helpers, and town hall cleaners, and clerical workers in local authority offices up and down the country. In her novel, *Benefits*, Zoe Fairbairns summoned up the image of a terrible Orwellian future:

The dying welfare state brought its own Newspeak as well: government's failure to link child benefit, unemployment pay and so on to the cost of living was *the fight against inflation*; putting children on halftime schooling was referred to as *giving parents a free hand*; closing hospitals and dumping dying relatives on the doorsteps of unwarned and distant relatives was *community care*; and a new political movement that saw remedies to the whole predicament, if only the nation's women would buckle down to their traditional role and biological destiny, was known quite simply as FAMILY.[7]

When her novel was published in 1979, it still sounded like fiction. By the time this book was written, it was beginning to seem more like the real thing.

State services and family relations

The political developments of the late 1970s and early 1980s have highlighted two of the main questions that have faced the women's liberation movement. How can the family – as we know and love and are subordinate within it – be transformed? And what role can the state play in this?

There are obvious ways in which state services and benefits can improve the quality of women's lives and help to change their role in the family. At the same time, the state contributes to female subordination, by the way in which benefits and services are organized, and the assumptions on which they are based. Furthermore, these can be manipulated by government as a political weapon against women.

This means the women's liberation movement is engaged in a three-way struggle: to defend state services and benefits, in their present imperfect condition, against governments committed to public expenditure cuts; to transform the assumptions and rules that govern them, and radically improve their quality; and to win new gains, in the form of additional benefits and services, as well as state funding for independent feminist initiatives.

The main focus of the campaign against public spending cuts, which has been led by the public service unions, has so far been to save jobs. Feminists are asserting the need for a new dimension to the campaign, involving a critique of the threatened services, and proposals for changing them. If school meals are to be defended, for example, the point is not simply to save the jobs of the women who provide them, but to improve the meals themselves, which have generally been heavily processed, over-cooked, unappetizing and – while more nutritious than the snacks that are replacing them – seriously lacking in nutritional value. And why should there be huge kitchens which are used for only a few hours a day? Could they not be opened in the evenings to provide low-cost meals for members of the local community?

Likewise, it is not enough to fight for a new public housing programme if it simply perpetuates the traditional pattern of privatized, 'nuclear' family life. Homes and communities need to be designed and equipped in order to facilitate change. This need not entail *forcing* people to change, nor is it an especially extravagant demand. It certainly requires committed public expenditure, but it is more a question of changing the habits of architects and planners.

A 1975 Department of the Environment circular, *Housing Needs and Action*, reported that over half the households in Britain consisted of only one or two people. The government concluded that more smaller homes were needed. But feminists have expressed reservations, after monitoring mass isolation endured by women in their homes.

Towards the end of the 1970s, the era of the tower block seemed to be over. Families with children were seldom allocated new sky-high homes although many remained in the upper storeys. The blocks were discredited, and often derelict – indeed in Merseyside and East London, blocks were actually blown up. For mothers, they had fulfilled the worst prophecies – but not simply because they had suspended them in mid air. According to the New Architecture Movement Feminist Group, women in tower blocks were 'more isolated than in any civilization in history'.[8]

It had proved to be an expensive form of public housing in which economies of scale were never realized. The desire to cut costs always excluded the very social spaces and services – for children, eating, shopping and washing – which could have mitigated the horrors of the high life.

The feminist campaign for maternity leave has produced a tangible new benefit from the state. The 1975 Employment Protection Act introduced six weeks' paid leave for women who had two years' service with their employers, plus the right to return to work up to twenty-nine weeks after the birth. A study by the Policy Studies Institute, published in 1980, showed that 45 per cent of women who were employed during their pregnancy received the statutory pay. However, the provision for reinstatement was found to have very little impact, with only 5 per cent of women who returned to their jobs doing so according to the new statutory formula. The Act laid down a string of conditions for women to fulfil in order to claim their right to reinstatement, and these were intensified by the Thatcher government's Employment Act of 1980. The legal obstacle course has no doubt deterred many women, but there are two further problems. There is no provision for men to take parental leave; and the great majority of women who qualify for reinstatement cannot take advantage of it even if they manage to jump all the hurdles – because they cannot combine their old job with their new child-care responsibilities. The PSI survey concluded:

Where women were disposed to return to work but did not go back, the chief reasons were the lack of anyone to look after the baby or the lack of accessible local jobs with convenient hours ... women's suggestions for change concentrated on the needs primarily for improved child-care facilities. . .[9]

Child care campaigners in the women's movement have pioneered a small number of nurseries, run along democratic, non-sexist lines; they have raised awareness about the need for child-care facilities, especially among trade unions. However, as we have seen, nurseries have usually been the first casualties of local authority spending cuts.

The Conservative government's attack on local government has serious implications for the women's movement. As an autonomous, locally based movement of heterogeneous elements, it has no party-political affiliations, nor any specific orientation towards constitutional politics. Yet some of the major practical innovations of women's liberation have been self-help endeavours at a community level, which supplement the functions of the welfare state, or represent a critique of traditional state practice. Women's Aid refuges and children's community centres both filled a gap in municipal provision. Their success was a result of the women's movement's engagement *in* and *against* the local state, in the course of which some local government practices were changed.

Feminist groups have thus found themselves entering into a dialogue with local authorities in order to gain access to funds and premises. They have seldom been able to engage directly through the channels of election and representation. The interaction has corresponded more closely to the movement's non-centralized form than the strictures and protocols of national politics. Moreover, it has produced concrete results, in the form of funded projects, run along feminist lines.

In the London borough of Lewisham, there has been a unique experiment, with the council setting up an official Women's Rights Working Party, composed of councillors and elected representatives from the local women's centre. The working party has investigated a wide range of issues, from the borough's employment policies and day-care provision, to the local display of sexist advertising. Its purpose is to recommend policy to the council.

As central government undermines the power of local government, this not only damages the quality of women's lives and destroys their jobs, but it also reduces the opportunities for feminist intervention in politics.

The call for financial independence, which is embodied in the fifth demand of the women's liberation movement, entails an attack on the rules that govern state benefits and pensions. These rules are based on the 'family wage' proposition, that the man is the main breadwinner for his wife and children, and feminists have been fighting to change them since the early 1970s. One target has been the rule that prevents married women workers from claiming extra benefit for their children and husbands while they themselves are receiving unemployment or sickness benefit (men automatically have this right). This rule is now due to change, but not because the government has been swayed by feminist campaigners: the EEC has directed that benefits should be awarded on an equal basis. The disgraceful 'cohabitation rule', which prevents a woman from claiming supplementary benefit if she is married to a man or thought to be living with him 'as husband and wife', has also fallen foul of European law, but no date has yet been fixed for abolishing it.

The married man's tax allowance (a large cash prize for the male taxpayer who has been through a marriage ceremony

96

more recently than a divorce) has been another target of the campaign for women's financial independence. At the time of writing there seems to be a consensus that the allowance should be abolished, but there are still arguments over how the money (some £27 billion) should be redistributed. The Conservatives seem to favour paying it back as an extra allowance to tax-payers who have 'a dependent spouse with home responsibilities'. Feminists suspect this will act as an incentive for men to keep their wives at home and perpetuate female dependence; instead they have been campaigning with the Child Poverty Action Group, and others in the 'poverty lobby', for the money to be used to increase the level of child benefit.

Child benefit was introduced by Labour, under some duress from the poverty lobby and the women's movement. It represents a real advance for women. As a tax-free, non-means-tested cash benefit paid directly to the mother, it guarantees her some financial independence and recognizes that the notion of the breadwinning father bringing home an adequate 'family wage' is now an anomaly for most households. Child benefit was a popular innovation – so popular, indeed, that during the election campaign Patrick Jenkin tried hard to claim that his own party was responsible for its introduction. But by 1980 the Conservatives had begun to edge away from it.

In his budget that year, Sir Geoffrey Howe announced an increase of 75p in the benefit, bringing it up to £4.75 a week per child. That was about 45p *less* than was needed to retain its purchasing power in the face of inflation, and it meant that over the year a two-child family would incur a net loss of some £73. On 25 November, in a speech to the Family Forum, Chancellor Howe fired his first shot in public against the *principle* of child benefit: It had replaced child tax allowance 'almost accidentally', he said, 'on the strength of the argument ... that children would be more likely to receive the benefit if there was a transfer from the wallet to the purse'. But the argument was 'not untainted with sex discrimination', he added disapprovingly, and, with a curious twist of logic, he went on to inquire whether it had been right to depart 'from the idea of the state dealing with the family as a unit headed by the father':

This may have had larger implications than anyone foresaw for financial reasons within the family. Does the mother feel greater independence because she is not dependent on the father for the children's support? Does the father feel less need to provide as much for the housekeeping and for the children?

Is child benefit to be branded an agent of family destruction? At that stage Howe would only hint: 'These questions are at least worth asking.'

The mixture as before

With the exception of child benefit, which made a small change in the distribution of resources within the family, none of the practical measures for which women campaigned in the 1970s has done anything to disturb the conventional pattern of family life. It has continued to be accepted as the norm that a woman should confine her sexual activity to one man, marry him or live with him as his wife, bear children, and remain with them in a single household, sealed off for most of the time – physically, socially and economically – from friends, neighbours and other relatives. Women have continued to be economically dependent on their husbands or cohabitees, and to be claimed as their exclusive sexual territory. They have continued to labour privately, each wife within her own four walls, to feed, clothe and generally sustain her own particular batch of human kind.

The sociologist Richard Titmuss has commented on the substitution of companionship in marriage for the sharp division of labour in the traditional patriarchal family.[10] When Geoffrey Gorer surveyed attitudes to marriage at the end of the 1960s, he too recorded a transition from complementary roles to companionship.[11] Couples expect to like each other and do everything together. Titmuss calls it the democratization of marriage. However, the balance of power in this new companionship has remained patriarchal. Wives are often busier and lonelier than ever. With a husband as a friend, they may have to eschew all others. Their access to the society of women is curtailed, or cut off altogether, and they find themselves with no time or place they can call their own.

It has suited some more than others. The divorce rate has soared, from 58,200 decrees in 1970 to 138,700 in 1979. The rate of remarriage has more than doubled in the same period – but a mid-life change of cast appears not to alter the plot. The structure of communities, the patriarchal character of the labour market, the philosophy of the welfare state, the ideology of the education system, the persistent influence of Christianity . . . all these factors and many more combine to ensure that family life proceeds as usual.

In 1978, the Study Commission on the Family was set up, headed by Sir Campbell Adamson, former head of the employers' organization, the Confederation of British Industry. In tune with the mood of the government, it hoped to corral the support of non-feminist women's organizations and a rather reluctant poverty lobby, and to help put the 'family perspective' on the political map. According to its pamphlet, *Happy Families*, published in 1980, marriage has become more popular than ever. It does not note that most people have little choice but to organize their sexual and domestic life around marriage.

The 1969 Divorce Reform Act exposed the instabilities of the institution of marriage in ways that took its architect, MP Leo Abse, by surprise. His chief intention in introducing the law had been to legitimize the children of men who had set up second families outside wedlock, but he could not solve this problem without causing another. Divorced men were expected to support their ex-wives, and this could be cripplingly expensive – not because divorcees lived in the lap of luxury, but because one man's wage was seldom enough to support one family, let alone two. The courts ensured that ex-wives got little enough if there was any matrimonial property to be shared out at the end of a marriage. Lord Denning decreed, in the case of *Watchel* v. *Watchel* in 1973, that a woman in these circumstances should expect no more than one-third. Nevertheless, the system failed miserably. Men could not pay, or did not want to pay. The state became involved in a massive mopping-up operation – paying out £419 million to wives of maintenance defaulters in 1980 alone. By the early 1980s, there was a growing campaign on behalf of divorced men, aiming to reduce their liability towards their first families. Leo Abse launched a new campaign to make divorce harder to get, and to put a stop to maintenance for ex-wives. There would be no solution while female dependence remained a primary characteristic of family life.

Since the late 1960s, many women have tried – individually and collectively – to break out of the conventional mould of family life. They have waged guerrilla warfare over the housework. They have 'nagged' and 'scolded' to get men to change their habits. They have fought for their own space within the household. They have 'reversed roles', leaving their husbands with the kids while they go out to work. They have lived communally with other men and women. They have set up networks of 'women's houses' in towns and cities throughout the country. All this has been intrinsic to feminist politics since the birth of the women's liberation movement.

At the same time, there are countless feminists who have married – to please themselves or their parents, or to 'legitimize' their children. And there are countless more who have set up home, nuclear-family style, in all details but the marriage certificate. As far as we can see, it is still the exception rather than the rule to find a household shared by feminists and 'sympathetic' men where housework, child care and other domestic responsibilities are really shared out *equally* between the sexes.

Marriage or quasi-marriage may be fraught with difficulty and contradictions, but for some it seems simpler, less threatening, or less consuming of time and energy than trying to break with convention. 'We once tried to share a house with another couple,' a woman told us, who married in the early 1960s and now has two teenage children, 'but you know, it's hard enough to work out a relationship with one man – this was almost like being married to three people at once!'

There is an impatience, too, among some feminists, with 'life-style politics'; there is a sense that there are more important things to worry about, other areas of life (work, politics, children) that are challenging and absorbing. Their men may be selfish, arrogant, lazy or unkind, or far too 'busy' to help at home – but, well, they are fond of them, or they 'love' them, or 'no one's perfect', and it seems easier to put up with the bad bits and shoulder the extra burden of domestic work, than to fight it out. The pressures to conform are mighty. 'I couldn't bear to be on my own', is a familiar refrain. 'I wish I could find a (reasonable) man' is another. . . And all after a good ten years of feminism. Much of this turns on the question of sex, and the relationship between feminist politics and the 'heterosexual imperative', which we examine in a later chapter, p. 211.

Of course, it would be easier to develop a clear political analysis of family life if it were altogether a bad thing. We could then call for the abolition of the family, and perhaps join with those radical feminists who prescribe a separatist life-style as the only correct way. But for the majority of women, this would be rather less appealing than the calls of Conservative politicians to restore traditional values and strengthen the family. For there *are* ways in which the family can be a source of care, affection, strength and security, as much as it can be a source of physical violence, psychic oppression and social control.

Separating out these interwoven threads is an important part of feminist politics. Women's liberation is founded on the principle that 'the personal is political', and family relations have been a consistent topic of discussion in women's groups. But they have not yet been brought out into the open and asserted as political in the same way as other aspects of the struggle. The successes that women have had in breaking with convention still seem like isolated incidents. They have yet to be celebrated as part of a continuum, or placed within a political framework; and the failures still seem purely – and painfully – personal. But these successes and failures are as much a part of the resistance of women as the defence of child benefit, the demand for socialized child care, or the right for equality at work.

Notes to Chapter 3

1 Sheffield Council memorandum 'Effect of 5% cut in spending on council departments', 1980.
2 *Under the Axe: London's Health Service Crisis*, NUPE, London 1978.
3 Ibid.
4 *Cuts and the NHS,* The Politics of Health Group Pamphlet no. 2. c/o BSSRS, 9 Poland Street, London W1.
5 Survey by Opit, *British Medical Journal*, vol. 1, 1977, p. 30.
6 Campbell, B. 'In a Family Way', *Time Out*, September 1979.
7 Fairbairns, Z. *Benefits*, Virago, London 1979, p. 38–9.
8 Brion, M. and Tinker, A., *Women in Housing*, Housing Centre Trust, London 1980.
9 Daniel, W. W. *Maternity Rights: the experiences of women,* Policy Studies Institute Report no. 588, London, June 1980.
10 Titmuss, R. *Essays on the Welfare State*, George Allen & Unwin, London 1958.
11 Gorer, G. *Sex and Marriage in England Today*, Panther, St Albans 1973.

4 Legislation

The Women's Liberation Movement protests against the term 'Sex Discrimination Bill' being used for what is only a limited equal opportunities Bill. The movement severely condemns obvious fundamental omissions of discrimination such as pensions, taxation, social security etc. We demand of the Government a comprehensive sex discrimination Bill so that women are no longer defined as dependants; and a Bill that provides for no less than genuine equality of treatment under the law for both sexes.

This resolution, passed by the National Women's Liberation Conference in Manchester on 6 April 1975, only hints at the range of views held by feminists in that period.

There was a strong current of opinion which held that the parliamentary battle was a side-issue, which would do little or nothing to help end female oppression: these women weren't opposed to it, but they were preoccupied with other matters. Some groups were eager for Parliament to legislate, believing with varying degrees of optimism in the efficacy of law. Some saw themselves carrying on the work of feminists who had campaigned for women's suffrage – taking their victory a step further by using Parliament to enshrine the principle of equality in a Sex Discrimination Act.

Few were in doubt that the Labour government's Bill, which was cruising through Parliament at the time, had serious weaknesses. Yet even fewer believed that (as the resolution suggests) any law could work the miracle of providing 'genuine equality of treatment'. The motion was proposed by a women's group in Watford, Hertfordshire, which in 1973 had launched the Women's Liberation Campaign for an anti-discrimination law. One of its members, Pat Howe, chained herself to the railings outside the House of Commons on 19 April 1975, as part of a National Day of Action, organized by her group, against Labour's Bill. But the demonstration attracted little support. Most women welcomed the Bill, warts and all.

Such differences as there were among feminists did not reflect the radical/socialist divide. The campaign for law reform had supporters on both sides. It was a popular cause, well publicized, which drew countless newcomers into the women's liberation movement. Moreover, it was a crucial stage in the development of feminist politics. It was an opportunity to remove some of the outer wrappings from the system which sustained inequality. Once that had been done, it was found that – like a parcel on April Fool's Day – there were layers upon layers beneath. Something of the kind was suspected by most women, but now they could get a clearer idea of how the monstrous item was constructed.

In this chapter we look at the campaign for 'equality' legislation, at how far the new laws have changed women's lives, and at the reasons why they have had such a feeble effect. Some of these reasons can be found in the laws themselves, others in the methods of law enforcement. We describe the emergence of a new campaign for 'positive action', which has grown out of women's experience of ineffective legislation. And finally we examine the changing relationship between the women's liberation movement and the machinery of party politics and parliamentary government.

Equality – good in parts

Labour's new Bill was a great deal better than women had been led to expect, after all the ups and downs of the seven-year fight for an anti-discrimination law. Joyce Butler, Labour MP for Wood Green, had introduced the first Private Member's Bill to outlaw discrimination against women in 1967. It had failed to get a second reading. Bills along the same lines were submitted every year after that, but it was not until 1972, when Edward Heath was Prime Minister, that a Bill introduced into the House of Lords by the Liberal peer Nancy Seear got over the crucial second hurdle. It might have gone on to become law had it not been referred (rather unusually) to a Select Committee of the Lords. This Committee heard an impressive range of evidence between June and December 1972, and eventually reported in the spring of the following year. Meanwhile, on 29 November 1972, Willie Hamilton, Labour MP for West Fife, submitted another, similar Bill to the Commons.

The two Bills now became the focus of a large and energetic campaign, uniting for the first time the new women's liberation groups and some trade unions with such long-established feminist organizations as the Fawcett Society (set up to continue the work of the suffragist Millicent Fawcett) and the Six Point Group (which belonged to the more militant tradition of the suffragettes). Both Bills were far less detailed and more narrowly focussed than the one which eventually became law.

At its second reading on 2 February 1973, Willie Hamilton's Bill narrowly missed a sudden death. As the feminist newsletter *Women's Report* explained at the time, 'Only the uproar on the crowded opposition benches and the massive support of British women (as manifested by the unabashed claps and jeers in the packed gallery) kept Speaker Selwyn Lloyd from killing the Bill for lack of time.' [1] A mass meeting followed at the old suffragette venue, Caxton Hall, where between three and four hundred women listened to speeches from MPs, women's liberation campaigners, trade unionists and others, under pre-1914 banners urging 'Dare to be free'. Then, at the call of May Hobbs of the Night Cleaners Campaign, they 'erupted into the night to march in torchlight procession to the House and 10 Downing Street'. It was a stirring occasion, with a scent of victory in the air. On 14 February, Hamilton's Bill completed its second reading, unopposed; but to the surprise and disappointment of many, it was referred to yet another Select Committee.

Neither Bill could succeed without some measure of support from the government. The strength of the campaign and the degree of enthusiasm inside Parliament made this seem a possibility. It therefore came as a bitter blow when on 14 May 1973, as Baroness Seear's Bill returned to the Lords, amended and strengthened from committee stage, Home Office minister Lord Colville announced that the government would not support it (nor Hamilton's, by implication), but planned instead to introduce proposals of its own.

The Tories' Green Paper was published in September 1973 and – as MP Renée Short declared at that year's Labour Party Conference – it was altogether 'flabby and toothless'. Education and training were omitted entirely, thanks to the intervention of Education Secretary Margaret Thatcher. There were wide exemptions in the provisions relating to employment: for example, it would remain lawful to discriminate 'Where it could be shown that for performance of personal services strong preferences among customers or clients make the employment of a man (or a woman) essential to the business.' There was nothing to stop discrimination by trade unions; the proposed Equal Opportunities Commission had no enforcement powers at all; and no

105

mention was made of penalties for offending employers, or arrangements for compensation. The Bill died an unlamented death when the Heath government fell in February 1974. Labour returned to power and introduced its own legislation, drawing on the findings of the two Select Committees, and going further than either Seear's or Hamilton's proposals. The Labour Bill embraced not only education, training and employment, but also housing and the provision to the public of goods, facilities and services, and, more important still, the concept of 'indirect discrimination', imported from the United States, which extended its influence in all these fields. Debate now homed in comfortably on the details: should there be an exemption for midwives? Should private clubs be included? Should new 'equal opportunities tribunals' be set up to enforce the law, instead of industrial tribunals? By this stage, many women wanted to give the Bill – which was finally enacted on 29 December 1975 – the benefit of the doubt. In any case, there was a strong feeling in 1975 that progress was being made, at least towards eliminating the more blatant forms of female disadvantage.

Along with the new Sex Discrimination Act, the Equal Pay Act, passed in 1970, came into force and an Equal Opportunities Commission was set up with a statutory duty to enforce these new laws. The 1975 Social Security (Pensions) Act introduced a new state pension scheme which made special provision for people who spent some time out of waged work because of their 'home responsibilities' and gave women a new chance to earn a full pension of their own. And the Employment Protection Act, passed that same year, gave women a statutory right to paid maternity leave, protection from unfair dismissal during pregnancy and the right to their jobs back up to twenty-nine weeks after the baby's birth. So the year designated 'International Women's Year' by the United Nations brought a shower of benefits – or so it seemed. It was not altogether unreasonable for women to assume they were making headway and that things would go on getting better.

The principle of equal rights now bore the official seal of approval and it ceased to be respectable to treat women less favourably than men – at least without making some effort to disguise what one was doing. The effect of having the principle of equality formally endorsed is hard to measure, but it must have helped to develop new expectations and a new sense of confidence among women, and it must have begun (however sluggishly) to change public opinion about what was 'natural' and immutable about the differences between women and men. The focus of argument shifted: open disputes about whether or not women were men's inferiors, worthy of unequal treatment, gave way to disagreements over what exactly constituted the equal rights that women were acknowledged to deserve, and how these could now be achieved.

On the other hand, the material circumstances of most women's lives remained almost entirely unchanged by the new legislation.

Equal pay – some more equal than others

As the resolution to the 1975 Women's Liberation Conference pointed out, the legislation did nothing to change women's unequal status in the fields of taxation and social security (except to a limited degree where pensions were concerned). By 1981 women had scarcely any more financial or legal independence than they had enjoyed in International Women's Year. The Inland Revenue still treated married women as though they had no separate identity from their husbands (unless they made a special application to be treated separately). Women who were married or thought to be cohabiting were still unable to claim supplementary benefit, because it was assumed that they were supported by a man. Men continued to dominate the higher-paid and skilled jobs and in 1980 they were still taking home, on average, 36 per cent more pay than women.

The Equal Pay Act said that a woman should be paid the same as a man if she was doing work that was 'the same or broadly similar' to his; at the very least, she should get no less than the lowest male rate in the lowest grade. The five-year gap between its enactment and its coming into force in 1975 was officially the period in which equal pay was to be 'phased in'. It was never expected to cost employers much: a 1970 Department of Employment report estimated that it would add only 3.5 per cent (on average) to employers' wage bills if they enforced the law by 1975.[2] In fact, those years were a gift for employers who needed time to work out ways of avoiding their obligations under the Act. The first government report on the implementation of the Equal Pay Act is worth quoting at some length because it lists many of the typical measures adopted to keep down women's pay.[3] One company, where 80 per cent of employees were women engaged on semi-skilled work similar to men's, set about separating women and men into distinct categories:

For example, the machine shop has had a female day shift and a male night shift; men are now being recruited for day work and women are being transferred to other departments. The more technical inspection jobs are being allotted to men and the women are being transferred to simple inspection tasks; central packing is becoming a male area, line packing is reserved for women; work in the finishing and paint shops and in the Stores, is to be a male preserve; this also applies to sign-writing, even though many women are considered to be more skilful at this.

White collar jobs are to be graded into three grades: the lower one predominantly women, the middle one mixed and the upper one predominantly for men. As a result of this reorganization it is expected that by the end of 1972 very little of the work undertaken by women will be even broadly similar to that of men.

All this was done 'with the acceptance of trade union representatives who are concerned about male unemployment'. In many areas, the Equal Pay Act was actually doing women more harm than good – and they were to suffer well beyond the end of the decade from this rigid segregation of male and female jobs, which depressed their pay and limited their opportunities. The company referred to above was by no means an isolated exception. A memorandum from the British Paper Box Federation, representing an industry of 26,000 employees, 70 per cent of them women, was quoted in the *Sunday Times* on 25 February 1973. It recommended to the Federation's member firms that if they had not made 'proper provision for an acceptable differential between the take-home pay for men and women, the following discriminatory factors [were] available: Long Service; Merit; Attendance Bonus; Willingness to work overtime to a given number of hours. . .' And, the memorandum went on, 'Jobs should be changed now where areas of conflict are likely to arise: i.e. the Lavatory Cleaner.'

When a research team from the London School of Economics embarked on a three-year project to study the effects of the new legislation, they found that sixteen out of nineteen organizations they were monitoring went on paying all female manual workers less than the lowest rate paid to men, until the Equal Pay Act came fully into force.[4]

So much for the five-year 'phasing-in' period. Once the Act was in force, a great many women were unable to benefit from it, there being no men with whom they could compare their pay. The most they could expect was that they should now be brought up to the lowest male rate, which was the minimum stipulation of the new law.

The Act was supposed to give women the right to claim equal pay not only if their work was 'the same or broadly similar' to a man's, but also if their work had been 'rated as equivalent' to a man's in a job evaluation scheme. These schemes had become quite common by the mid 1970s. They involved assessing each job for its value, according to particular criteria: how much skill did the job require, for instance, and how much responsibility did it carry? The job would then be placed in what was thought to be the appropriate grade, and paid at the agreed rate for that grade. It was (and is) common practice for employers and unions to cooperate over job evaluation, jointly agreeing the criteria and negotiating the value of each job.

The problem for women arose over which criteria were chosen and how they were applied. As we explained in Chapter 2, the notion of skill is by no means neutral or fixed, but is part of a political process in which certain workers have fought for better pay over more than 150 years. One outcome has been that greater value is routinely attached to heavy or dirty jobs, which are normally done by men, than to jobs requiring manual dexterity or non-stop concentration (such as assembly line work), which are more often done by women. It women are not in a strong bargaining position, which they seldom are, opinions of this kind prevail, leaving them on their own in the lowest-paid grades, still unable to claim equal pay. There is a provision in the Equal Pay Act for discriminatory wage structures to be referred for amendment to the Central Abritration Committee, a statutory body set up in 1970. But this net can only catch the more blatantly unequal arrangements.

On 10 February 1975, a directive was issued by the EEC, defining the principle of equal pay set out in the Treaty of Rome (to which Britain is a signatory). It clearly states that equal pay should be given to women and men doing the same work or work of equal value. Britain's Equal Pay Act has proved hopelessly inadequate as a means of enforcing the EEC Directive and Britain has been judged in breach of the Rome Treaty by the European Court. The Act leaves untouched the majority of unfair job evaluation schemes, and fails to provide for women whose jobs are not subject to formal evaluation.

The kind of absurdity that can arise out of this failure to deal with the question of equal value is illustrated by the case of Leicester community worker Sue Waddington. Ms Waddington made a claim in 1976 for equal pay with a male playleader whom she had employed to run an adventure playground which she herself had set up. His pay, determined by the national scale for youth leaders and community centre wardens, amounted to 14 per cent more than hers, which was fixed under a separate national pay scale for social workers. She lost – on the ground that her job carried more responsibility than his and was not therefore 'broadly similar'![5]

In any event, it is no simple matter to introduce the principle of 'equal pay for work of equal value'. It is a political minefield. Whose job shall it be to judge the value of work? Industrial tribunals (of which more later) are ill-equipped for the task by any standards. The Central Arbitration Committee has won some respect, but a single, central statutory body cannot be expected to evaluate jobs at every workplace. Some would consider it unwise to intervene in the bargaining process between unions and employers – of which job evaluation is often a crucial part – because of the danger of undermining unions' position as the chief defenders of the workers' living standards. But unions, as we shall see in Chapter 5, are imperfect protagonists as far as their female members are concerned. Such are the dilemmas which arise when the law is wheeled in to compensate for the shortcomings of a male-dominated trade union movement.

As the 1970s came to a close, still no satisfactory formula had been found. In 1981 the Equal Opportunities Commission produced (belatedly) a set of quite helpful guidelines on job evaluation; unfortunately no one is obliged to follow them. It has been suggested that the powers of the Central Arbitration Committee be extended so that it can, in some circumstances, help to introduce job evaluation. But this requires an amendment to the law, for which nobody holds out much hope while the Conservatives remain in power.[6]

The failings of the Equal Pay Act were fairly obvious from the start. Optimists, however, had imagined that the Sex Discrimination Act would give it the backbone that it lacked. It has taken longer to appreciate the shortcomings of that piece of legislation.

Sex discrimination – a bad case of loopholes

As we explained earlier, the Sex Discrimination Act was born with something of a silver spoon in its mouth. People looked kindly upon it and expected it to do well. It was left to a small band of sceptics in the women's liberation movement to reject it for the chinless wonder that it really was.

In theory, the Act makes it unlawful to treat a woman less favourably than a man would be treated in the same circumstances, just because she is a woman. (It applies, conversely, to men.) It covers the fields of education, training, employment, housing and the provision to the public of goods, facilities and services. It makes it unlawful, too, to treat a married person less favourably than a single person (though not vice versa) in the fields of training and employment.

The Act embraces not only straightforward, 'direct' discrimination, but also 'indirect' discrimination – defined as imposing a condition which can be met by more people of one sex than the other, and which is not 'justifiable'. An obvious example would be an employer's requirement that applicants for a job should have 'O' level Physics, even though the job can be done perfectly well without it. Since far more boys than girls take 'O' level Physics, the requirement amounts to an unjustifiable condition which can be met by more members of one sex than the other.

The Act may seem far-reaching at first glance; but it is also exceedingly complicated. It is ringed around with 'ifs' and 'buts' and shot through with loopholes. It is often very difficult for an individual to discover whether she is a victim of unlawful discrimination. If she has applied for a job and failed to get it, how will she know if she has been turned down because of her sex? If she asks for a mortgage and is turned away, how can she find out whether the mortgage company has rejected her simply because she is female? And it is up to *her* to prove the point.

In 1978, Mrs Nasse, who worked as a clerical officer for the Science Research Council, applied for promotion but was passed over in favour of two people whom she considered less well qualified than herself. She suspected discrimination on grounds of her marital status – having heard that the SRC considered married women to be lacking in mobility and therefore unsuitable for promotion. In order to prove her case, she applied to an industrial tribunal for disclosure of confidential documents relating to the other candidates. Disclosure was ordered, but the SRC fought it all the way to the House of Lords, where it was finally ruled that she would not be allowed to see the documents, but that the industrial tribunal should look at the relevant ones first, and then order discussion of any that it considered necessary for a fair hearing.[7] This was not altogether unhelpful, but the right of women to see documents which may help to prove discrimination against them remains indistinct. (And, of course, discrimination is not always documented.) The position might be improved if the Act were worded differently, so that the individual applicant simply had to show that she had been treated differently and to her disadvantage, with the burden of proof on the respondent (the employer, for example, or the mortage company) to show that the treatment *did not* amount to unlawful discrimination. While the burden of proof remains on the individual complainant, it is relatively easy for employers and others who are practising sex discrimination to cover their tracks.

Even where a woman has successfully brought a case under the Sex Discrimination Act, her victory has rarely improved conditions for other women. Employers can just go on behaving as before, until the next individual brings another complaint – and her victory, in turn, affects her situation alone. This is true of most cases of direct discrimination. However, a successful complaint against *indirect* discrimination may have a wider impact, as the case of Belinda Price shows.

Belinda Price, a single mother of two, wanted to return to full-time employment at the age of thirty-five, having spent several years at home while her children were young. She applied for an executive officer's job in the Civil Service, and although she had suitable qualifications she found that entry to executive officer grade was restricted to people aged twenty-eight or under. She brought a complaint of indirect discrimination, claiming that the age bar amounted to a condition which could more easily be met by men, since so many women take a break from paid employment in their twenties and early thirties, to look after young children. There was ample statistical evidence to support her claim. The Civil Service argued that all women could go out to work in their twenties if they wanted to, it was a matter of 'choice'; but the Employment Appeals Tribunal ruled that

it should not be said that a person 'can' do something merely because it is theoretically possible for him [sic] to do so; it is necessary to see whether he can do so in practice.[8]

112

As a result, the Civil Service has raised its age bar to forty-five, opening the rank of executive officer to many more women than before. So the benefits in this case spread far beyond the individual litigant.

However, remarkably few formal complaints of indirect discrimination have been made since the Act came into force (eighty-nine altogether – less than 10 per cent of the total). Not that such breaches of the law are rare. When the London School of Economics' Equal Pay and Opportunities Project monitored nineteen employing organizations, sixteen cases of possible indirect discrimination were identified. These included age bars; restriction of certain jobs to people who had served a formal apprenticeship, where this was not necessary for the job; and requirements that employees be geographically mobile or undertake lengthy periods of residential training in order to qualify for promotion. None had become the subject of a formal complaint. Reporting the results of the LSE Project in 1979, Mandy Snell, one of the researchers, commented:

Indirect discrimination is a complex concept and there was little awareness and even less understanding of its implications among women, unions and employers. This situation is not confined to the workplace; unions at a national level, the media and many women activists have failed to recognize the potential importance of this provision of the Act.[9]

Falling between two stools

A major weakness of the Sex Discrimination Act is the separation of its sphere of influence from that of the Equal Pay Act. The latter covers pay and all other benefits and conditions which are included in an employee's contract; the former deals with non-contractual matters. Thus the principles of sex discrimination cannot – absurdly – be applied to pay, nor to many other conditions of employment.

This has raised problems in a series of cases where women working part-time have sought equal pay and benefits with full-timers. Patricia Durrant, who in June 1977 joined the North Yorkshire Area Heath Authority as a full-time clinical psychologist, tried to claim expenses to cover her move to that area from a similar, but part-time, job in Derby. The Authority refused, saying that removal expenses were available to full-timers only and Ms Durrant's former part-time status disqualified her. She claimed parity with a man doing similar work who had received expenses for moving from one full-time job to another. However, she lost her claim when the Employment Appeals Tribunal ruled in 1979 that if the man had moved, as she had done, from a part-time to a full-time job, he too would have been refused removal expenses. Ms Durrant tried at the same time to claim that the restriction of removal expenses to full-time workers amounted to indirect sex discrimination, because the vast majority of part-timers were female. But she was not allowed to do that because the removal expenses were a contractual term of employment and so fell under the Equal Pay Act![10]

In another case, Jeanette Jenkins, a part-time worker with Kingsgate (Clothing) Ltd, claimed the same hourly rate as full-timers doing the same job for the same company. All the part-timers at Kingsgate were female, all the full-timers male. She fought her case as far as the House of Lords, only to be told that her part-time status amounted, under the terms of the Equal Pay Act, to a 'material difference' between her case and those of the full-timers, which entitled her employer to keep her on unequal pay. She finally appealed to the European Court, which heard the case in November 1980. It was estimated at the time that some four million women could be affected by the decision, which had taken five years to be reached. In the end the judgement was so indistinct that the EOC claimed it as a victory for women, while *The Times* interpreted it as a defeat. The European Court ruled that a women's part-time status did not amount to a 'material difference' which made unequal pay lawful, unless the employer could show that he lost out financially because she worked part-time.[11] Had the two Acts been joined together as a single code, the confusion might not have arisen.

It is worth recalling that these laws were drafted by politicians and civil servants (mainly men) who were lodged very near to the heart of the established order, and who had been forced to respond to outside pressure (mainly from women). Roy Jenkins, then Home Secretary, Anthony Lester QC and Dipak Nandy, the men who were largely responsible, were well meaning liberals who had taken care to study the example of US equal opportunity law, and to turn out a product which was, if anything, an improvement on the American model. But their guiding principle was not 'How can we make sure those bastards don't get away with it any more?' (which might have been the feminist approach); but 'How far can we go without causing too much trouble?' It wasn't a priority for them to close loopholes, minimize exemptions or install the strongest possible means of enforcement, but to avoid anything approaching a showdown with the entrenched powers of the CBI and the TUC. Their product was then fed into a system of courts and tribunals controlled, in the main, by men with similar attitudes (or worse). There have been enough decisions in favour of women to prevent a national scandal, but not enough to disturb the time-honoured practice of treating women less favourably than men, or to upset the traditional balance of power between the sexes.

Problems of enforcement

Between 1 January 1976 and 31 December 1979, a total of 3,099 applications were made under the Equal Pay Act, and 839 under the employment section of the Sex Discrimination Act. Of these, 39 per cent were heard by industrial tribunals. The rest were settled out of court or abandoned, largely with unknown results. A study by Jeanne Gregory has shown that the intervention at this stage by ACAS (Advisory, Conciliation and Arbitration Service), which is prescribed by the law, has unnecessarily deterred many women from pursuing their claims.[12] ACAS officers, who are predominantly male, contact the applicant and the employer after a complaint has been lodged: their primary task is to avert a tribunal hearing, not to help the applicant obtain her legal rights. Gregory reports this woman's experience as typical of many:

He [the ACAS officer] said that if you take a case to the tribunal the onus is on you to produce evidence and prove your case. If you lose the case you have to pay the costs and you can't ask for a reference from your employer if you leave. He said the number of cases which go through successfully is virtually nil. All this information succeeded in putting me off. He also asked me who had told me I could make a complaint about sex discrimination and I told him the Job Centre had. He said they shouldn't do that.

The officer was wrong on several counts: a woman who takes a complaint to an industrial tribunal incurs no costs of her own unless she chooses to employ a lawyer; only in exceptional cases, where the tribunal takes the view that a complaint is 'frivolous or vexatious', is the applicant ordered to pay the costs of the other side. While relatively few cases succeed, the total cannot be described as 'virtually nil', as the tables on p. 140 confirm. And it is the duty of Job Centres to provide complaint forms to women who want to take action under the Sex Discrimination or Equal Pay Act. Another applicant commented to Gregory:

If a lot more help, advice and understanding had been available I think I could have been successful. As it was I didn't really know what I was doing or how to go about it, and the ACAS chap could have been a lot more helpful, if only by not interrupting me half way through everything I tried to say.

Of the applications that have gone ahead to tribunal hearings, well under a third have been upheld. As the tables show, the number of cases has declined significantly over the years. The Equal Pay Act has evidently outlived its usefulness, having mopped up the more outrageous cases remaining after 1975. The Sex Discrimination Act still has some potential: the decline in applications under that law (which is less marked) may reflect a lack of confidence in its ability to produce useful decisions.

No exhaustive study has been made of tribunal proceedings under the two Acts, but the signs are not promising. A great majority of those who chair the tribunals (who have to be lawyers) are male; there is seldom more than one woman on a tribunal. Tribunal members are not experts in equality legislation: they are supposed to be lay amateurs, applying their common sense. But neither do they receive any training to help them understand the predicament of women workers – and so it is hardly surprising if they display traditional attitudes about male and female roles. One chairman, in his written decision rejecting an equal pay claim by a housemother at a school for handicapped children, observed:

A housemother is engaged to look after the younger boys and carry out domestic duties. A housefather is engaged to lead the growing boy to a better approach to life and help him in his problems. The roles are largely those of a mother and father in ordinary life; they are both important, but they are different ... for those reasons we find that the applicant is not engaged on like work with a man ... full of admiration as we are for the work which she is doing...[13]

Against odds such as these, female applicants usually have to plead their case without qualified legal assistance, and withstand, more often than not, the arguments of lawyers hired by the other side. Legal aid isn't available for tribunal proceedings;

the most a woman can claim (in 1981) is £45 worth of preliminary legal advice. A large proportion of applicants are represented by trade union officials. In 1979, for example fifty-seven equal pay claimants, 73.1 per cent of the total in that year, had union representatives. However, the correlation between trade union representation and success is not encouraging. In 1979, 10.5 per cent of equal pay claimants represented by their unions were successful, compared with 40 per cent of those who represented themselves.[14]

The two Acts have serious internal weaknesses, as we have seen; and the machinery for enforcing them through ACAS and industrial tribunals is not designed to give women positive help in obtaining justice – rather the contrary. But these are not the only reasons why the new laws have had so little impact. The patterns of male and female employment are too deeply entrenched to be disturbed more than superficially by legislation alone. But even superficial disturbance is minimized by the fact that most women either don't know about their rights, or dare not pursue them. And neither the trade union movement nor the Equal Opportunities Commission has put sufficient effort into overcoming their ignorance or their reluctance.

In her report of the LSE Equal Pay and Opportunity Project,[15] Mandy Snell claims that women are still concentrated in low-paid jobs with little hope of preferment 'largely because so little use has been made of the rights and powers conferred by the Acts, rather than because of the content and wording of the Acts themselves'. It is clear, she says,

that the absence of action and negative action by employers, unions, women and the Equal Opportunities Commission has been the major factor responsible for the limited effectiveness of both Acts at workplace level.

The LSE researchers may have underestimated the intransigence of the underlying structure of the labour market, but their observations about the law are, nonetheless, relevant. In more than half the organizations they studied, they found cases of non-compliance with the Equal Pay Act, and had managers admit to them that they were continuing to discriminate against women. In most cases the women were unaware that the laws were being broken. This was attributed to the wide extent of job segregation, to a high degree of managerial secrecy, to women's lack of involvement in pay bargaining, and to the fact that management could easily practise sex discrimination without the victims finding out. Even cases where women were aware of non-compliance with the law, they were sometimes unwilling to take action:

They feared unpleasantness or negative reactions from fellow workers or management... Some women could not face going to a tribunal.

Some were deterred by 'the difficulty of proving a case' or 'the feeling that it was not worth the trouble'. Many feared lack of support, or even hostility from male trade unionists.

For example, union representatives in one organization dismissed women's complaints of discrimination with the statement that it was 'management's right to select whoever they want'.

In other words the laws cannot be properly enforced unless women have the power and the will to put them to use. For that they require legal knowledge, organization and money – none of which they possess.

Goods, facilities and services

We have dwelt so far upon the application of the new laws to pay and opportunity in employment. For although there has been very little action on this front, it has certainly overshadowed the few, poor stirrings there have been in other areas.

Cases under the non-employment sections of the Sex Discrimination Act have to be taken to the county court. Between 1975 and 1980, no more than two dozen cases actually got that far. In a test case which went to the Court of Appeal in November 1980, June Quinn of Leicester obtained a ruling that Williams furniture store had discriminated unlawfully when it asked her husband to act as guarantor for a hire purchase agreement. Ms Quinn asked the store whether they would have required a similar guarantee for her husband if his material circumstances had been the same as hers; they admitted that they would not.[16] By the end of the 1970s this type of overt discrimination in the granting of credit, mortgages and tenancies had become quite rare – which was progress of a kind. Nevertheless, stores and credit companies have retained the privilege of refusing credit to anyone, on their own undisclosed terms. If they wish to discriminate against women on the quiet, they can usually do so without fear of reprisal. The same is true of mortgage companies, for whom it remains common practice to lend *less* money on the basis of a wife's earnings than on a husband's.

By the early 1980s, mortgages were so hard to obtain that most prospective buyers were grateful to get anything at all, and were not inclined to complain.

Pubs which refuse to serve women with pint mugs of beer have been taken to court and found guilty of unlawful sex discrimination. Sheffield's Wellington Inn has been ordered to pay £10 damages for refusing to allow a young woman called Gay Rice to play snooker. But private clubs are exempted from the Act, which means that a vast range of 'facilities and services' continue to be out of bounds for women. London's gentlemen's clubs, the working men's clubs of the North, and countless political, sporting and recreational clubs are free to exclude women altogether, or to allow them in sometimes, on special conditions. When Wakefield City Working Men's Club banned Sheila Capstick, a long-standing member, from playing snooker, it provoked a popular campaign against one of the bastions of male pre-eminence. The Equal Rights in Clubs Campaign for Action was launched after the Capstick ban in 1979, and challenged the restrictions on women's membership and participation in the four thousand clubs affiliated to the Club and Institute Union. ERICCA is fiercely opposed by the CIU, which ignored the demands of two hundred women and male supporters at its April 1980 annual conference in Blackpool. So entrenched was their antipathy to female incursion that they hackled and gave a slow handclap to *Morning Star* reporter Frankie Rickford when she went into the conference room. ERICCA is campaigning against the immunity granted to private clubs in the Sex Discrimination Act.

Where the law has not made specific exemptions, judges have sometimes helped to create them – as in the case of El Vino of Fleet Street.

El Vino is a little wine bar perched between what used to be the home of Britain's newspaper industry (until it moved out to cheaper premises) and the law courts of the Strand. Its clients are, by and large, superannuated public school boys who eke a fat living out of the press and the Bar. It serves good wine and mediocre sandwiches, and cherishes the tradition of forcing 'ladies' to drink only while sitting down. Photographer Sheila Gray took El Vino to court, alleging sex discrimination; but on 26 May 1978 Judge Ruttle declared at Westminster County Court that her application had failed. El Vino, he said, treated women *differently* from men, but not *less favourably*. There was often a frightful jostling at the bar; and on some occasions staff had to cross the bar room and fish out wine bottles from a rack near floor level, which sometimes meant reaching past customers' legs (egad!). Quoting Lord Denning in the Court of Appeal, Judge Ruttle said:

It would be very wrong to my mind if this statute were thought to obliterate the differences between men and women or to do away with the courtesies and chivalry we expect mankind to give womankind...[17]

In a later case, Lord Denning himself departed from this view and ruled in *Jeremiah* v. *Ministry of Defence*[18] that 'chivalry and good administration' could *not* be a defence against alleged sex discrimination. But in 1981 El Vino was still allowing men to choose whether they stood up or sat down, while giving women no choice in the matter at all. Sheila Gray did not appeal, but another case is to be taken to the Court of Appeal, by lawyer Tess Gill and journalist Anna Coote, backed by the Equal Opportunities Commission. The result is anxiously awaited at the time of writing.

Nor did twelve-year-old Theresa Bennett have any choice about joining Muskham United, her local football club. The Nottingham Football Association and the Football Association Ltd barred her because she was a girl – and she sued them. In the Appeal Court, Lord Denning ruled that it made no difference whether she was as good as any boy of her age. The Sex Discrimination Act exempted 'any sport ... where the physical strength, stamina or physique of the average woman puts her at a disadvantage to the average man'. In other words, Ms Bennett was not to be judged on her own ability, as any boy would have been, but by the *average* ability of all women of all ages.[19]

So what have we to show from our experience of a law prohibiting sex discrimination in the provision of housing, goods, facilities and services? A handful of colourful cases which may have helped to publicize the intention of the Act, but which have been mainly unsuccessful. A little more circumspection on the part of those who wish to continue treating women as second-class citizens. In a few areas real changes which have extended opportunities for women ... but on the whole life has gone on much as ever.

As in employment cases, women may feel they are being treated unfairly, but they are seldom aware that they are victims of sex discrimination. Moreover, it is even more difficult to take a case to a county court (where non-employment cases have to go) than to a tribunal. It is an alienating and expensive procedure. Legal aid is seldom granted. Judges, on the whole, take a traditional view of male and female roles and so interpret the law narrowly. And – perhaps most important – there is no base from which women can organize to enforce these sections of the Act. The trade unions may have had only a limited effect in enforcing the employment section of the Act, but at least they hold out an opportunity for women to overcome male resistance and use their combined strength to claim their rights.

Discrimination in education

In the field of education, the Sex Discrimination Act has had practically no impact at all. Schools continue to educate girls quite differently from boys, narrowing their horizons and restricting their job opportunities (we shall look more closely at this in Chapter 6). In the first six years, only *one* case has been taken to court under this section of the Act.

Helen Whitfield, a pupil of Woodcote High School, Croydon, Surrey, wanted to participate in a 'craft' course which covered woodwork, metal work and design technology. The school refused: the course was for boys and a separate course in 'home economics' was provided for girls. Helen's mother threatened legal action. Later, when a boy dropped out of the craft course, Helen was offered a place, as a special concession. But she didn't want to be the only girl in a class of boys and turned the offer down. She and her mother pursued their legal action, alleging that if the school admitted boys automatically to the course but did not admit girls unless they made a special application, that amounted to 'less favourable treatment' under the terms of the Sex Discrimination Act. When the case came to court in December 1979, Helen's lawyers called expert witnesses to testify (among other things) that a craft course provided better prospects than a home economics course because it was more likely to lead on to skilled employment. Judge Perks, in Croydon County Court, disagreed. He decided that Helen had suffered no damage, and that she never genuinely wanted to take the craft course 'but acted throughout under her mother's influence and was used as a weapon, or perhaps an ally, in her mother's campaign for women's rights'.[20]

Thus schools throughout the country have been given the green light to carry on providing 'vocational' courses for girls and boys on an effectively segregated basis. Occasionally, one or two rather unconventional girls have asked to be let into a 'boys-only' course and, to avoid trouble, the school has usually admitted them. However, courses in woodwork, metal work and other technological subjects retain a strong 'boys-only' image which is enough to deter the vast majority of girls.

In its guidance to schools, the Equal Opportunities Commission has pointed out that opportunities for pupils to study non-traditional subjects 'should be real opportunities and not token gestures... While many schools operate an apparent choice, the grouping of the subjects and the timetabling arrangements can discourage pupils from selecting a subject which is non-traditional.'[21] The pattern could be broken if schools provided both 'craft' and 'home economics' courses to girls and boys on a genuinely equal (and possibly compulsory) basis. Had Helen won her case, they might have been encouraged to do something of the kind.

A major problem with this section of the Act is that it can be extremely difficult and risky to take a case to court. Since minors cannot take legal action on their own, a girl who wants to pursue a complaint must have the full cooperation of a parent or guardian. Few children would be keen to stand out from the crowd by challenging their school in court, and probably even fewer parents (having been brought up in some awe of educational authorities) would want to 'make trouble' in a daughter's school. They may worry that it would damage her chances of achieving good results, or earn her a poor reference which could count against her later on (teachers' references are usually kept secret). Or they may feel thoroughly daunted at the prospect of going to court. A special 'cooling off' period is required, in which parents must first write to the Secretary of State for Education and wait two months (to see if anything changes) before going ahead. This may act as a further deterrent.

Since this section of the Act has not yet been properly tested in court, it is impossible to predict how judges will interpret it, in anything but the clearest-cut of cases. Most schools have ceased to display blatant sex discrimination and the practices which need to be challenged are therefore of a more subtle variety, harder to prove. So the parents would need expert help to pursue a complaint. They can apply for assistance to the Equal Opportunities Commission, but this may be refused – the EOC being far from bold in such matters. They can apply for legal aid, but their chances of getting it are slim. In view of what Judge Perks had to say, it is ironic to note that if Helen Whitfield's mother had *not* been a campaigner for women's rights, she would not have taken up the case at all – and the dubious practices of Woodcote High School would have remained entirely unchallenged.

Until another parent or until the Equal Opportunities Commission decides to challenge the educational establishment in a persistent and uncompromising manner the Sex Discrimination Act will remain a dead letter in this field. There is little chance of the teachers' unions taking up the fight in any meaningful way. They believe in defending their members' autonomy as professionals, and tend to resist attempts to interfere with what goes on in the classroom.

It certainly would have helped matters if, from the day the new equality laws were enacted, there had been a large, bold, vigorous organization, with a free hand and a generous budget, whose purpose it was to monitor the progress of the legislation, to ensure that it was brought to everyone's attention and enforced as effectively as possible; and to campaign for necessary amendments to the law and other measures to promote equality, in the light of new experience. Instead, there was only the Equal Opportunities Commission.

The EOC – 'a passionate caution'

Set up in a great rush so that its launch could coincide with the new laws coming into force, the EOC opened the doors of its Manchester headquarters on 29 December 1975 – amid frenzied cries of 'Personchester!' and other hilarious jokes from the nation's media people. The powers and duties conferred upon it by the Sex Discrimination Act sounded rather impressive.

In general, it has a duty to monitor the working of the Sex Discrimination and Equal Pay Acts, to combat discrimination and to promote equal opportunity. In particular, it has the power to conduct formal investigations where it suspects that sex discrimination is being practised. The scope of these inquiries can be broad, covering a whole region or industry, or narrow, looking into the conduct of a particular organization – such as a factory, school or credit company. In the course of a formal investigation it can compel people to supply relevant information; it can order a course of action to prevent further breach of the law; it can issue a 'non-discrimination notice' requiring

123

the offender to stop breaking the law; and if that doesn't do the trick it can apply to court for an injunction, which carries the threat of fine or imprisonment if it is not obeyed.

The EOC has power, too, to give financial and legal assistance to individuals who are pursuing complaints under the two Acts – especially if the case involves a key principle and will serve the purpose of testing the law. It has a duty to see that the law is properly enforced; to conduct research into relevant areas; and to recommend to the government necessary changes – including amendments to the Equal Pay and Sex Discrimination Acts, and reforms to end discrimination in other fields not covered by those laws (such as tax, immigration and provisions for retirement).

In addition, it is responsible for chasing up certain kinds of discriminatory behaviour, such as advertisements which convey an intention to discriminate unlawfully; in cases where a person has been instructed or encouraged to discriminate unlawfully; and in cases of persistent discrimination, where patterns of inequality are so firmly entrenched that no woman is likely to get as far as raising a complaint.

One might be tempted to imagine that with powers such as these, with 170 employees, with an annual budget of £2 million, and with fourteen Commissioners meeting on a regular monthly basis, the EOC would be blazing a fair old trail – striking fear into the hearts of the powerful men at the very mention of its name. ('My God, Basil, they're on to us – we'll have to let the women through!... Take down that Pirelli calendar and get Miss Jones a cup of coffee at once!') It has not been quite like that.

In the first five years of its life, the Equal Opportunities Commission gave financial and legal assistance to some two hundred cases which went before industrial tribunals, and about two dozen which went to the county courts; it gave legal advice to a further fifty or so. It backed more than sixty appeals to higher courts, including five to the European Court of Justice. It sponsored eighty research and educational projects. It issued detailed proposals on a number of areas outside the scope of the two Acts, including taxation, social security, maternity rights and child care. It produced guidelines for employers, employees, schools and advertisers on how to enforce the law. And it built up an impressive library which was officially opened to the public in 1980.

As the idea of equal rights has become more respectable in

the late 1970s, so the EOC has become a little more confident, and with the passing of time we have seen the gradual accumulation of tangible achievements. By the early 1980s, it has thus escaped being a full-scale disaster. But when examined in the light of its statutory duties and powers, its record is abysmal.

By 1981, the EOC had launched no more than six formal investigations, completed one and issued one non-discrimination notice. Formal investigations are not easy to carry out: the EOC must jump through a long row of legal hoops, allowing for a series of delays and appeals, before getting into full swing. Nevertheless, they are potentially a wide-ranging and effective weapon – if the political will is there to use them, and if sufficient expertise is developed to proceed as quickly and efficiently as the law allows. The EOC has never had that political will, and so has never built up the necessary expertise. The Commission for Racial Equality, no ball of fire itself, managed to open forty-four formal investigations, complete more than ten and issue more than eight non-discrimination notices in the first three and a half years of its life (having been launched in June 1977).

The EOC's first formal investigation, into the organization of secondary schooling in Tameside, near Manchester, ended in *débâcle*. The Commissioners who conducted the inquiry were outmanoeuvred by local authority officials and in the end were unable to make any finding of unlawful discrimination. The second, into equal pay and opportunity at the Electrolux domestic appliance firm in Luton, Bedfordshire, has begun to rival *No Sex Please, We're British* as the longest-running comedy show. It was first announced in February 1977 – and then only after Mr Justice Phillips in the Employment Appeals Tribunal had said that there *ought* to be a formal investigation. The grading structure at Electrolux is highly complex and sensitive, as is the relationship between the different unions who organize at the plant. One of the local union officials was especially hostile to the investigation. It was all too much for the EOC. An interim report and a non-discrimination notice dealing with equal pay were published in 1979. In 1981, the final report has still not been published.

The first major case the EOC took to an industrial tribunal was on behalf of a school teacher, Ms Castle, who had been refused a senior job at a Surrey school because of a rule which said that the second mistress (or master) should not be of the same sex as the deputy head. The rule, introduced nationwide by the Burnham Committee, was designed to maintain even numbers of male and female teachers in senior posts and, since top jobs tended to go to men, it had helped to preserve a minimum quota of these for women. The case was won, the Burnham rule declared unlawful.[22] The EOC claimed it as a victory against protective quotas 'which excuse people from facing the full consequences of equality'. Such was the spirit in which the EOC embarked upon its career. Not until the end of the decade did it start to recognize some merit in the principle of 'positive action' in favour of women (which we shall discuss later on).

In 1976 the EOC launched an informal inquiry into five hundred leading employers – the biggest exercise it has ever conducted in the field of employment. It consisted, quite simply, of a questionnaire to management, asking them what they had done about equal pay and opportunity. Naturally, the employers did not care to cast themselves in a poor light, and the EOC made no effort to check their testimony against the experience of their female employees. The results, published a year later with much huffing and puffing, were predictably bland and uninformative.

In the field of education, the Commission has engaged in endless discussions with figures in the education hierarchy and has published some fine-sounding guidance, but has done nothing to change traditional practices in most schools.

Prevarication has attended almost all of its activities. To cite just two examples, a small booklet on child care, '*I want to work but what about the kids?*'[23] went through seventeen months of drafting and redrafting before the Commissioners could agree on a final version. (The deputy chairwoman found the phrase 'collective child care' distasteful and insisted that it be changed to 'group child care'.) The Commission has always abhorred confrontation, and has shrunk from making strong statements in public – preferring to negotiate and conciliate behind the scenes with fellow members of the establishment.

Women have ceased to expect much action from the EOC; in fact, they are pleasantly surprised when it produces anything at all – even at a time when the government is waging a massive attack on the rights and living standards of working women. Back in 1975, there were hopes that the EOC would champion the cause of women and fight to enforce the laws. But it was only an illusion.

The EOC was set up according to the same unwritten rules

by which most commissions and 'quangos' are established. These rules are designed first and foremost to satisfy the interest groups which carry most weight with the government, and only secondly to enable the organization to perform its statutory duties. So the Labour Party's Women's Officer, Betty (now Baroness) Lockwood became chairwoman – although she insists upon being called 'chairman' – and Lady Elspeth Howe, a prominent and rather well-connected Tory, became her deputy. It kept the two parties happy, but was not the best recipe for a strong, determined leadership.

There was a battle over whether the TUC and CBI should have two or three places on the Commission. In the end they won three each, making an industrial block which has usually outweighed all other alliances and interest groups. The education establishment had to be satisfied next, then Scotland, Wales and the Home Office itself, which incidentally made all the appointments. The idea that the Commission might be filled by individuals most noted for their enthusiasm and ability to work for equality was not entertained. It was intended to be (and is) a disunited group of the 'Great and the Good', who have prior and sometimes conflicting allegiances, who are busy with other commitments and usually see their work on the Commission as peripheral to their lives and who approach their statutory task with a passionate caution.

When advertisements went out for staff to fill the Manchester office, they appeared to present ideal opportunities for energetic young women with impressive qualifications and a high level of commitment to the work in hand. The mix proved disastrous. One Commissioner complained in 1978: 'There are too many people [on the staff] who are committed to the women's cause, so they can't think straight. They just go barging through.' There have been massive defections. In 1978 staff turnover was 38 per cent – more than three times that of an average office. One senior officer explained in her resignation letter that she was leaving because of 'a total disillusionmont with the lack of direction and commitment to decisive action by EOC Commissioners in all areas of the EOC's work'. The fact that the Commission had four Chief Executives in the first five years of its life suggests the quality of management and the degree of internecine strife there.

Inevitably, it has been in areas which are least politically sensitive that the Commission has made most progress. There are no major disagreements between political parties, or between the TUC and CBI, or between feminists and non-feminists, as to whether job advertisements should have a nondiscriminatory form, or whether credit companies should treat women as favourably as men. Consequently, in these and other areas outside employment and education, the EOC has a fairly uncontroversial record of diligence. Meanwhile the TUC representatives on the Commission have guarded their own traditional sphere of influence as assiduously as the CBI appointees have looked after their fellow-members' interests. The EOC has therefore confined itself mainly to individual casework in the employment field; anything more radical would be bound to get caught in political cross-fire. (The EOC's guidelines for employers could not be published until *seventeen* different drafts had passed back and forth between staff and Commissioners.)

From the day it was born, the EOC has lived in constant terror of the government's axe – and rather than build strong allies among women, making itself indispensable to them, so that no government would dare touch it, it has just gone on cowering. It is sensitive in most of its dealings and nervous to the point of paranoia about media attention. But that characteristic, too, was programmed into it from the start, by the arrangement of its funding and the careful selection of Commissioners. For, as with the 'equality' laws themselves, the EOC was designed to *contain* the problem of sex discrimination, not *solve* it.

It is neither representative of women, nor accountable to them. MPS would find it easier to keep an eye on the work of the Home Office – and that's hard enough – than on the EOC. Neither MPs nor members of the public can sit in on Commission meetings, or get sight of any of its unpublished documents. There has never been any question of its being answerable to a constituency of women. Its quasi-independence from government purports to make it more effective. Instead, the relationship has made it behave like a poor cousin on the annual visit to the Big House: dull, overdignified, obsequious and desperately afraid of missing the next handout [24]

Within the women's movement, some efforts have been made to compensate for the shortcomings of the Equal Opportunities Commission. The Rights for Women Unit of the National Council for Civil Liberties, the Equal Pay and Opportunity Campaign, and Rights of Women (ROW) have worked hard in their various ways – helping individual women, producing guides to the law, proposing amendments, lobbying Parliament and holding seminars and workshops to teach people how to enforce the legislation. The first two have concentrated their attention on the unions, believing this to be the proper channel for promoting equal pay and opportunity in employment.

All three have operated on a tiny fraction of the Commission's budget. Between them they have seldom had more than two salaried workers and two dozen volunteers, and this has inevitably limited their scope and effectiveness – although much of what they have lacked in money they have made up in the quality of their operations. In a major investigation for the *Sunday Times*,[25] Patricia Ashdowne-Sharpe commented in 1977 that the NCCL women's rights officer seemed to be doing more to enforce the legislation than the whole of the EOC!

From time to time these small organizations have received grants from the Commission for specific projects, but this hasn't kept them going for long. And once the EOC came on to the scene, other potential sources of funds, such as charitable trusts, were keen to divert their own funds to other causes. It has never been easy to raise money by individual subscription, because so few women are well-off and most of those who are have difficulty appreciating the urgency of the problem.

It is worth imagining what might have happened if, instead of setting up the EOC, the government had made £2 million a year available to feminist organizations and trade unions, for a range of activities aimed at promoting equal opportunity.

The need for 'positive action'

Women who fought for the vote in the early 1900s saw it as a means of improving their position in society generally, but until they won it they could only guess at how little or how much it would help to change their circumstances. In the same way, women who have fought for equal pay and sex discrimination laws, and then experienced them in practice for a few years, have been able to appreciate more fully the extent of their oppression and to work out further strategies. By the early 1980s it was clear that laws *against* unequal pay and sex discrimination would do nothing to tackle the entrenched patterns of inequality that had built up over centuries. In some quarters – notably the NCCL and the TUC – people have begun to insist that *positive* measures are needed in order to compensate for past discrimination.

In the United States, this principle has been accepted at an official level since 1970. Many US employers have been obliged by law to implement what are known as 'affirmative action programmes', aimed at increasing the numbers of women in jobs done mainly or exclusively by men. Those who hold government contracts have to show that they are already employing women at all levels in equal proportions with men, or that they are making a 'good faith' effort to do so. If they fail, they risk losing their contract. In order to prove they are making a 'good faith' effort, they usually have to introduce an 'affirmative action programme'.

The basic idea behind 'positive' or 'affirmative' action is that women are constrained by more than just overt discrimination ('We don't hire women in this job'). A woman may be deterred from coming forward because she feels the job is not for her. She may lack confidence in her ability, she may have the impression that the job is intended for a man, she may not have had the opportunity in the past to develop the necessary qualifications, or the job may be organized in such a way that she cannot easily make it fit in with the rest of her life. These are not personal failings so much as products of an unequal system, in which strong habits have been developed about the way women and men are perceived and treated. They can be overcome if certain measures are adopted which help women change themselves and which encourage them to think they can do the job. Which measures are appropriate will depend on the nature and circumstances of each job. A 'positive action programme' is a package of measures which are considered to be appropriate to the organization in question. It usually includes a set of goals and timetables, with the intention of achieving certain levels of female employment by certain dates in the future (for example, that 25 per cent of trainee drivers in a company will be female in five years' time, and 50 per cent in ten years' time). It is not expected that changes will occur overnight, but if the goals are not met within the required time, then the programme ought to be reviewed and strengthened. The programme might include such measures as aiming job advertisements specifically at women and publishing them in women's magazines; reassessing the skills and qualifications required of applicants, to weed out any which favour males and are not strictly necessary for the job; scrutinizing selection procedures; and providing special training to enable women to

130

qualify for promotion. It is written out in detail and is usually monitored by a team representing management and employees.

In some US organizations, women have made substantial gains as a result of affirmative action. For example, a programme set up in 1972 by the Bank of America aimed to fill 40 per cent of jobs at officer grade with women by 1978; in fact the goal was exceeded by 3 per cent. General Motors introduced a programme which increased the proportion of female students at its engineering college from 0.6 per cent in 1970 to 32 per cent in 1977.

Positive action is no panacea. It has proved more effective where there are groups of articulate, middle-class women who are prepared to fight to ensure that programmes are properly implemented. It has had no apparent effect on the gap between male and female average pay (which is even greater in the United States than in the UK) and it has done little to change patterns of employment among lower-paid blue-collar workers. Nevertheless, in some areas it has helped to change attitudes and to provide new opportunities for women. As a strategy, it is important for feminist politics because it shifts the focus of the campaign for equality towards a recognition of the system which sustains male supremacy, and suggests that men themselves must actively participate in the process of change. It is a useful device for raising awareness.

Gradually, the idea of 'affirmative action' has begun to attract attention in Britain. In the early 1970s it was widely believed – even among some feminists – that if women were to be equal they should be treated *the same as men*; anything else would demean them, or inhibit their progress, or be unfair to men. This was the philosophy behind the EOC's challenge to the Burnham quota system for senior teachers. Nevertheless, when the Sex Discrimination Act was drafted, an allowance was made for women to be treated differently in some circumstances. The Act says that certain training organizations may provide women-only courses for jobs which are monopolized by men, and special training for women returning to employment after raising their families. Employers may encourage women to apply for jobs traditionally done by men, and provide single sex training for them. Trade unions, employers' organizations and professional associations may take steps to increase the levels of female participation. These provisions were largely ignored for some years. But by the end of the decade, it was becoming increasingly clear that unless they were utilized women would make no progress at all.

In September 1980, a resolution was passed by the Trades Union Congress which called for 'positive action in favour of women' to help break down job segregation and raise the level of women's pay. The dismal record of the Equal Pay and Sex Discrimination Acts helped to win the assent of Congress. It was necessary to reassure delegates that positive action in favour of women need not entail discrimination *against men* – for example, it would not mean that a woman could be hired for a job who was less well qualified than a male applicant. Two months later, the TUC held a special conference to discuss draft guidelines for positive action programmes which might be negotiated by unions.[26] (It is interesting to note how vigorously – and with what comparative success – men resist any threat of discrimination against themselves, as though this were an even greater evil than continuing discrimination against women. Some of the most celebrated cases brought under the Sex Discrimination Act have been fought and won by men.)

With funding from the EOC, the National Council for Civil Liberties launched a positive action project in 1979. Its purpose was to introduce pilot schemes in two or three different workplaces, in collaboration with unions and management, so that the idea could be tested in practice. Thames Television was the first company to show interest, and barrister Sadie Robarts was employed by the NCCL to investigate patterns of employment at Thames and help the company to devise a plan for extending opportunities for women. An important early consequence of her intervention was that women at Thames formed a group and began to meet regularly to discuss their employment conditions and to find ways of improving them. This provided a strong impetus for a positive action programme.

In 1981, Ms Robarts made her recommendations to the Thames Board of Directors. She advised them to appoint a senior director with special responsibility for implementing and monitoring positive action over a five-year period. A women's employment officer should be appointed within the personnel department, and a Positive Action Committee formed, comprising management, unions and the Women's Committee, to have regular discussions of the positive action programme. The Thames workforce should be analysed by sex, and targets set for recruiting women to jobs where they have been underrepresented. Records should be kept of all jobs applications, appointments and promotions. Job advertisements should be written and published in such a way as to ensure their appeal to women, and unnecessary qualifications which favour one sex should be eliminated from job descriptions.

The company should publish a code of practice for interviewers; educate its managers and supervisors about the implications of the equality legislation and women's employment problems; provide more technical training courses and 'voluntary attachments' (by which employees can move from one department to another); and improve career development and planning for all employees, particularly women. There should be an immediate commitment by the company to increase funding for child care assistance and, in the longer term, a feasibility study of setting up a crèche within the company.

At the time of writing, although Thames has not begun to implement these recommendations, there are some signs that it may make a start. There is wider agreement at Thames Television, and more generally among individual unions and the TUC, women's organizations, some employers and the EOC, that positive measures are needed. However, when it comes to putting theory into practice, there are serious difficulties. For a start, there is no law in Britain to force employers to introduce positive action: the Sex Discrimination Act merely says that if anyone does it, it won't be illegal. There is no threat of government contracts being withdrawn (as in the United States). So where will the incentive come from?

So far, no more than half a dozen organizations in the UK have seriously contemplated positive action. There has been a pilot project at one of the national clearing banks. The London borough of Camden has drawn up a set of plans and two other London boroughs have started discussions on the subject. The Sainsbury food chain has made efforts to hire women as butchers (having experienced difficulty recruiting men in that area) and by 1979 were employing 141 women – 19 per cent of the total – as 'meat trades assistants'.

Some employers have declared themselves 'equal opportunity employers' and have even published policy statements. ICI, for example, has announced that 'in the past job opportunities for women employees have tended to follow traditional career patterns associated with their own sex. The Board now considers that this concept is too restrictive. . .' But it has been left mainly to women to take action: the Board believes, it says, 'that women have a responsibility to prepare and present themselves for the opportunities available and that they should be encouraged to do so'.[27]

Rank Xerox has gone as far as to instruct its managers in 1978 to 'develop programmes appropriate to the national circumstances designed to ensure equal opportunity in employment'. Each unit should

aim to have a considerably higher proportion, compared with most companies, of women in what have hitherto been regarded as 'male' jobs. Each unit will therefore be asked to set its own targets and maintain a clear record of progress achieved.[28]

Rank Xerox's policy declaration is longer and more sophisticated than that of any other private company in the UK. But even there it isn't clear *whose* energy and enthusiasm will ensure that the policy is carried out at unit level. Will managers be demoted, will workers threaten industrial action, if targets are not set high enough, or if targets are not met? There are no signs of any practical progress at all at Rank Xerox.

Here is the crux of the problem. Employers will take action when it suits them – as indeed it has suited Sainsbury's to hire female butchers. (One can see why Thames Television is prepared to pioneer the field: television is one of the few expanding industries in the UK in the early 1980s.) If they believe positive action to be cost effective they may pursue it – that is, if they don't entertain traditional prejudices about women doing 'men's jobs'. But if they fear it will make any kind of trouble for them, in terms of profits, efficiency or industrial relations, there is no reason why they should not simply carry on as before. There is no kudos attached to positive action; there are no MBEs for employers who make special efforts to promote women, no 'Awards to Industry' for training women in traditional male spheres. There are no legal sanctions against those who take no action.

The spur will have to come from the people who stand to gain by it, namely from women workers. They can only exert effective pressure on management if they are well organized. The trade unions have gone so far as to commit themselves to the principle of positive action. How far will they be prepared to go to carry it through – especially as times get tougher? If women are to have more opportunities in a shrinking job market, that can only mean there will be fewer opportunities for men. Will men give way gracefully or put up a fight in defence of their own interests? How far will women have to organize independently in order to promote positive action?

We have seen that the women's liberation movement has had little influence over the way the 'equality' laws were drafted, and even less over the design of the Equal Opportunities Commission. It might have been different if there had been a strong force of women within Parliament. Law-makers are not generally inclined to undermine their own interests, and the British Parliament is unmistakably packed with men.

Isolation at the centre

In February 1974, twenty-three women were returned to the House of Commons – three fewer than in 1970. They represented 3.6 per cent of the total of 635 MPs. In October 1974, when Harold Wilson called a second election to consolidate his majority, the number of female MPs rose to twenty-seven. Of the 161 women who stood as candidates that time, six were defeated for every one who scored a victory – while the failure rate for the 2,252 male candidates was only 3.7 to one. In May 1979, when Margaret Thatcher became the first female Prime Minister of Britain, nineteen women were returned to Parliament, the lowest proportion in twenty years.

This is, of course, no accident. In her book *Women in the House*,[29] Elizabeth Vallance identifies a wide range of social and political constraints on women. They are not encouraged from an early age (as men are) to be bold with their opinions, to articulate them in public, or to seek out power. Parliament's hours of business have been arranged for the convenience of male barristers, not women with young children. Selection committees in the constituencies still tend to assume that women cannot deal with certain 'heavy' political issues. It is possible, too, that 'the ritual and ceremonial of the House, its slow, ponderous processes, its interminable committees and talk rather than action, [does] not appeal to women whose experience is largely practical, pragmatic and here and now'.

Moreover, it seems that women who 'make it' in Parliament have not paved the way for others as they have done in many walks of life: 'A few outstanding individuals may make their own way and achieve great personal success,' says Vallance, 'but this does not accrue to women in general. Each time, it appears, the ground has to be ploughed anew...' Margaret Thatcher's arrival as Prime Minister 'is most unlikely to pave the way for women any more directly than Margaret Bondfield's achievement did over forty-eight years ago. In 1930 there was one woman in the Cabinet, and in 1978 there was also one.'

If the feminist tradition has been weak in Parliament, this is partly because the women who are in it have always been so isolated. When feminists have organized around parliamentary politics, they have done so as lobbyists only – until very recently. There have been few attempts to increase the numbers of women in the House and there have been no efforts to combine lobbying with organization of feminist support for sitting female MPs.

Getting women into Parliament did not figure among the aims of the women's liberation movement in the 1970s. Abhorring leaders, hierarchies and all man-made power structures, feminists have seen little merit in fighting such a battle. Some have taken the view that all MPs are elitist time-servers, out of touch with the needs of ordinary people, and that women who join their ranks are bound to be corrupted – so there is no point encouraging them. Those who put themselves forward have commonly been dismissed as 'opportunists'. There has also been the awkward question of whether one favours a woman on account of her sex before one rates her in conventional political terms. Few feminists have felt they have any common cause with Tory women; but there has remained the problem of whether a woman with feminist views at the centre or right of the Labour Party is preferable to a man with left-wing credentials and a wife at home looking after the kids.

More important has been the general alienation of the women's movement from parliamentary politics. It is one thing to write letters to MPs, sign petitions and carry torches down Whitehall – to beat on the front door from the outside. It is quite another to go round the back and fight one's way inside – past forbidding doormen, through long corridors of protocol and compromise, up grubby, hypocritical stairs, into uncomfortable ante-rooms of self-advertisement – to seek out the place where power is supposed to lie, but seldom can be found. So women have continued to lobby a male-dominated legislature, which has had little understanding of their needs and no intention of making them a priority.

By 1980 there were at last some signs of a growing feminist presence within the Labour Party. There was a new determination to get women's voice heard within the structure of the party as well as within Parliament. Increasing numbers of women in their twenties and thirties were making the Labour Party the main focus of their political activity *as feminists* as well as socialists. They were generally on the left, supporters of increased democracy within the party. And they were demanding that special measures be taken to increase female participation.

A new unity

In the autumn of 1980, the newly formed Women's Action Committee of the Campaign for Labour Party Democracy launched 'a major campaign to give women political equality' and issued a list of objectives. They wanted the women's section of Labour's National Executive Committee to be elected by the party's annual women's conference; they wanted resolutions to be carried forward from the women's conferences on to the agenda of the party's national conference; they wanted 'positive discrimination' on parliamentary shortlists; a reformed parliamentary day, a National Women's Department at the Labour Party's headquarters, positive discrimination on NEC study groups, and the party's Women's Advisory Committee to be elected by the women's conference.

In June 1981, resolutions embodying these aims were put to the National Conference of Labour Women: they were defeated but on some the vote was very close, and considerably closer than the previous year when similar motions had been proposed. The composition of the conference had altered noticeably in the space of three or four years. By 1981 there was a large contingent of young, left-wing feminists. As part of this trend, there are more women – and more feminists – prepared to stand for Parliament. Their opportunities have been enhanced by the new system of mandatory reselection of MPs, introduced after Labour's 1980 national conference.

Elizabeth Vallance points out that a new sense of unity has already begun to develop among Labour women MPs – and the spur for this was the challenge they faced from a series of anti-abortion Bills between 1975 and 1979. 'This unity was, according to many of the women involved, at least in part the product of male apathy. Even the men who were willing to support them saw the issue as not important enough to devote a great deal of time to. And it did take a great deal of time simply not to allow the stages of these Bills to go through almost by default.' When the abortion debate was in full swing in 1976,

137

the women gathered in the Chamber one evening, waiting to intervene:

At one stage there were twelve of them sitting, as they do not typically do, together, on the back benches awaiting the Speaker's sign. This apparently was too much for some of the men who came into the Chamber from elsewhere in the Palace . . . to view this unholy alliance, [the men were] laughing and making suggestive remarks, perhaps more than anything to cover their own trepidation.[30]

Vallance suggests that women MPs are becoming less apologetic about concentrating on 'women's issues' instead of proving themselves in the big, strong, masculine arenas of economics, industry and foreign affairs. Why should women have to steer clear of feminist contention, or risk being stigmatized as emotional and tendentious?

Isn't political debate always tendentious, they ask, doesn't it always involve talking about what you know, and isn't it often extremely emotional? No one castigates a union-sponsored MP for putting his members' case. No one suggests he is not being objective or only talking about what he knows. This response seems largely to be reserved for women, talking about women.

Mary Kaldor, the disarmament campaigner, published an astute critique of the 'parliamentary career' in the *Guardian* (22 June 1981) which illustrates why so many women – however talented and politically active they may be – are reluctant to stand for Parliament. When she was a prospective parliamentary candidate, she says people were always saying to her 'I hear you're going into politics':

What a funny phrase, I thought, since I have been 'in politics' all my life. What they meant, of course, was going into a well-paid job, with a career structure, a job which is called 'politics'. And the fact that this 'politics' is a career separates Westminster from the rest of politics – constituency parties, community activities, single-issue campaigns. The chasm . . . is entrenched by the sexual divisions in society. So long as we think men ought to have careers, it will be difficult to end the isolation of Parliament.

She maintains, nevertheless, that women *should* stand, and she remarks that when she was standing for selection in the London constituency of Dulwich, she got to know two of the other female candidates rather well:

Perhaps because we were women, we became friends. Kate Hooey, who was eventually selected, and I thought we should turn the job into a collective enterprise so we could all do it together, helping each other with the difficult questions and spreading the issues around. Nevertheless, the situation was competitive. We were competing for a job which we might have for life. We were getting trapped into a male situation... As long as being an MP is a career, and that means the combination of good pay, tenure, and patronage, Parliament gradually gets sealed off from other activities: a separate male institution...

It is possible to imagine that if the influence of the women's movement – so evident in Mary Kaldor's critique – were to continue to spread and to bring more women into the House of Commons, parliamentary politics might start to be transformed. If women accounted not for *3* per cent of MPs (as at present) but for 20, 30 or 50 per cent, we might even see the beginnings of a useful legislative programme.

Applications to industrial tribunals under the Equal Pay and Sex Discrimination Acts

**Table 6
Equal Pay Act**

Year	Applications made	Applications heard (as % of total)	Applications upheld (as % of those heard)	Applications dismissed (as % of those heard)
1976	1,742	709 (40.7%)	213 (30.04%)	496 (69.9%)
1977	751	363 (48.3%)	91 (25.06%)	272 (74.93%)
1978	343	80 (23.3%)	24 (30%)	56 (70%)
1979	263	78 (29.6%)	13 (16.66%)	65 (83.33%)
TOTAL	3,099	1,230 (39.7%)	341 (27%)	889 (73%)

**Table 7
Sex Discrimination Act**

Year	Applications made	Applications heard (as % of total)	Applications upheld (as % of those heard)	Applications dismissed (as % of those heard)
1976	243	119 (48.9%)	24 (20.16%)	95 (79.83%)
1977	229	77 (33.6%)	17 (22.07%)	60 (77.92%)
1978	171	67 (39.18%)	14 (20.89%)	53 (79.1%)
1979	180	61 (29.5%)	16 (26.22%)	45 (73.77%)
TOTAL	823	324 (39.3%)	71 (22%)	253 (78%)

Notes to Chapter 4

1 *Women's Report*, vol. 1 (2), January–March 1973.
2 'Cost of Equal Pay', in *Employment and Productivity Gazette*, January 1970.
3 First report on the implementation of the Equal Pay Act, from the Office of Manpower Economics, HMSO 1972.
4 Glucklich, P., Povall, M., Snell, M. W. and Zell, A. 'Equal Pay and Opportunity' In *Department of Employment Gazette*, July 1978.
5 *Waddington* v. *Leicester Council for Voluntary Service*, EAT, 1976.
6 Both proposals in this paragraph were put forward by the Equal Opportunities Commission (in 1981) and by the National Council for Civil Liberties (in October 1977).

7 *Nasse* v. *Science Research Council*, House of Lords, November 1979.
8 *Price* v. *Civil Service Commission*, EAT, July 1976.
9 Snell, M. 'The Equal Pay and Sex Discrimination Acts: their impact in the workplace', in *Feminist Review*, vol. 1(1), London 1979.
10 *Durrant* v. *North Yorkshire Area Health Authority*, EAT, April 1979.
11 *Jenkins* v. *Kingsgate (Clothing) Limited*, European Court of Justice, March 1981.
12 Gregory, F. 'The Great Conciliation Fraud', *New Statesman*, 3 July 1981.
13 Industrial tribunal chairman Sir Martin Edwards, quoted in Coussins, J. *The Equality Report*, NCCL, 1976.
14 *Department of Employment Gazette*, April 1980.
15 Snell, M. op. cit.
16 *Quinn* v. *Williams Furniture Ltd*, Court of Appeal, November 1980.
17 *Gray* v. *El Vino*, Westminster County Court, May 1978.
18 *Jeremiah* v. *Ministry of Defence*, Court of Appeal, October 1979.
19 *Bennett* v. *the Football Association and the Nottinghamshire Football Association*, Court of Appeal, July 1978.
20 *Whitfield* v. *the London Borough of Croydon and Woodcote High School*, Croydon County Court, December 1979.
21 *Do You Provide Equal Educational Opportunities?* EOC, Manchester.
22 *Castle* v. *Surrey County Council*, industrial tribunal, September 1976.
23 *'I want to work but what about the kids?'*, EOC, Manchester.
24 See also Coote, A. 'Equality and the Curse of the Quango', *New Statesman*, 1 December 1978.
25 Ashdowne-Sharpe, P. 'Women's Rights – the missed opportunity', *Sunday Times*, 20 February 1977.
26 The TUC published a discussion document, *Equal Opportunities: 'Positive' Action in Women's Employment*, in May 1980.
27 Quoted in Robarts, R. *Positive Action for Women, The Next Step*, NCCL, 1981.
28 Ibid.
29 Vallance, E. *Women in the House*, Athlone Press, London 1979.
30 Ibid.

5 *Unions*

From the early stages of the women's liberation movement, efforts have been made to forge links with the trade unions. Indeed, this has been a key strategy of the socialist-feminist element of the movement. It is seen as a way of reaching women who are not yet acquainted with feminist politics, as an organizational base for feminist campaigns, and as a means of anchoring women's liberation in working-class politics – which is essential to those who regard feminism as an integral part of the struggle for socialism.

There has also been a general trend, beginning in the 1960s and continuing throughout the 1970s, alongside the development of the women's movement, of massive numbers of women (especially white-collar workers) joining unions for the first time. For many women, then, the start of trade union activity has coincided with, or has prompted, an introduction to feminist ideas.

In 1961 there were four male trade unionists for every female union member. By 1980, the ratio dropped to barely two-to-one. Female membership increased during that period by 110 per cent – more than twice the rate at which women joined the labour force (an increase of 48.5 per cent). Within the same years, the number of men in the workforce remained fairly stable, while they increased their union membership by only 17.6 per cent.

The unions have held out considerable promise. They have power in the workplace. They have a hot-line to government (under Labour, at least). Their business is to represent workers and help them to win better pay, benefits and conditions. The British trade union movement is perhaps the most experienced and influential in the Western capitalist world. Through the unions, women have a chance to enlist male support in order to fight with them, rather than fighting alone.

Many radical feminists – and others too – have considered the trade union movement a bastion of male power which is

143

inimical to women's liberation. Socialist feminists have not been under any great illusions about the extent of male dominance in the unions: it has been plain to see that men are in control of almost all the top positions, both in individual unions and in the TUC; it is also clear that they control most of the key decision-making posts throughout the trade union structure; and the special needs of women workers are very low down on the list of union bargaining priorities. The fact that socialist feminists have been determined nevertheless to engage in trade unionism is an expression of their approach to politics generally. They see it as necessary to organize within the unions, to campaign through them and to struggle to change them – at the same time.

In the course of the 1970s, women have begun to discover what a slow, difficult business it is going to be to change the unions. They have made some inroads, and they have achieved some material gains. But, just as they have had to discover, through campaigning for equality at work, that inequality is deeply built into the structure of the labour market, so they have learned, through their involvement in the unions, that female powerlessness is not a surface problem, but a profound and intractable one.

In this chapter we look at the record of the trade union movement in fighting to improve the position of women since the early 1970s. We examine the reasons for women's continuing powerlessness, and we assess recent attempts by the TUC and individual unions to increase the participation of their female members.

The impact of feminism

During the 1970s the unions notched up some notable gains for women. Each one has its own favourite examples – and it is worth recounting a few to indicate the range of their activities. APEX, the office workers' union, made a string of successful applications to the Central Arbitration Committee, which led to the scrapping of low-paid 'women's grades' in several large companies, including the tobacco giants, Imperial and Gallaghers. TASS, the white-collar engineers' union, conducted a campaign under the slogan 'Men's pay for women', which went beyond the scope of the Equal Pay Act and demanded that women should be paid the rate that a man would be paid for doing the same job; according to the TASS salary census, between 1975 and 1980, the pay of female clerical workers increased on average from 74.4 to 81.3 per cent of the male average – which was considerably better than the national figures. The National Union of Public Employees negotiated maternity pay agreements for two large groups of public sector workers, which went well beyond the statutory awards. The General and Municipal Workers' Union has won several important victories at industrial tribunals and at the Employment Appeals Tribunal in equal pay and sex discrimination cases (including two that were abandoned as no-hopers by the EOC). ACTT, which organizes film and television workers, commissioned an exhaustive study of female employment in those industries, published in 1975, which became a classic reference point for feminists and trade unionists, as well as a valuable bargaining counter for women in the ACTT.[1] Britain's first 'positive action' agreement, at the London Borough of Camden, was negotiated by the national and local government officers' union, NALGO, and the same union has produced a series of negotiating guides for its members, *Negotiating for Equality, Workplace Nurseries* and *Rights for Working Parents*[2] – all with a distinctly feminist tone.

The influence of the women's liberation movement is easy to trace. Feminists have taken jobs in unions' expanding research departments, and have played a part, as lay activists, in the development of policy. Small, but conspicuous incursions of women into manual trades have been directly inspired by the women's movement, and these have brought tiny contingents of feminists into such solidly male enclaves as the building workers' union, UCATT, and the electricians' union, the EETPU. At the TUC's annual conference of women workers, the feminist presence has grown visibly stronger year by year. There have been growing numbers of younger delegates with prior experience in women's groups, and at the same time older delegates and women in traditional blue-collar jobs have been voicing their demands in increasingly feminist terms. Since the mid 1970s, the cultural and political gap between the women's liberation movement and women in the trade union movement has narrowed considerably. The impact on TUC policy has been unmistakable. When the feminist campaign around the Working Women's Charter reached its height in 1974, the TUC set about revamping its own charter, *Aims for Women at Work*. Its motives were not entirely admirable: it wanted to head off the initiative of the charter campaign, which had an unofficial

145

base, a grass-roots orientation and an ambitious list of demands, including a national minimum wage. Nevertheless, the TUC was obliged to include most of the same points in its own charter, which was published in 1975 and updated in 1978 to include a pro-abortion statement. The feminist campaign for child care, which began in the early seventies, eventually found expression in the TUC's *Charter for the Under-Fives*,[3] published in 1978, which called for a 'comprehensive and universal service' of care and education for children from 0–5, with 'flexible hours to meet the needs of working parents'.

A resolution carried at the 1979 TUC Women's Conference brought the feminist debate on domestic labour into the trade union debate on the unemployment crisis. It called on the General Council

to campaign for a shorter working week for all waged workers to offset the effects of unemployment and to campaign among male trade unionists to use the extra time available to spread the burdens of housework and child care.

At the 1981 TUC Women's Conference, a resolution was passed which recognized 'that the unequal division of work in the home is one of the main obstacles to equal pay and employment opportunities, and to the full participation of women in the trade union movement'. The conference called 'upon the General Council and the Women's Advisory Committee to launch a campaign to raise consciousness amongst male trade unionists about the importance of taking an equal part in housework and child care.' And later that year, the TUC Congress passed a resolution which recognized that the 'outdated concept of the family wage' was a basic cause of rising unemployment among women.

The 1979 conference launched a TUC charter for equality within trade unions, which set out proposals for 'positive action' to encourage female participation in the unions. The 1980 Women's Conference espoused the cause of positive action in employment and education; this was confirmed by the TUC Congress in the same year and endorsed in more detail in 1981.

The idea of positive action has been imported from the United States, via the British women's movement and, as we noted in the previous chapter, it marks something of a watershed in feminist politics. It expresses an understanding that ending discrimination against women is not going to achieve equality, and that special measures have to be taken to tackle the underlying causes. The TUC has held a special conference on positive action and has drawn up a very useful set of guidelines for introducing positive action in employment. The government officers' union, NALGO, the finance union, BIFU, and the film and television workers' union, ACTT, have begun to work towards setting up positive action programmes in a handful of workplaces. But the commitment of the unions to positive action in employment has yet to be widely demonstrated in practice. The unions' official approval of the principle of applying positive action to their own organizations provides a real chance for feminists to make headway in their efforts to transform the character of trade unionism. We return to the subject later in this chapter, p. 160.

One of the most dramatic manifestations of union support for women's demands was the TUC's official demonstration against the restrictive abortion Bill introduction into Parliament by John Corrie, Conservative MP for Bute and Ayrshire North. When some 80,000 women and men marched from Marble Arch to Trafalgar Square on 31 October 1979, it was the largest trade union demonstration ever held for a cause which lay beyond the traditional scope of collective bargaining; it was also the biggest ever pro-abortion march.

It came as the culmination of four years' hard labour by the feminist National Abortion Campaign, which had been launched in 1975 to defend the 1967 Abortion Act. As the 1970s wore on, attacks on the 1967 Act became more concerted and in response, individual unions began to pass pro-abortion resolutions at their national conferences. This was often at the instigation of feminist members already active in NAC or other pro-abortion groups. At the 1975 TUC Women's Conference, when James White's notorious anti-abortion Bill was before Parliament, the medical practitioners' union (a section of ASTMS) put forward a resolution which pledged support for abortion 'on request'. It was moved by a young doctor who was a founder-member of NAC, and it was carried by a large majority. Later that year, Terry Marsland, deputy general secretary of the tobacco workers' union, took a similar motion to the TUC Congress – and that, too, was passed.

James White's Bill fell for lack of time, as did its successor, introduced the following year by William Benyon. But further trouble was anticipated. At the 1978 TUC Women's Conference, a delegate from the National Union of Journalists, who was a member of NAC's steering committee, moved a resolution from her union which called upon the TUC to organize a national demonstration in defence of the 1967 Act, in the event of another restrictive Bill. It was passed overwhelmingly. Once again, Terry Marsland carried a similar resolution through Congress. So when John Corrie brought his Bill into the new Parliament, under a Tory government which had no inclination to defend the 1967 Act, it was time for the TUC to fulfil its pledge.

When the big day came, the TUC had arranged for General Secretary Len Murray and a group of General Council members to head the procession as it moved off down Park Lane, and inevitably this meant it would be led almost exclusively by men. A contingent of young radical feminists staged an angry protest. Women, they insisted, without a shade of respect for the official grandeur of the occasion, should lead the march. Len Murray, by all accounts, was beside himself with rage. So was Marie Patterson, chairperson of the TUC Women's Advisory Committee and one of the two women on the General Council, who had the place of honour at his side. Many other senior trade unionists railed against the folly of the protest. ('After all we've done for you ... don't expect to be so lucky next time!') If feminists wanted TUC support, they were going to get it on the TUC's own terms. Such an open challenge was considered an intolerable breach of protocol and there was no question of giving way. For the women in NAC who had worked so hard for this moment it was an excruciating ordeal to be caught between elements of mutual distrust and intolerance in the two movements they wanted to bring together. Only the impressive size of the demonstration, which took more than four hours to file into Trafalgar Square, could sweeten the atmosphere.

It was indeed a big success and it clearly confirmed that public opinion was leaning towards a woman's right to choose. (There remained, however, some strong support for making it more difficult to obtain abortions late in pregnancy.) Corrie's Bill ran out of time in Parliament; the government did not give it any more, and it fell. Male trade unionists would cite the event for some time to come as evidence of their commitment to the women's cause.

The defeat of Corrie's Bill has been one of the trade unions' few *major*, *tangible* achievements for women. They have passed many excellent resolutions and they have won some impressive piecemeal gains for their female members. But we have yet to see convincing signs that they have the capacity to mount an effective challenge to the traditional distribution of jobs and pay between women and men.

No action on low pay

Point Two of the TUC Charter for Women at Work demands 'complete equality of job opportunity for women with men'. Point Four calls for 'an end to all pay discrimination against women workers'. For some groups of women, unions have negotiated a real improvement in their basic wages, relative to men's. But as we have seen, the overall gap between female and male take-home pay has narrowed by less than ten pence in ten years. The extent to which women's jobs are segregated from men's has increased during the 1970s. And there is evidence that the trade unions have in some instances deterred women from pursuing claims under the new 'equality legislation'. The laws were intended to compensate for past failures of collective bargaining: had the unions succeeded in negotiating adequate pay and conditions for their female members, there might have been no need for Parliament to step in. The unions backed the campaign for legislation, but at the time many trade unions argued that the laws were an unnecessary intrusion into their own territory: wages and conditions were a matter for collective bargaining: they did not want the autonomy of the unions undermined by courts or tribunals or quangos: and anyway the laws wouldn't work.

A resolution carried by the 1975 TUC Congress declared that the Equal Pay Act could not close the gap between the average earnings of men and women:

The aim of this Congress is that a woman should be paid the wage a man would be paid if he were doing the job. This will only be achieved by intensive industrial campaigns for higher wages for women.

These intensive campaigns have not yet taken place.

At the same 1975 Congress, TUC General Secretary Len Murray tried, successfully, to head off left-wing opposition to the new 'social contract' between the unions and the Labour government, and to the £6 pay limit which was part of its first phase. He argued that this was neither a wage freeze nor an anti-working-class policy. . .

Our voluntary policy of a £6 a week increase will help, and it will work, because it can be operated without disunity. It is fair and socially

149

just, in that the greatest benefit goes to the lowest-paid ... the policy before you is an attack on low pay.

The trouble with this approach to low pay was that there were no means of ensuring that the low-paid actually got the £6. Many poorly organized workers (including women and in particular part-timers and homeworkers) did not have the bargaining strength to win more than a fraction of it. Many got nothing at all. It was a strategy for holding down wages at the top of the ladder, not for increasing those at the bottom. It was a bonus for employers, an empty promise for many of the lowest-paid and weakly organized workers, and it was bound to build up trouble for the future, since it was seen as no more than a temporary interruption of the traditional function of trade union bargaining – which was to safeguard differentials between weaker and stronger groups of workers, between the 'skilled' and the 'unskilled', between women and men.

The statistics show that women's pay did improve in relation to men's between 1975 and 1977 (see p. 78). This was partly because there were still some blatant cases of unequal pay which could be swept up under the new Equal Pay Act, and these settlements were exempted from the limits of the 'social contract'. It was also partly because certain groups of lower-paid women did get pay rises which increased the overall female average, while there was a temporary brake on stronger groups of (male) workers who might otherwise have got more than £6. It was a brief respite.

In June 1976, when the TUC held a special congress to ratify Phase Two of the 'social contract' (this time a 5 per cent pay limit), the problem of low pay seemed almost forgotten. Lord Allen of the shop workers' union, USDAW, who chaired the congress, declared:

We all know that differentials have been squeezed ... what we are saying is that in a freer situation ability must be rewarded, skill must be rewarded, effort must be rewarded.

The TUC came out in favour of a 'planned return to free collective bargaining' in which priority would be given to the 'satisfactory restoration of differentials'. Kevin Halpin, one of the leaders of the rank-and-file Liaison Committee for the Defence of Trade Unions, later summed up the disdain for 'soft' struggles which were all that remained on the bargaining table when demands for pay were fettered. The social contract had inhibited negotiations, he told *Morning Star* readers on 4 February 1977; shop stewards were 'reduced to arguing about such things as soap and towels and redundancy'. By the end of that year, the gap between female and male pay had begun to widen – a trend which continued for the rest of the decade. 'Free collective bargaining' was unlikely to help low-paid women while their bargaining power remained weaker than the traditionally higher-paid and predominantly male sectors of the workforce. An incomes policy would be no help to women while it was based on restoring or maintaining differentials, and it would be no help to anyone except employers while its effect was simply to hold down the wages of the higher-paid.

The issue of low pay returned to the headlines during the 'winter of discontent' of 1978/9. NUPE had tabled a demand for a minimum basic rate equivalent to two-thirds of the average male wage, plus a 35-hour week – which suggested that it was at least trying to grasp the nettle of female disadvantage. On 22 January 1979, 80,000 came out in support of a National Day of Action for the Low Paid, and shortly afterwards the unions organizing public service workers launched a programme of industrial action, to protest both at low pay and at Labour's cuts in public spending, which threatened jobs and the quality of the services. The Tory press made a meal out of it, ensuring the defeat of the Callaghan/Healey government in May 1979. It did nothing much for the low-paid. At Dowing Street in the small hours of 10 February, a deal was struck between James Callaghan, Len Murray and the general secretaries of the four unions whose members were involved in the action. The demands for a 35-hour week and a minimum earnings guarantee were abandoned; the public service workers were given £1 'on account' and it was agreed to instigate a comparability study with a view to increasing their pay in line with the private sector. Terms of reference were drawn up which left plenty of scope for the new Standing Commission on Pay Comparability, set up under the chairmanship of Professor Hugh Clegg. NUPE suggested that the Commission should compare women's pay with men's pay rather than with that of workers doing similar jobs in the private sector (where, if anything, they were less well organized and lower paid). This fell on deaf ears.

Clegg reported in August 1979. He recommended pay increases for cleaners, kitchen assistants and domestic assistants (who were all female and already the lowest paid) of between 2.9 and 4.9 per cent. For ambulancemen, storekeepers, caretakers, refuse collectors, heavy plant operators and other male workers in higher grades, he recommended increases ranging from 9.7 to more than 20 per cent. It amounted to a massive betrayal of the low-paid women who had been involved in industrial action during the 'winter of discontent'. By the time the seeds of that betrayal bore their bitter fruit (in the form of actual pay awards) Margaret Thatcher was in Downing Street, the unions were demoralized and there was no hope of any effective protest.

The problem of powerlessness

As the economic crisis deepened, the unions became increasingly preoccupied with saving their members' jobs and defending the purchasing power of wages. Nobody came out into the open and *said* that men's interests should be looked after first; but it was widely accepted among trade unionists that the fight against female disadvantage was not a top priority in a period of recession. Nurseries have been closed down, maternity rights have been curtailed. A higher proportion of women than men joined the dole queue in eight out of ten years between 1970 and 1980. But although some unions have voiced a protest, defensive action in these areas has been negligible. It seems that women's economic equality has to be a no-cost benefit, which can only be sanctioned in a period of economic growth, because redistribution of wealth between women and men is not seriously considered.

The most obvious cause of the failure to improve the lot of women is that women themselves still have no real power in their unions. They have little or no control over the making or implementation of policy. They are still severely under-represented on their unions' executive committees, among full-time officials and on delegations to the TUC. As the table on p. 167 shows, in 1980 the 657,000 women who belonged to Britain's two largest unions (the Transport and General and the General and Municipal Workers') had not a single female executive member between them; and if the two major public sector unions (NALGO and NUPE) wished to achieve the same proportion of female full-time officials as female members, they would need to hire 150 more women. In spite of the massive increase in female membership since the 1960s, this pattern of male dominance has remained entrenched at almost every level of the union structure – from regional councils to the shop-floor, from industry-wide negotiating teams to specialist committees (except those concerned with equality).

It isn't just that women have failed to fill key posts in the unions; they have remained absent from a whole range of union activities. Polls conducted by MORI for the *Sunday Times* show that although female union activity increased in the late 1970s, more than one in four women still had no record of union activism by the end of the decade.[4] (This means they have never been involved in industrial action, nor held union office, nor attended union meetings.)

'What can women expect if they don't get involved?... They've got no one but themselves to blame ... women are their own worst enemies...' – familiar refrains, but are they accurate? What are the real reasons for women's continuing powerlessness?

Men, too, often find themselves powerless in their unions, cut off from the centres of activity and authority. Evidently, there are difficulties about the way trade unions are organized which affect both sexes. For example, there are increased bargaining advantages to the unions as they grow in size; but the larger they become, the harder it gets for them to meet the needs of all their members. At the same time, the scope and complexity of their business has grown steadily, with the changing structure of industry and the worsening economic climate constantly demanding new strategies. If solutions to general problems such as these were found, they would no doubt help women improve their position. But that would not be the end of the matter. For it is still men, not women, whose voice is heard, whose strength is felt, whose investment in the organization yields greater dividends.

There are no formal bars to female participation and there are few overt acts of discrimination against women. So we need to look deeper – at the history of trade unionism, at the structure of paid and unpaid labour, and at the way these have shaped the different traditions and attitudes of female and male workers.

As we have seen in Chapter 2, the character of British trade unionism has its roots in the early craft unions, developed during the nineteenth century by skilled male workers to protect their own interests. Women were at that time excluded both from skilled work and from the means of organization. Then, as now, they did mainly unskilled and semi-skilled work at much lower rates of pay than men.

In the latter half of the century, new trade unions were developed for workers outside the traditional crafts; but for these, women were at best a problem, to be accommodated in some special way, and at worst a menace, to be driven out of the labour force. As Henry Broadhurst put it to the 1875 TUC, one of the aims of a union was to

bring about a condition ... where [men's] wives and daughters would be in their proper sphere at home, instead of being dragged into competition for livelihood against the great and strong men of the world.[5]

Cheap female labour (a consequence of women's exclusion from organization) was regarded by men as a threat to their jobs. However, rather than ensure that women were paid more, men tried to control their access to the labour market by keeping them out of the unions.

Women began to set up their own organizations to fight for better pay and conditions, and in 1906 the National Federation of Women Workers was established, with some 2,000 members and Mary McArthur as its first president. Effective and militant, it built up its membership to 80,000 by the end of the First World War. But by that stage there had developed a strong feeling that the separatist 'experiment' should come to an end. Mary McArthur argued at the Federation's national conference in 1920 that it should merge with the National Union of General Workers, to become 'a great industrial organization of men and women, in which women are not submerged but in which they take as active part as the men'.[6]

At first, the Federation kept its own executive council and became a 'district' of the NUGW, with special officers to cater for women. In the next three years, however, the separate women's district and the National Women's Committee were abolished. All signs of separate identity swiftly disappeared and the number of women's officers fell from sixteen to one. By 1930 the voice of women was so thoroughly silenced that the NUGW did not send one female delegate to the TUC Congress. (Almost half a century was to pass before the union – now the General and Municipal Workers' – stirred itself to make good the damage and actively encourage women to participate in its affairs.)

In other unions women were silent too. Whether they would have been more effective if they had remained separate is difficult to judge. They were not deliberately suppressed. They believed their future lay in fighting alongside men on equal terms and they did not foresee how hard that would be.

Just as the silence of women in the unions has stretched into the last decade of the twentieth century, so the principle which has justified and encouraged it has remained firmly embedded in trade union philosophy. This is the idea that men have the right to earn a 'family wage', which we have already described (p. 57). Although it has never borne much relation to working-class life – since women have continued to do paid work to support their families – it has helped to perpetuate the unequal division of labour between women and men, with men retaining economic control within the family and women bearing the full burden of unpaid domestic work.[7]

As long as the myth of the family wage persists, there is bound to be a conflict of interest between women and men in the trade union movement. For if men see themselves as breadwinners-in-chief, how are they to view the prospect of women gaining equal opportunity and equal access to all jobs, with equal pay and job security? Especially at a time of recession, when jobs and money are in short supply, they will probably conclude that there will be less to go around for themselves. (Some argue that employers' profits are the rightful source of the extra pay and benefits that are due to women. We may agree in principle but that does not dispose of the problem immediately, and women will not 'wait until the revolution'.)

Thus, for men to champion women's cause wholeheartedly requires a degree of altruism that has no part in the tradition of British trade unionism. The unions' chief purpose has always been (and still is) to look after their members' interests. Self-protection is their business. Pure altruism, requiring self-denial without hope of future gain, is not. Of course there have been brave acts of comradeship, but that is another matter. The thousands who turned out to support the Grunwick strike in 1977-8 (for example) felt that the struggle of those Asian workers was their struggle too – it was, after all, a defence of the general right to organize. Men have not identified with the struggle of women in the same way. Instead, seeing it as a threat, they have dug in their heels and with the passing of time they have developed increasingly diplomatic ways of doing so.

This conflict of interest has lain beneath the surface of the trade unions' fight for equality like a wrecked tanker – polluting the waters and impeding all passage. Nobody has wanted to admit that it is there. Men have often recognized it only sub-consciously, acting upon it instinctively more than deliberately. Women may have been reluctant to look too closely at the reasons men have not supported them. It isn't easy to confront a conflict of interest with men at work while trying to build a domestic life which is based on an assumption of common interest. Women themselves are often affected by the 'family wage' propaganda, even though it diminishes their status as workers, undermines their claim to equality and contributes to a feeling that the trade unions are not primarily *for them*.

So what of men's support of women's abortion rights? Unlike the fight for equality at work, the defence of the 1967 Abortion Act has entailed no threat – present or future – to men's material circumstances. Indeed, a great many men have been spared financial hardship and social embarrassment by the 1967 Act. And there has so far been no danger of women gaining control over their fertility, as they still have to obtain the consent of two doctors before terminating a pregnancy. This is not to say that self-interest has been the only motive behind men's support of abortion rights, but there has been no serious conflict of interest between women and men over the issue.

We have shown in Chapter 2 that women's experience of paid employment is radically different from men's. They do different jobs and earn a lot less money. Their employment is less likely to be continuous. They work shorter hours and they often have part-time jobs. When they go home from their work they begin another job, whose hours are unlimited and for which they receive no pay. If they have children, the job of parenthood carries with it full-time cares and responsibilities, which often intrude into their paid employment. None of these factors is inevitable or immutable; they are a result of the unequal division of labour between women and men; and they all have a bearing on women's relationship with the trade unions.

In his analysis of a 1980 MORI survey, Peter Kellner demonstrates the impact of child bearing and rearing on working patterns and union membership. A smaller proportion of women aged between 25 and 34 work than among any other age group between 18 and 55; a smaller proportion of 25- to 34-year-old women who have jobs work full-time than in any other age group; and a smaller proportion of those in this age group who work full-time belong to a union than those in any other age group. The cumulative result of these biases means that one man in two aged 25–34 has a full-time job and belongs to a union – compared with *one woman in twenty* in the same age range. Kellner concludes:

As a result, the typical male union member in his late thirties or forties has had work and union experience over twenty years; whereas for the typical female union member, work and union experience will be nothing like as continuous. It follows that wherever buggins' turn applies, buggins is seldom a woman.[8]

Here women are caught in a vicious circle. There is strong evidence that they would work if they could in their late twenties and early thirties, but they are largely deterred by the lack of adequate child care facilities. The problem of child care *could* be a priority in trade union bargaining. However, it is not – and according to another recent MORI poll, only 19 per cent of female (and 15 per cent of male) trade unionists thought their union 'should do more to meet the needs of workers with young children'. Women who cannot work because of child care problems don't join unions until the problems cease to affect them, so they are unlikely to demand policy changes which could radically improve their freedom to go out to work and participate fully in union activities.

Since collective bargaining has traditionally reflected male, not female, experience, and men have seen themselves as wage-earners, playing only a minimal part in the day-to-day lives of their families, they have seldom seen fit to use their power in the unions to win improvements which do not relate directly to the workplace. Their bargaining strategy has never expressed any responsibility as *active* parents, because they have had none.[9] The male view has remained the dominant view of what matters most in a trade union context, since women have had insufficient power to assert other priorities.

The consciousness-raising effect

The reasons for women's low pay and powerlessness range well beyond the economic relationship between workers and employers. The day-to-day concerns of working women, different from those of men, because of their different role in the home, are not a familiar part of trade union language; there are no established channels for talking about them; there is no bank of experience on which to draw for tackling – in a trade union context – the particular problems that confront women.

For us, these points were vividly illustrated when, in the autumn of 1980, we interviewed two groups of women factory workers in the north-west of England. In both factories, the women saw each other every day at work, but had never before met together as a group. Therefore, although they experienced low pay and powerlessness, they had had little opportunity to articulate them as grievances, less still to work out what to do about them. As they began to discuss the link between their jobs and their pay, and their participation in their union (the GMWU), their attitudes swiftly changed.[10]

Early in one of the discussions, which took place in a glass factory on the outskirts of Liverpool, one woman expressed strongly her view that it would make no difference if there were more female shop stewards at the plant. 'Why should it?' she demanded; 'the union treats you the same whether you're a man or a woman. I mean, I'm paying my 35p the same as any man. They've *got* to treat you equal!'

Jobs in her factory were divided into nine grades; the women were concentrated in the lower four. She said she thought her job – which involved stamping the glasses as they came off the assembly line – was graded too low. 'We're in grade three, but we ought to be in grade seven. Machine operators are in grade six and it's an easier job. In our room, when the machines are running smoothly, the operators can sit there all morning and read a paper, while I put in four and a half hours continuously, like a robot.' She didn't know who had devised the grading system, but guessed that management alone had been responsible. She was surprised to hear that it had been negotiated with the unions. Could her union get her on to a higher grade? At first she shook her head: 'They've tried.' But then she decided they hadn't tried hard enough: 'Well they can't have, can they, because we're still on grade three!'

One of her colleagues said at first that she thought men should be paid more than women, but later after discussing the problem of redundancy (two of the women were afraid their husbands would lose their jobs), she changed her mind, explaining: 'Nowadays you get a lot of women on their own, and women left working when their husbands are put out of work. I never really gave that thought before.'

In the second factory, which made pharmaceuticals, the women out-numbered the men by more than four to one, yet the men ran the union. The women were paid no more than the lowest male grade, although they worked more intensively than

158

most of the men. One of them explained that they barely had time to get to the canteen and back for their ten-minute tea break: 'You run the length of the factory, up four flights of stairs, run right down to the canteen, get a drink, sit down, scald your tonsils and you've got to be back on the line before the buzzer goes again. But the men, they saunter in and saunter out. If *we're* late back, it's marked down on the lost time paper, but they're not as hard on the men. The management bend over backwards towards the men.'

Asked why, she said the men 'stuck together' in a way that the women didn't. The men themselves, who joined the discussion later, agreed that they were strong in the union because they got together more often. 'The women are tied on the line and they can't stop,' said one. 'There's plenty of time during the day when we can meet up. Quite often all the men are in the same cloakroom.' Couldn't the women get together at lunch time? Apart from practical difficulties – they were on different shifts and (as one said) the married women had to go out shopping – it hadn't occurred to them to congregate in that fashion. The men had got into the habit of meeting in the cloakroom during the day just as they gathered in the pubs at night. The women were not in the least downtrodden or disinclined to unity; they had simply lacked the opportunity to meet and exchange views.

Not only did they miss out on informal gatherings, but they also had problems getting to official union meetings. One of the female stewards at the pharmaceutical factory explained: 'A lot of women have to go home and cook tea for their husbands. Or they can't get out because they've got to do their washing or their ironing.' Some said their husbands would disapprove if they knew they were going to a pub for a union meeting; and who would look after the children? (Who indeed?)

Most striking of all was the link between the prospect of 'responsibility', which deterred so many women from union office, and the role they played at home. It was not simply that the women had less time: they were reluctant to add to the mental and emotional burden – of looking after other people, having to remember to do things, always being on call – which they already carried with their domestic responsibilities.

Many of our impressions were confirmed by Jane Stageman's study of women trade unionists in the Hull area.[11] With a grant from the Equal Opportunities Commission, Stageman set out to discover why women did not participate more fully in trade union affairs, and what might encourage them; 108 women from five union branches (spanning the public and private sectors, servicing and manufacturing) answered questions about what they thought would increase the level of women's union activity. As the table on p. 168 shows, one vital practical measure came top of the list: 'holding meetings in work time'. This was followed closely by measures to increase women's sense of involvement ('making union matters easier to understand' and 'making more information available about how unions work'). More than half said they would participate more if they had 'more interest in union affairs' and if they had 'fewer home responsibilities'. Next, they thought participation would be encouraged if opportunities were created for women to 'get together and discuss matters of interest to them'; if they felt 'more confident'; and if they knew that women could be 'as competent as men in union affairs'.

Experiments with positive action

Throughout the 1970s, there were fierce arguments in the trade union movement about whether or not special steps should be taken to increase women's activity. Should there be special conferences for women, special courses, special committees, special seats? Or would these amount to tokenism, would they ghettoize women's issues? Would it be an insult to women to treat them as something other than the exact equals of men?

Some white-collar unions made vigorous efforts to disband the TUC Women's Conference (inaugurated in 1925) on the ground that it was a ghetto and an anachronism. The last serious attack came in March 1977, when the Civil and Public Services Association and the National Union of Journalists moved a resolution that the conference be discontinued, chiefly because of 'the fact that women can now claim equal rights with men ... [and] the trade union movement's opposition to discrimination and progress made towards fuller participation by women members in the general work and direction of the movement.' Such expressions of faith were mingled, in the proposing speeches, with more sophisticated arguments: there were no 'women's problems' as such, said one delegate; education and child care were the concern of men as much as women. Against the motion, it was argued that women would continue to need a special platform until they really were equal, and the conference was saved by a decent majority. The delegates went on to vote for 'at least seven additional seats for women on the General Council' of the TUC. (There was no action on that until 1981 – and then only five seats were added.)

In the late 1970s, support gathered for positive action in the unions – as feminist influence grew and it became increasingly hard to deny that here, as in the field of employment opportunity, women could make no progress unless special efforts were made to shift entrenched patterns of discrimination.

The white-collar engineers' union, AUEW (TASS), acted earlier and more thoroughly than most, appointing a national women's organizer in 1974. TASS has had a network of women's sub-committees ever since 1922, when the all-female tracers' union merged with the engineers' and draughtsmen's union (then the AESD). Unlike the women who joined the National Union of General Workers in 1920, the tracers insisted on maintaining a degree of separate identity within the larger organization (perhaps because theirs was a distinct craft). In the early 1970s, TASS began to recruit clerical workers in engineering firms, which led to an increase in its female membership from 3.3 per cent in 1968 to 15 per cent in 1979. Its leaders realized that the membership drive would be assisted if the union made a positive effort to cater for the special needs of women workers. This coincided with a growing awareness of the women's liberation movement and sympathy with some of its more pragmatic demands. Thus, the women's sub-committees at national and divisional level, each with a special seat on its parent body, were given a new significance. The union began to run annual weekend women's schools, and to produce an impressive range of literature on women's issues. TASS has developed a large and vocal contingent of female activists.

The National Union of Public Employees commissioned a study of its structure from Warwick University. In their report, published in 1974, Bob Fryer, Andy Fairclough and Tom Manson of Warwick's sociology department argued:

We do not believe that the [existing] under-representation has anything to do with 'women's nature' or lack of interest in the affairs of NUPE... It has to do first with the position of women in the wider society and at work. All women come through a process which emphasizes domestic activity as a prime virtue, especially supportive of and secondary to the activities of men ... The structure of the union can either be designed to alleviate the effects of such disadvantages

161

or else it can operate on the basis of accepting subordination as a 'fact of life' which is only confirmed by the low degree of female participation in the union at all levels.[12]

On their advice, NUPE reserved five seats for women on its national executive council from 1975 onwards.

The local government officers' union, NALGO, set up a National Equal Opportunities Committee, urged its twelve districts to do likewise and began to publish a regular equal opportunities bulletin. Two other white-collar unions, APEX and ASTMS, established similar networks of national and regional committees in the mid 1970s; and by 1980 the two largest blue-collar unions, the Transport and General and the General and Municipal, had begun to set up equal rights committees in their regions. The TUC and a number of individual unions began to provide crèches at their larger meetings; some branches set about negotiating work-time meetings specifically for the benefit of female members; and at least one office committee bargained successfully for baby-sitting payments to cover union meetings outside working hours.

In 1979, the TUC endorsed a ten-point charter, *Equality for Women within Trade Unions*, which urged unions to take positive steps such as these to increase women's participation. It recommended special seats on national and local bodies where women were under-represented, special advisory committees, paid time off for union meetings in working hours, child care arrangements for meetings, special encouragement for women to attend union training, and non-sexist union publications. It was mildly worded, leaving unions free to ignore it if they wished. Nevertheless, it provided a legitimate base from which campaigns for positive action could be launched.

Most promising of all was the spread of women-only meetings and courses (or, put another way, the introduction of consciousness-raising into the trade union movement). By the end of the decade, these were being provided regularly by several unions – notably the GMWU and TASS – as well as by the TUC. Jenny Owen, who was responsible for setting up TUC weekend courses for women in Manchester and Liverpool, described the response of her students in terms that no feminist who has spent time in a women's group could fail to recognize: 'It works every time. At the end of two days they're high on the experience of being together – and they all say what a difference it makes to have just women on their own.' A NUPE

162

women's school that we visited in Kent was attended by twenty-five women – nurses, caterers, cleaners, a road sweeper, a gardener and others. They all said they found it invaluable, they'd learnt a great deal and they wanted to come back again. 'We couldn't have spoken freely if men had been here,' said one. Another explained that she'd discovered for the first time that other women shared her ideas and feelings: 'I used to think it was just *me*!'

In the Yorkshire region of the GMWU, plans were being made in the early months of 1981 to set up a series of factory-based discussion groups for women only – the first such project to be launched in Britain. The region had been active on the equal rights front for at least four years, holding regular meetings of its equal rights committee and special training courses for women. It had learnt not only that women found it immensely valuable to get together, but also that the great majority of female members could not take up the opportunity while meetings were held outside working hours and away from the workplace. The solution was to take the opportunity into the workplace, by training women in the GMWU to lead discussions among groups of their own workmates, in working time. The planning stage has not yet been completed at the time of writing. Only a tiny minority of women in any of the trade unions have had a chance to attend a women-only meeting or training course; fewer still have been able to repeat the experience even once, let alone on a regular basis.

Rocking the boat

As these and other new measures have been introduced, they have inevitably encountered some resistance. Poor communication is a serious obstacle – especially in the larger unions where members are scattered around small workplaces, with no centralized bargaining structures. The two groups of GMWU women whom we interviewed in the North-west had never heard of their union's national women's officer, Pat Turner, nor did they know that their own region employed an equal rights officer and had recently held a regional equal rights conference. Marjorie Harrison, who conducted a study of women in ASTMS, found that letters from the ASTMS National Woman's Advisory Committee were often blocked by unsympathetic branch secretaries:

It was discovered that some Secretaries were not passing on the information at all and others, instead of reading from the letter (which was deliberately low-key), were mentioning almost in passing that 'two women's libbers want to come and talk to you about women's lib', which got the reaction it was geared to receive – rejection.[13]

Harrison also found that while the Women's Advisory Committee had scored some considerable successes on 'social issues' such as the defence of abortion rights and the campaign for child benefit, its impact was minimal when it came to industrial matters such as pay and maternity leave – because it had no direct links with the officials responsible for negotiations. In ASTMS as in many unions, there has remained a strong distinction between 'women's issues' and industrial matters over which men retained firm control.

NUPE's allocation of special seats on its executive council is said to have encouraged the election of three additional women who stood in competition with the men – so in that respect the experiment has been a success. However, links remained weak between NUPE's ordinary female members and the women on the executive, and the latter seemed to exert little influence when it came to policy-making on issues of special concern to women. This was partly because NUPE lacked a network of women's committees, which would have spurred on the executive members and made them more accountable. To rectify this the union began to set up women's committees at divisional level in 1981.

In the giant Transport and General Workers' Union, progress has been especially slow. The union has always been proud of its internal democracy and when its 1979 biennial delegate conference voted to set up regional equal rights committees, it could not *instruct* the regions how or when to do so. The results have been patchy. Officers in charge of each region were free to invite whom they pleased to attend the inaugural meetings. Some went into action right away, others dragged their feet for eighteen months or more. The huge membership of the T&G made it prohibitively expensive to mail directly to shop stewards from head office – let alone directly to members. Consequently, most of its female members have been unaware of what is going on and have had no say in the development of equal rights committees in their areas.

Women who have reached positions of prominence in their unions have not always been the best supporters of new measures to encourage female activism. Some, who had fought for most of their lives to 'make it' on men's terms, have grown comfortable as token women near the top, and lost sight of their sisters' need for a helping hand. Others have held on to their commitment, but have been driven, in their relative isolation, to degrees of paranoia and over-caution. At the 1980 TUC Congress one delegate wanted to protest from the platform that the General Council had allotted only five additional seats to women, instead of the seven demanded by the TUC Women's Conference. She canvassed support beforehand from three senior female trade unionists, two of them members of the TUC Women's Advisory Committee: all begged her to say nothing, explaining that women were lucky to have been given any extra seats at all, and it was best to keep quiet in case the men had a change of heart: 'Don't rock the boat.' Similarly, the delegates who brought pro-abortion resolutions to the TUC Women's Conferences in 1975 and 1978 were both strongly urged by members of the Women's Advisory Committee to withdraw them – for fear that they would cause a split in the ranks. That fear was proved unfounded.

It is not the women themselves who are to blame so much as the character and structure of their organizations, which have tended to isolate and intimidate them. The problem will only diminish if stronger women's networks are developed in the unions, if more women emerge in senior positions, and if union hierarchies keep in much closer touch with the grass roots.

From the evidence available so far, it is clear that the more positive action a union undertakes, the faster its female members progress towards fuller participation; and the more aware women become of their powerlessness – and their potential – the more they demand. On the same evidence, it is clear that women are a long, long way from equal participation and equal power; and it will be a long, long time before they cease to make special demands on the trade union movement. ('Okay brothers, we think you've got the hang of it now. Let's scrap the men's conference and merge it with ours!')

At least by the end of the 1970s, unions had begun to acknowledge that the causes of women's inactivity were deeply rooted. And women had begun to talk openly about the links between their lack of power and their own domestic arrangements. At the TUC's conference on positive action in November 1980, one delegate demanded: 'When will *our* unions start telling *our* members to do their fair share of work at home, so that *our* members can get out to meetings?'

For the future, the hope lies in bringing the techniques and policies of women's liberation into the centre of the trade union movement. Women trade unionists need to *develop the habit* of gathering together, discussing their common experiences, setting them in a political framework and, on that basis, working out ways of achieving their needs. They will have to insist on making the inequality of domestic labour a primary concern of the trade unions. Only if men are obliged to stop claiming the right to be breadwinners-in-chief, and to see themselves as equal, active parents and home-makers, will they start to view their interests from a new perspective. And perhaps then they will cease to fear and resist the advance of women in the field of paid employment.

The question then arises: what can the unions do collectively to advance the cause of the low paid and of parents, and (in particular) of women? Of course, trade unionists aren't just workers. They are people who have children and homes. They are members of communities who have lives to lead outside their factories and offices, and whose needs as workers are inseparable from needs which arise from other parts of their lives. How can this be reflected in the bargaining process?

The trade unions, and especially the left of the labour movement, cherish the tradition of 'free collective bargaining' as a sovereign right of the working class and as chief defence against the exploitation of employers and the control of government. Yet the traditional priorities of union bargaining – focussing on the wage and on the maintenance of differentials – have not helped to lift women out of low-paid ghettos, or to alleviate their domestic responsibilities. On the contrary, the process we know as 'free collective bargaining' is primarily a defence of the interests of male workers. A 'social contract' between unions and government, which is based on flat-rate pay limits or maximum percentage increases, offers no improvement.

For all workers, but especially for women, the benefits, services and facilities provided by the state (the 'social wage') are as vital as the wage – and these need to be vastly improved. At the same time, if women are to change the structure of the labour market, which is crucial to their fight for equality at work, they must have a strong voice in the way industries and services are designed and run, and in the way jobs are organized. What this amounts to is a need to *politicize* and *feminize* the trade unions. Bargaining priorities must be transformed,

166

both at the level of negotiations with employers, and at the national level, where unions have a key role to play in bargaining with government for the kind of social and economic planning that will redistribute wealth between women and men, and within the family, as well as across society.

Table 8
Women in the unions

Figures in brackets show how many women there would be if they were represented according to their share of the membership

Union	Membership			Executive members		Full time officials		TUC delegates	
	Total	F	%F	Total	F	Total	F	Total	F
APEX (Professional, Executive, Clerical, Computer)	150,000	77,000	51%	15	1(8)	55	2(28)	15	4(8)
ASTMS (Technical, Managerial)	472,000	82,000	17%	24	2(4)	63	6(11)	30	3(5)
BIFU (Banking, Insurance, Finance)	132,000	64,000	49%	27	3(13)	41	6(20)	20	3(10)
GMWU (General & Municipal)	956,000	327,000	34%	40	0(14)	243	13(83)	73	3(25)
NALGO (Local Govt Officers)	705,000	356,000	50%	70	14(35)	165	11(83)	72	15(36)
NUPE (Public Employees)	700,000	470,000	67%	26	8(17)	150	7(101)	32	10(22)
NUT (Teachers)	258,000	170,000	66%	44	4(29)	43	3(28)	36	7(24)
UNTGW (Tailor & Garment)	117,000	108,000	92%	15	5(14)	47	9(43)	17	7(16)
TGWU (Transport & General)	2,070,000	330,000	16%	39	0(6)	600	9(96)	85	6(14)
USDAW (Shop, Distributive, Allied)	462,000	281,000	63%	16	3(10)	162	13(102)	38	8(24)
TOTALS	6,022,000	2,265,000	38%	316	40(150)	1,569	76(595)	418	66(174)

All figures are approximate and the most recent that were available in November 1980.

167

Table 9

Factors which 108 female respondents from the five union branches believed would encourage participation in union activities

Personal	No.	%	Union	No.	%
Fewer home responsibilities	51	55	Meetings held in more convenient places	34	37
Giving up other activities	15	16	Meetings held at a different time	11	12
Feeling more confident	41	44	Meetings held in work time	59	64
Going to meetings with someone I know	34	37	Make union matters easier to understand	57	62
My husband agreeing to me being active in the union	11	12	Provide childcare facilities so I could come to meetings	5	5
Knowing that women can be as competent as men in union affairs	37	40	Make more information available about how unions work	52	56
Male union members giving me a chance to air my views	25	27	Organize more social events	14	15
Having a greater interest in union affairs	52	56	Running education courses	22	24
Nothing would make it easier	10	11	Creating opportunities so women could get together and discuss matters of interest to them	43	46
Other	4	4	Other	3	3

Sources: *Hear This, Brother: Women Workers and Union Power*, Anna Coote and Peter Kellner, New Statesman, 1981.

Notes to Chapter 5

1 Benton, S. *Patterns of Discrimination*, ACTT, 1975.
2 *Negotiating for Equality, Workplace Nurseries, Rights for Working Parents*, NALGO, 1 Mabledon Place, London WC1.
3 *Charter for the Under-Fives*, TUC, Congress House, Great Russell Street, London WC1.
4 Kellner, P. 'The Working Woman: her job, her politics and her union' in *Hear This, Brother*, New Statesman 1981, p. 33.
5 Quoted in Boston, S. *Women Workers and the Trade Union Movement*, Davis Poynter, London 1980, p. 16.
6 Ibid, p. 150.
7 Land, H. *The Family Wage*, Eleanor Rathbone Memorial Lecture, University of Liverpool 1979.
8 Kellner, P. op. cit., p. 30.
9 Campbell, B. and Charlton, V. 'Work to Rule – Wages and the Family', in *Red Rag*, 1978.
10 See also Coote, A. 'Powerlessness and how to fight it' in *Hear This, Brother*, New Statesman, 1981.
11 Stageman, J. *Women in Trade Unions*, Hull University, 1980.
12 Fryer, R., Fairclough, A. and Manson, T. *Organization and Change in the National Union of Public Employees*, NUPE, London 1974.
13 Harrison, M. *Women in ASTMS*, Warwick University, 1980.

6 Learning

We are told that there is little or no sex discrimination in most British schools. According to three separate surveys, a majority of teachers say they are opposed to it, that they personally do not engage in such practices, and that they treat students fairly and provide girls and boys with equal educational opportunities.[1] In spite of being treated 'equally' girls have continued to do badly at school – especially in maths, science and technology. Between 1970 and 1977, girls increased their share of GCE 'O' level passed in physics by only two and a half percentage points, from 20.1 to 22.7. Their share of 'A' level physics passes increased even more slowly, from 16.7 to 17.9 per cent. For every girl who enrols to study non-advanced engineering and technology in further education colleges, there are some 44 boys. In universities, girls account for less than a third of science undergraduates and for just under five per cent of undergraduates in engineering and technology.

This persistent 'under-achievement' is explained by Mr R. R. Dale, writing in *Educational Review*.[2] 'A preponderance of androgen is responsible for the relative aggressiveness and unruliness of the male,' he declares, 'and the reverse for the comparative submissiveness and obedience of the female.' He goes on to argue that man's 'natural' aggressiveness gives him a stronger drive towards success. Another prominent educationalist, Mr J. A. Gray, points out in a book on girls and science, *The Missing Half*,[3] published in 1981, that experiments on rats have shown a link between 'the presence of testosterone [a male hormone] in the neo-natal period' and spatial ability. This, says Mr Gray, suggests an inherent difference in spatial ability between human females and males. In a nutshell, spatial ability is what a rat has if it is good at dealing with two- and three-dimensional shapes; in humans it is put to use in certain applications of maths and science. So much for the second demand of the women's liberation movement, which calls for 'equal education opportunity'. The opportunity is there, apparently, but girls (or girl rats, in any case) are naturally disinclined to take advantage of it. It's the way they are made. . .

As women have fought for equality at work and for an equal voice in the unions, they have found themselves contending with a social and economic system which has been constructed by men to express and sustain male power. Laws against discrimination can do no more than ruffle the surface of this system, which has designated women as unpaid domestic labourers, and effectively barred them from mainstream union activity and higher-paid, skilled jobs. But women are not simply excluded by force. They are *taught* their place. The training is long and thorough. Lessons are accumulated hour after hour, year after year, and they are assimilated deep into the subconscious. Some of the learning is formal and institutionalized; much of it occurs informally, as ideas are passed from one generation to the next, through the media, by word of mouth, by signs and gestures.

This is the construction of feminine psychology, to which we referred in Chapter 1. It is central to the process of female subordination. It prepares women for their own appointed role, and leaves them poorly qualified to perform any of the roles that men have reserved for themselves. It ensures that women acquire certain knowledge and skills, but not others, and it equips them with a sense of what is appropriate and possible for women in general, and thus for themselves. The notion that British education treats girls and boys fairly and equally, and that girls are *naturally* worse at some things than others, is part of a constant battle, fought on many levels, to pre-empt and quell female resistance to the supremacy of men.

In this chapter we look at institutionalized learning, at the formal and informal ways in which girls and boys are schooled in their respective roles. In the next, we examine some of the teaching that goes on outside the education system, through different manifestations of our culture.

Women who are engaged in education – as teachers, students, publishers of school books and so forth – have been active in the women's liberation movement from its inception. Women's groups devoted to equality in education, the elimination of sexism from school texts, and the promotion of women's studies, have proliferated since the early 1970s. A bi-monthly newsletter, *Women in Education*, was launched in Manchester in the autumn of 1973. The same year, the October issue of *Shrew*, the magazine of the London women's liberation workshop, produced the first thorough survey of sexist children's literature.[4] On 23 February 1974, in London, eighty-five women attended the first national feminist conference on education.

Activities such as these have multiplied as the years passed. In themselves they amount to a remarkably intensive and productive educational exercise. As women have learned in more detail how the education system operates, so their own policies towards it have developed. The very experience of trying to introduce feminist ideas into an allegedly liberal education establishment, and meeting constant rebuffal, has been instructive. Early in the decade, the emphasis of feminist campaigning was on equal access for girls to the education boys received and equal treatment within it, as well as on proving once and for all (or so it was thought) that girls were not inherently inferior. This was an important step; however, it has gradually become evident to more feminists that what girls need is not access to boys' education, but for education to be redefined and transformed, and then to be made available to both sexes on an equal basis, in such a way as to intervene against inequality.

Did we fall or were we pushed?

During the 1960s and 1970s, feminists on both sides of the Atlantic made considerable progress towards a new understanding of sex differences in learning. Thanks to Eleanor Maccoby, Carol Jacklin, Carol Dweck, Alison Kelly and others, evidence has mounted to counter the arguments of Messrs Dale, Gray and others that males are *naturally* better suited than females to certain academic disciplines.[5] First, the effect of hormonal differences on the mental processes of females and males has been shown to be slight – so slight that it cannot possibly account for the gap between girls' and boys' performances in science subjects.

Secondly, researchers have demonstrated that girls and boys are treated very differently from the moment of birth – in an infinite variety of ways, ranging from the tone of voice with which their first movements are greeted and the sex-typed colours of baby clothes and blankets, to role models presented by adults, older children and media characters, and rewards and punishments meted out for different forms of behaviour. Thus, whatever differences girls and boys may have been born with, these provide no more than a flimsy platform upon which society has constructed the powerful ideologies of 'femininity' and 'masculinity'.

Thirdly, experiments in schools have shown that with a little extra encouragment, girls can swiftly increase their spatial skills, bringing themselves into line with boys. And fourthly, attention has been drawn to evidence that girls display superior verbal skills, a fact which suggests that certain testing techniques (such as multiple choice questions) have artificially enhanced the achievements of boys.

While the theorists have been hacking their way through the undergrowth of prejudice, the great forest of educational practice has remained almost entirely undisturbed. Young women and men have continued to emerge from schools and colleges with different skills, qualifications, self-images and aspirations.

The arrival of the Sex Discrimination Act has made virtually no impact, except in prompting a few schools to admit girls to 'craft' courses traditionally reserved for boys – and then usually only in exceptional cases, where girls apply for the privilege. In most schools, girls continue to be taught 'home economics', which equip them for a lifetime of marriage, motherhood and household drudgery, while boys learn woodwork, metalwork and technical drawing, in preparation for skilled employment. For every boy who passed 'O' level cookery in 1977, there were 61 girls; for every girl who passed 'O' level woodwork, there were 166 boys.

Teaching materials have continued to reflect and reinforce traditional sex roles. In the early 1970s, Ladybird Books revamped their 'Peter and Jane' reading scheme, transforming Jane from a passive little cissy in a white dress to a 'modern Miss' in jeans and tee-shirt; however, the new Jane keeps her feet firmly on the ground and looks on in admiration as her brother climbs trees and scores goals on the football pitch. Penguin's 'Breakthrough Reading Book', *Things I Can Do* (1970) shows a little girl sweeping with a broom ('I can be good'), while two little boys let rip with the androgen ('I can be very bad. I can fight.'). A book entitled *Tudor Britain*, in the Evans Brothers series of 'History topics and models' (reprinted 1974), contains no female characters at all, except for the 'queen' and the 'master craftsman's wife'; it gives directions for building Elizabethan houses and furniture, but suggests that 'the girls in the class should dress dolls in Tudor costumes'. These are typical examples of texts still used in schools in the early 1980s.

Reporting her study of school text books in *Learning to Lose*

174

(1980),[6] Marion Scott notes that women's contribution to production and their role in society are rarely given proper acknowledgement: 'For example, in Third World countries women play a crucial role in farming but this was certainly not the impression which would be gained from the [geography] books...' In some books, says Scott, women are dealt with in a separate section or chapter, where coverage is usually superficial and often ill-informed:

A discussion of women's part in the labour market in the twentieth century ... ends in an uninspired discussion of fashion (Robson, 1973). I also noticed a tendency to assume that by the twentieth century women had overcome most of the problems of inequality.

Illustrations in science text books rarely feature females – and then only to demonstrate typically 'feminine' pursuits, such as blowing bubbles, mixing puddings and vacuuming. All this is rounded off with a blushing misconception of female sexuality. A typical sex education guide warns boys that they 'should not for a moment think that girls have no sexual physical sensations at all':

These sensations are different from yours in that they tend to be rather vaguely spread throughout the body and seem to most girls just general yearning feelings – rather like looking at a beautiful sunset and wanting to keep it but not knowing how.[7]

In most schools, careers guidance teachers have continued to channel girls and boys into traditional sex-typed occupations.

Dale Spender, who was responsible for one of the surveys we reported at the beginning of this chapter, has carried out, along with other feminists, extensive research into the way teachers behave. It has been discovered that teachers mete out preferential treatment to boys on an astonishing scale, without realizing that they are doing so. They spend more time talking to boys, and allow boys to talk more. By taping lessons, Spender has found that 'in general ... teachers spend about two-thirds of their classroom interaction time with boys'. Girls have to wait longer to get the teacher's attention. Teachers are more likely to see boys as individuals and to differentiate between them: 'Whereas some teachers can readily provide the names – and frequently idiosyncratic and biographical details – of the boys they teach, they have difficulty providing the same information on girls.' It is a maxim in teaching to 'begin with the experience of the learner', yet it is usually male, not female, experience that teachers make the subject matter of their lessons. The majority of teachers of both sexes say they prefer to teach boys. They tend to enhance the achievements of boys, while underrating those of girls, and they *expect* boys to do better. Says Spender:

I have found that there are occasions when the same feature is cause for commendation when thought to be the work of a boy, and cause for penalty when thought to be the work of a girl. Elaboration of presentation is one such feature, with teachers commenting on its excellence when they believe it to be the work of a boy, and dismissing it as superficial and time-wasting when they believe it to be the work of a girl.[8]

Why do teachers say they treat girls and boys equally when they evidently do not? It is not that they are deceived or being deceptive but because they operate in a social system which 'perceives preferential treatment for males as the norm, as the status quo, and therefore find such practices *fair*.' Spender reports that when teachers have been asked to try to re-allocate their attention more equally, they find it very hard to give more than 40 per cent of their time to girls, and are then beset by feelings of guilt that they have been treating boys unfairly. 'A teacher who spends more than approximately one third of the time with girl students is perceived by herself and the students as spending too much time with the girls.' On the other hand, when students are told what is happening and encouraged to confront the problem of preferential treatment of males, it has been found not only that girls are quite capable of asserting themselves and challenging the boys, but also that the boys themselves are less likely to complain.

Only rarely are trainee teachers made aware of these patterns, or encouraged to modify their views or behaviour. The subject of sex-typing has not yet begun to feature in the average teacher-training syllabus, and so the preferential treatment continues unchecked. Margaret Maden, head of Islington Green comprehensive school, acknowledged at a 1980 conference that she had been surprised to find, after taping her lessons, that she had been paying considerably more attention to the boys than to the girls.[9] Most members of her profession have not bothered to find out whether they do or not.

Of course, the intransigence of the education system acts as a brake on progress elsewhere. Educators are busy all the time, *actively* producing and reinforcing attitudes which perpetuate inequality and sexism. Even though there have ceased to be any formal bars against women becoming astro-physicists or motor mechanics, schools still manage to ensure that girls are alienated from such 'masculine' occupations.

Liberalism and the patriarchal norm

During the 1970s, British educationalists have moved slowly towards a new assessment of 'educational deprivation'. The introduction of comprehensive schooling was based on the premise that all children should have equal opportunity. Steps have been taken to compensate for the environmental inequalities suffered by poor, working-class children – by setting up 'Educational Priority Areas' and allocating extra resources to them (albeit chiefly in the form of more money for teachers). It has gradually been acknowledged that the 'under-achievement' of West Indian and Asian children is not due to innate inferiority, but to the failure of the education system to take account of their different backgrounds, or to accommodate their special needs. Thus 'multi-cultural' education has been unleashed on some schools – a white concept and a mixed blessing, aimed primarily at bringing black kids up to standards already set by whites.

Meanwhile, no special measures have been introduced to help girls, in spite of clear evidence that they consistently 'under-achieve'. By the late 1970s, the idea that girls' talents are 'under-utilized' was gaining some credence, and this was being expressed in terms of 'society's loss' of potential scientists and technologists (in the 1980 Finniston Report on engineering, for example).[10] But there has been a marked reluctance to do anything about it – especially anything that involves more than a superficial questioning of sex differences.

The British education system cannot be seen as a blank sheet on which changes in society have been noted over the years. As Raymond Williams has observed, we have inherited an educational model which 'was essentially created in the nineteenth century, following some eighteenth-century models and retaining elements of the mediaeval'. Far from being neutral, it incorporates a set of beliefs which have grown out of those times. All that has happened in the twentieth century is that amendments and additions have been made where it has been necessary to respond to social change and possible to do so without upsetting the basic structure of beliefs.

Large numbers of women have been involved in the development of the education system, but only as practitioners, not as policy-makers or administrators. Research by Eileen Byrne has demonstrated that 97 per cent of the people involved in the 'government of education' are male.[11] Thus, the principles on which the system is based have been devised by men. Its concerns and disciplines have been selected and designed from a male perspective, and underpinned by the values of a patriarchal culture. Today, they are widely accepted as objective, immutable and true.

Science, for example, has superseded religion as the fount of truth, and scientific methodology is generally assumed to be intrinsically objective, correct and unchallengeable, even though scientific 'truths' are disproved at regular intervals. Ruth Hubbard has pointed out that scientists habitually select evidence to back up their theories and discount evidence that threatens them:

Science ... is made by a process in which nature is filtered through a coarse-meshed sieve; only items that scientists notice and structure into a cohesive system are retained. Since scientists are rather a small group of people – predominantly male – and mostly economically and socially privileged university-educated males at that, there is every reason to assume that like all other human productions, science – and biology – reflect the outlook and interest of the producers.[12]

The interests of the white, male middle class are enshrined in the education system and remain undisturbed by gestures to mitigate the disadvantage of working-class and non-white students. The rules of nineteenth-century liberalism are deployed in defence of the status quo. What is normal is 'fair'. Attempts to change what is normal are condemned as 'social engineering' – the Big Bogey of the educational world.

Feminist researchers are finding that the alienation of female students from the study of science is intricately bound up with their sense of themselves as female and their idea of what constitutes 'femininity'.[13] It would not be unreasonable to assume that if schools made it their business to challenge conventional ideas about female roles and 'femininity', and set about changing the 'masculine' image of science, then the girls' alienation would decrease. However, as we know, it is still the dominant view in society that the female is the centre of the family, and that her function of wife and mothers takes precedence over any other. The men who govern the education system comfortably assert that it is the duty of schools to *reflect* social values, not to change them. What they overlook is that schools have been engaged in a massive exercise of social engineering for well over a century.

Eileen Byrne and others have argued for a single 'core' curriculum, common to all schools, to be followed by pupils up to a certain age. Their purpose is to stop girls dropping out of subjects such as physics before they have had a chance to find out about them.[14] Their opponents raise the spectre of 'Big Brother' imposing drear and dangerous uniformity, and carol the virtues of 'individual choice'. Likewise, suggestions that sexist books should be banned, or at least energetically discouraged, are met with accusations of 'censorship'. (We return to the censorship debate in the next chapter.)

Liberal individualist arguments such as these are reinforced by another mainstay of the British education system: the manmade concept of professionalism. Teachers know best; their professional status embodies truth and authority; their freedom to conduct themselves as they wish in the classroom is sacrosanct and must be defended – by employers as well as unions – at (almost) all costs. It certainly takes precedence over the freedom of young people to question conventional wisdom and draw their own conclusions as they learn.

Such developments as there have been in recent years have tended towards more rigid control and direction, although these have remained under the cloak of liberalism. In her autobiography *The Tamarisk Tree 2*, published in 1980, Dora Russell suggests that there has been a 'glaring shift of values' in education since the 1960s. (To us it seems more as if dominant values were briefly challenged – and then reasserted.) The ideas that Russell herself pioneered in the 1920s – that education should encourage self-discovery and self-expression in a non-competitive, egalitarian atmosphere – enjoyed a certain popularity in the 1960s, but soon fell back into disrepute with the onset of a new utilitarian stringency. She quotes Shirley Williams, speaking as Education Secretary in 1978 of the need for a 'coordinated approach by schools, teachers and industry'; and a 1976 directive from the EEC urging member states to provide 'appropriate preparation for working life at all stages of general education'. By the mid 1970s, as Russell says, teachers had become 'producers', ex-pupils the 'product':

Children in school must therefore be regarded as the 'raw material' to be processed into manufactured articles.[15]

Had Russell's own values prevailed, schools might have responded more readily to new ideas from the women's movement. But a system which is supposed to groom young people to meet the requirements of industry will refrain from disturbing traditional sex roles. Modern industry is itself an expression of the patriarchal values that prevail in schools, and it depends as much on the continuing unpaid domestic labour of women as on a steady supply of waged labour.

Cuts in education

The entrenched conservatism of the education system has been hardened considerably by the economic recession. Between 1974 and 1980, government expenditure on education fell in real terms, with the worst cuts coming at the end of the decade. Under Margaret Thatcher's government local authorities had their rate support grant from central government cut by £600,000 million between April 1979 and April 1981 – and the largest slice of the grant (36 per cent) was usually spent on education. Schools have found that they cannot replace essential textbooks when they have worn out with use. One million fewer books were purchased by schools in the first three months of 1980 than in the same period in 1979. Capitation allowances (the money given to schools for each pupil) have halved in value in many areas, and at the same time they are expected to cover more items than before. The following reports are typical of many published in October 1980 in *Where*?, the magazine of the Advisory Centre for Education:

Leicestershire school: Net capitation increase is 5 to 6 per cent against an inflation rate of about 20 per cent. Telephone bills and teachers' travelling expenses chargeable to county hall pegged to 1979/80 level; any increased spending must come out of the capitation allowance.
Solihull school: Our capitation is relatively low. For sixth-form A-level students it has risen from £15 a head in 1974 to £24.60 in 1980. [Inflation in the meantime had been almost 300 per cent.]
Trafford school: Actual cut of 20 per cent, but estimate approximate 50 per cent reduction in real terms over 2/3 years. Capitation now only provides basic materials; specialist crafts have been discontinued; no new books can be bought.

Any thoughts there might have been of replacing teaching materials on the sole ground that they were sexist were soon abandoned.

Adult and further education were hard hit by spending cuts,

too. These provided the main opportunities for women to make good their inadequate schooling, or prepare themselves to re-enter employment after raising their families. One of the first victims of local education cuts were discretionary grants, usually awarded to students in the arts, and in the para-medical and social services fields. (According to a 1979 report from the Equal Opportunities Commission, the latter two fields were 'areas to which mature women are attracted and where they can use the expertise gained in the rearing of children and the care of families generally'.[16]) College crèche facilities were another early target, putting post-school education out of reach of many women with pre-school-age children.

As the recession deepens, schools feel they are hard-pressed to maintain the educational standards they know and love; the prospect of change becomes associated with deterioration rather than progress, and this inhibits criticism of the status quo. Where the idea of combating sexism is not actively resisted, it is nowhere near the top of the list.

The need for positive action

Even in a more favourable climate, however, the outlook may not be much brighter. For if schools are to stop reproducing sexist attitudes, and seriously set about promoting equal opportunity, they will need to do a lot more than to buy in new teaching materials and instruct their teachers in the evils of sex discrimination. Children arrive in school with attitudes and aspirations ready-formed; and throughout their formative years they continue to learn, from their families, from the media and from their day-to-day experience, that women and men have different functions and different aptitudes.

There are conflicting theories about how children adopt sex roles. 'Social learning' theories suggest that they are moulded by external forces: they act in a manner which is socially acceptable in order to obtain rewards and avoid punishment. 'Cognitive' theories suggest they are more active participants in the process: once they have established a sense of themselves as female or male, they select forms of behaviour which seem appropriate to their gender. Alison Kelly points out in *The Missing Half* that if the 'cognitive' theorists (whom she favours) are correct, then it will not help simply to offer children alternative forms of behaviour ('Girls can be scientists; so can boys') as though sex distinctions were unimportant.

To attempt to eliminate sex distinctions may make children more conformist to those distinctions they can establish, and may even cause them anxiety over their gender roles...[17]

It follows that children should be brought to realize as soon as possible that it is not their behaviour which makes them into boys and girls, but their physical (genital) formation.

They should also be encouraged to see cross-sextyped behaviour as not only pleasing to adults around them, but as competent behaviour for their own sex. This suggests that, in the short term at least, we should be aiming not towards a neutral or sex-free conception of behaviour, but towards reversed or dual-sex typing.[18]

Kelly confirms that the principle of affirmative (or 'positive') action, which we have already explored in the context of employment, should be applied to education. Indeed, positive action is necessary even if the 'social learning' theorists are correct, in order to compensate for the influences girls encounter outside school hours.

The idea does not cut much ice in education circles. It is new; it costs money; it threatens to upset the apple-cart. For what is positive action if not 'social engineering'? The parents may not approve and, anyway, the teachers are already doing their best... A small crack in the surface has nevertheless appeared in the Manchester area, where Alison Kelly and Judith Whyte have obtained a grant from the Equal Opportunities Commission to experiment with intervention strategies in a number of local schools. Their aim is to put new ideas and positive tactics into practice and see whether, after four years from the start of the scheme, more girls have been encouraged to take up science and technology. Their strategies include making science more relevant to the experience of girls; accentuating the skills which girls have already developed, playing down aspects of science which they find especially difficult; presenting more female role models; discouraging opting out; and experimenting with single-sex classes where it seems that girls are inhibited by the presence of boys.

The scheme, entitled 'Girls into Science and Technology' (GIST), was launched in September 1979; it is the first experiment of its kind in Britain. If it shows results, there are hopes that similar strategies may be employed elsewhere. It may also help to puncture traditional ideas about education – for although it is ostensibly geared to bringing girls up to male standards of achievement, it sets about the task by introducing into schools new, female-defined values. GIST is a small beginning. It is not only in science that girls are disadvantaged; to right the balance in their favour, positive action is needed at all levels, as an integral part of the education system. Feminist teachers in two north London schools introduced a more general positive action experiment in 1980–81. They have been given funding by the EOC and the Inner London Education Authority to assess the project, with a view to extending it to other schools (another small but encouraging sign).

In addition, schools will have to change their own patterns of employment, which reproduce within almost every school in the country a standard pattern of inequality. Eighty-nine per cent of infant and primary school teachers are female. Male teachers predominate in secondary schools and in senior posts – more often than not teaching maths, science and other typically 'masculine' subjects. In 1976, women accounted for 59.5 per cent of the full-time teaching force, but filled only 38.4 per cent of the headships. More than three-quarters of all female teachers are in the lowest-paid jobs (scales 1 and 2), compared with less than half of all male teachers.[19] Among non-teaching staff, the division of labour is even more pronounced, with male caretakers in positions of authority over teams of female cleaners, and 'dinner ladies'.

Few children would identify this as sex discrimination. Nevertheless, they all learn from it. They gain the impression, for instance, that caring and servicing are functions of the female and that authority is ultimately vested in the male. For most of them, this reinforces what they have already learnt at home. In particular, the exclusively female regime in primary schools is likely to have a far-reaching effect on female and male patterns of learning. As Elinor Kelly explains in her contribution to *The Missing Half*, primary school teachers frequently demand obedience, silence, passivity and conformity from their pupils – all features of traditional female behaviour:

Many boys as a result of this process, which risks alienating them from school, are actually being trained to a degree of independence and initiative which encourages analytic thinking later in life. By contrast the girls, by conforming to femininity, are discouraged from originality and experimentation.[20]

Any serious attempt to help girls (and boys) realize their full potential will have to include a concerted attack on job segregation in schools; and this must be carried through to all levels of the education hierarchy. Ideally, a positive action programme in employment, combined with intervention strategies in teaching, along the lines of the GIST project, needs to be introduced into schools and colleges throughout the country. And neither will succeed unless the need for positive action – and all that that entails – becomes a central part of the curriculum in teacher training.

A feminist model of education

Even then, we shall have covered only part of the necessary distance. It is not enough simply to adjust the education system in order to enable girls and boys to compete on equal terms. While the aims and methods of teaching continue to reflect patriarchal values, the education system will continue to stifle the development of children and sustain male control. The component parts of the system need to be dismantled and rebuilt. Schools are intensely hierarchical institutions; learning takes place in a stratified order, and in an atmosphere of competition, in which students strive towards standards of 'achievement' built on male-defined criteria. A girl who drops out of physics is defined as an 'under-achiever'; yet she may have rejected it for valid reasons – for instance, because it seems to her to bear no relation to everyday life. Her striving to relate science to humanity is an 'achievement' of another kind, just as a boy's view that cooking is 'cissy', or his lack of interest in language, is another form of 'under-achievement'. Educational values must be redefined.

Teaching has become a process by which 'experts' hand down information to the uninitiated. As Dale Spender suggests in *Learning to Lose*, a feminist approach would be quite different:

If students deny their own experience and accept that of the experts then hierarchical structures are strengthened on many fronts: if, however, they do not accept the judgement of the experts, then a novel form of interaction ... can emerge. This has become the basis of understanding within consciousness-raising groups.[21]

A feminist model of education is non-hierarchical and non-competitive, because it seeks to change, rather than reproduce the present structure of society. 'In order to reproduce the social hierarchical order,' says Spender, 'a fundamental educational principle demands that most people fail – sooner or later.' Standards of excellence by which success and failure are judged are not objective, but have 'their origins in a culturally specific view of the world':

Feminist educational ventures have 'proven' by the cooperation they have structured and fostered that the concepts winners and losers are meaningless and useless. If the traditional educational system is as inadequate as some critics claim and most evidence suggests, then there is an alternative model, which stresses cooperation, available. Such a model will not, however, reproduce the existing divisions and inequalities within society.[22]

It will be an uphill battle to redefine and reorganize education along such lines. A recognition that it is necessary to do so has developed in the course of the 1970s, as feminists have experienced the resistance of the education system to their demands, and observed the limits of each small, piecemeal advance they are able to make. But their achievements so far should not be underestimated. Slowly, they have been changing attitudes and broadening their influence. Many of their ideas have become current in education circles even if they are not accepted. Most secondary school girls now have access to information about women's changing role in society, even if they still see marriage and motherhood as their main goals. These developments carry a momentum of their own, which leads to a clearer perception of what needs to be done: that is to refurbish the image of 'free education' (tarnished by a reaction to the 'alternative' culture of the 1960s), reassert the values of Dora Russell, and go beyond that to create a model of learning which actively contributes to the liberation of women.

Notes to Chapter 6

1 Clarricoates, K. 'Dinosaurs in the Classroom' in *Women's Studies International Quarterly*, 1:4, 1978; Spender, D. *Men's Education – Women's View*, Writers and Readers, 1981; Stanworth, M. *Schooling and Gender: A Study of Sexual Divisions in the Classroom*, Women's Research and Resources Centre, 1981.

2 Dale, R. R. 'Education and Sex Roles' in *Educational Review*, vol. XXII, no. 3.

3 Gray, J. A. 'A Biological Basis for Difference in Achievement' in Kelly, A. (ed.) *The Missing Half*, Manchester University Press, 1981.

4 Women's Liberation Workshop, *Shrew*, vol. 5(4), October 1973.

5 See Dweck, C. S. and Coetz, T. E. 'Attributions and Learned Helplessness' in Harvey, Ickes and Kidd (eds.) *New Directions in Attribution Research*, vol. 2, Halsted, New York, 1978. Dweck, C. S. 'Learned Helplessness and Legative Evaluation', *Educator*, vol. 19(2), 1977. Fennema, E. 'Influences of Selected Cognitive, Affective and Educational Variables on Sex-Related Differences in Mathematics Learning and Studying', *Women and Mathematics: Research Perspectives for Change*, NIE Papers in Education and Work, no. 8, 1977. Fennema, E. and Sherman, J. A. 'Sex-Related Differences in Mathematics Achievement and Related Factors: A Further Study', *Journal for Research in Mathematics Education*, no. 9, 1978. Fox, L. H., Fennema, E. and Sherman, J. *Women and Mathematics: Research for Change*, NIE Papers in Education and Work, no. 8, Washington D.C. National Institute of Education, 1978. Maccoby, E. E. and Jacklin, C. N. *The Psychology of Sex Differences*, Stanford University Press, 1974.

6 Scott, M. 'Teach Her a Lesson; Sexist Curriculum in Patriarchal Education' in Spender and Sarah (eds.) *Learning to Lose*, The Women's Press, London 1980.

7 Jackson, S. 'Girls and Sexual Knowledge', in *Learning to Lose*, ibid.

8 Spender, S. Unpublished paper delivered to a seminar in Copenhagen in 1981.

9 Speech at National Housewives' Register conference, St Albans, October 1980.

10 *Engineering Our Future*, report of the Committee of Inquiry into the engineering profession (Chairman Sir Montague Finniston), Cmnd. 7794, HMSO, January 1980.

11 Byrne, E. *Women and Education*, Tavistock, London 1978.

12 Hubbard, R. 'The Emperor Does Not Wear Any Clothes: The Impact of Feminism on Biology' in Spender (ed.) *Men's Studies Modified: The Impact of Feminism on the Academic Disciplines*, Pergamon Press, London 1981.

13 See Kelly, A. (ed.) *The Missing Half*, op. cit.
14 Byrne, E. *Working the System: A Strategy for Action*, paper presented to the Feminist Summer School, Bradford, obtainable from Women's Research and Resources Centre, 190 Upper Street, London N1.
15 Russell, D. *The Tamarisk Tree 2*, Virago, 1980, p. 204.
16 EOC, *The Effects of the Government's Financial Policy on Educational Provision*, 1979, from EOC, Overseas House, Quay Street, Manchester M3.
17 Kelly, A. 'Science Achievement as an Aspect of Sex Roles' in *The Missing Half*, op. cit., p. 81.
18 Ibid.
19 *Promotion and the Woman Teacher*, a National Union of Teachers Research Project, published jointly with the EOC, 1980.
20 Kelly, A. 'Socialisation in Patriarchal Society' in *The Missing Half*, op. cit. See also Maccoby, E. 'Women's Intellect', in Hinton, K. (ed.) *Women and Science*, SISCON project.
21 Spender, D. 'Educational Institutions: Where Cooperation is called Cheating' in *Learning to Lose*, op. cit., p. 44.
22 Ibid, p. 47.

SOMEWHERE ON FLEET STREET...
THE THINKING MAN'S DAILY.

7 Culture

Looking beyond the institutions of formal learning at the tangled and uncomfortable relationship between the female sex and the media, we can detect a pattern which is similar to that in education. Men control the means of expression – from the press and broadcasting, to advertising, film, publishing and even criticism – by occupying dominant positions within them, and by using the power this gives them to convey the ideas and values of a patriarchal order. Women are excluded from the formulation of policy and the execution of business. An intensive war is waged against women, to degrade them as human beings, to deny their ideas and achievements, and to suppress their own perspectives on the world.

The women's liberation movement has exerted some influence on the media since the early 1970s, and has encountered some formidable resistance. It has taken most of a decade for feminists to measure the extent of male control, to assess the nature of it, and to work out strategies for overcoming it. The process is still under way at the time of writing.

To illustrate some of the general problems, we focus on an area we both know well: the news media. The treatment of women in this field has been a target of feminist campaigning from the early seventies. *Women's Report* kept up an exasperated commentary on Fleet Street's excesses in its column, 'Thanks and a free consciousness-raising session to . . .' *Spare Rib* did the same in its regular feature 'Tooth 'n Nail'. In July 1973, *Women's Report* offered 'Thanks . . .'

And seventeen blows with a wooden Japanese abacus to Robert Lacey, intrepid editor of the Sunday Times Look! Section. Only the redoubtable Mr Lacey could decide that the way to break down sexist barriers against female mathematicians was to (wait for it girls) HOLD A BEAUTY CONTEST TO FIND THE PRETTIEST MATHS STUDENT!!![1]

Even the redoubtable Look! pages of the *Sunday Times* could not stoop to that in 1981. Nor could the *Daily Mirror* report a debate between Margaret Thatcher and Barbara Castle as it did on 1 October 1974, when political editor Terence Lancaster informed his readers: 'Redhead took on honey-blonde yesterday.'

In October 1975, the National Union of Journalists' Equality Working Party (which has close links with the women's movement) published *Images of Women*,[2] subtitled 'guidelines for promoting equality through journalism'. The guidelines point to different ways in which women are ignored, trivialized and stereotyped in newspaper reporting, and suggest alternatives where possible. They deal with grammatical conventions, such as the use of 'he' and 'his' to describe human beings of either sex:

This ... gives an impression that women are absent, silent, or simply less important than men ... 'they', 'their', 'them' and 's/he' can often be used instead...

They urge journalists to avoid 'the gratuitous display of women's bodies' as well as 'clichéd references to "dumb blondes", "nagging-wives", "the fair sex", the "little woman" ', and 'sex-typing of jobs, except where reference is specifically to men'. The tone of the first edition is cautious, even defensive. 'Some of you may laugh,' says the Working Party's introduction:

Some may find our suggestions odd, unnecessary or extreme. But these guidelines are a serious attempt to show how everyday words and phrases ... help to form and perpetuate a discriminatory, patronizing attitude to women.

By January 1977, the second edition displays a more confident tone, reflecting a shift in public attitudes. This time, the introduction cites clause 10 of the NUJ's Code of Conduct:

A journalist shall not originate material which encourages discrimination on grounds of race, colour, creed, gender or sexual orientation.

In theory NUJ members who break the Code can, at the end of a long complaints procedure, be fined or suspended from membership – and suspension can mean the loss of their jobs. A big threat.

The efforts of the Equality Working Party and the influence of the Code of Conduct, together with campaigns outside the NUJ by groups such as Women in Media, have helped to raise the consciousness of many individual journalists – and, in some newspapers, have even altered the style of reporting. However, the guidelines continue to be widely ignored and the NUJ has so far failed to enforce its Code of Conduct. By 1981 only *one* complaint under clause 10 had been pursued right through the complaints procedure, and it ended without a reprimand. Yet there has been no shortage of material that encourages 'discrimination on grounds of race, colour, creed, gender or sexual orientation'.

It has not been easy to engage in ideological battle with Britain's newspaper barons. Their well-paid editors and columnists leap briskly into print with warnings of *Pravda*-style conformity or McCarthy-style witch hunts, at the first hint of any effort to interfere with their glorious 'free' press – just as in education, the vocabulary of liberalism is used to defend the status quo, and the dominant assumption is that what is normal is fair. When it comes to the crunch, journalists – like teachers – usually defend the 'professional' autonomy of their colleagues. Well-meaning, socialist-inclined men who have jobs on the *Mirror* and the *Daily Star*, and local papers which model themselves on Fleet Street's popular tabloids, shake their heads and shrug their shoulders earnestly: of course they loathe the tits and bums and the trivialization, but what can they *do*? They have to earn a living, after all. The less well-meaning ones accuse their feminist colleagues of 'losing their sense of humour', or 'getting things out of perspective'. Many women in journalism are induced to share these attitudes.

By the end of the decade, Fleet Street had its own equivalent to *Women's Report*'s 'Thanks . . .' column: 'Naked Ape', every Monday in the *Guardian*. That is progress of a kind. But 'Naked Ape' provides regular reminders that even the *Guardian* itself can print horrors like this, by a Peter Dobereiner, in November 1980, on the subject of a golfing holiday:

On no account consider taking along wives or mistresses. Women can be admirable creatures in their own way but the female who is content to pull your trolley for 36 holes a day without speaking, without deserting to the shops, without wanting to pinch the car for excursions to the beach, without complaining about the service and without generally fouling up a golf trip has not been born.[3]

And what the *Guardian* can still do, the *Daily Express* can still do better. When pilot Judith Chisholm completed a round-the-world-flight in November 1980, the *Express* revealed that underneath her canvas, fur-lined jump suit, 'the blonde' had been wearing 'a pair of frilly black pants and bra'.[4]

Mercifully, such crude and offensive reporting has now be-

191

come less common – doubtless due to the influence of the women's movement. In the 'quality' newspapers, it is rare to find women referred to in terms of their 'vital statistics' or the colour of their hair, or even (gratuitously) in terms of the number of children they have. The tabloids use clichés like these less frequently, too. Some newspapers have learned to report feminist issues *without* any mention of 'bra-burning'. And women's pages occasionally give extended and sympathetic coverage to campaigns of the women's movement.

However, these are often printed alongside soft-porn photographs of women in underwear, thinly disguised as 'fashion reports'. And the *Sun* and the *Star* show no signs of reconsidering their policy of printing huge pictures of 'lovelies', 'dazzlers', 'sizzlers' and 'tantalizers' – allegedly servicing a daily need of their readers. Indeed, it was during the 1970s that the idea of a 'newspaper' became inseparable, in the minds of many millions of British readers, from the idea of naked female breasts.

The male perspective on news values

During this period, the traditional values of news reporting, and the balance of power between women and men in the newspaper (and broadcasting) industry, have remained almost entirely unchanged. In a sense, this has more dangerous implications than the unashamed policy of exploiting women carried out by the tabloid newspapers. For while those have been hard at work building false images of women, they have been joined by the rest of the news media, in a combined effort to keep *real* women out of sight altogether.

A spot check on two national newspapers reveals that on 28 January 1981, the news pages of the *Guardian* included reports of 237 named individuals, of whom 19 were female. The *Sunday Times* on 25 January featured 14 women among 181 named individuals. (Names occurring twice or more are counted only once for each story in which they appeared; business, sport and feature pages are not included.) Who are the women who make the 'news'? Out of the 33 named in the two newspapers, the largest number are politicians; 12, including 9 references to Margaret Thatcher and Shirley Williams. Next are women-as-victims, mentioned because they have died or incurred some injury (10). There are 6 names of women-attached-to-men (without whom they would not have attracted the publicity). Finally there are 5 non-politicians who were mentioned because of their work; of these 3 are actresses.

Of the 109 news stories carried by the two newspapers, 3 make no mention of human characters at all; 4 are all or predominantly about women; 12 give equal coverage to women and men; 47 are predominantly about men, and 43 are all about men.

The pattern remains typical of news coverage throughout the media – especially in the 'serious' newspapers, and on radio and television. A 1980 study of one local station, Radio Nottingham, has found that men's voices occupy seven-eighths of the two-and-a-half-hour morning news programme.[5] Women are featured more regularly in the 'popular' press, but these are almost invariably 'wives', 'mums', 'brides', 'mistresses', victims of crime or misfortune, TV stars, or 'sizzlers'. Reports are written from a male perspective, almost obliterating female experience. When a woman, a man and two children died together in a caravan fire in January 1981, the *Daily Mirror* told its readers: 'An RAF officer and his family were found dead. . .' Women as autonomous human beings rarely feature anywhere in the news media. Their multi-faceted experience as women (individually and collectively) is seldom reported at all – and almost never from a female perspective.

A standard response to criticism of this kind is that women don't get mentioned as often as men because they don't do as many important things. That is true enough – if one accepts the Fleet Street definition of what is important. Where does that definition come from? Who has decided what is 'news' and what is not; what is a 'hard' story and what is a 'soft' one; what is central and what is peripheral? Who has set the standards by which certain everyday events, but not others, have become 'human interest stories', worthy of public attention?

The prevailing values of the news media have not fallen from heaven into the laps of editors: they have been manufactured over the years by successive generations of middle-class newspapermen, who have handed them down, intact, to their counterparts in radio and television. So solidly have these values been established that it has become hard to imagine any other way of conveying information. Most journalists sincerely believe that there is such a thing as 'objective' or 'unbiased' reporting, when in fact the most they can do is to communicate events as fairly as possible, from their own point of view, according to the journalistic conventions they have learned, and in a manner which is acceptable to their editors. For their readers, listeners and viewers, the product of journalism *becomes the real world* – even though it is nothing more than one cockeyed version of it.[6]

More women have gradually become involved in journalism but they have never been able to set the pace, or imprint their character on the news industry. They have always lacked the power to challenge the dominant view of what matters, or develop a tradition of reporting which consistently interprets events through their eyes.

To make it in journalism, women have to strive to be as good as men, according to male standards. This is not easy, and so women have remained, throughout the 1970s, in a minority in journalism, occupying the lowest-paid and least influential jobs. A 1977 survey by the National Union of Journalists found that among 314 journalists employed on seven newspapers in the North of England, 279 were men and 35 were women. All editors and deputies were male; all sports specialists were male; all photographers but one were male; there were 69 male and 11 female sub-editors; 42 male and eight female features/ specialist writers; and 99 male and 23 female reporters. That pattern has changed very little – nor is it substantially different in other parts of the country, or in radio or television. Our spot check on the *Guardian* and *Sunday Times* in 1981 found a total of 11 female and 74 male by-lines.

With the arrival of women's movement has come a growing awareness that certain items are being left off the news agenda. The media have made minor adjustments but have managed all the while to identify women as a sub-category of a male universe – both in the style of reporting and in the allocation of space. Thus, a news report will inform us that 'many people, including women' have been injured in an accident. News editors feel free to insist that one story about women is quite enough for one day. Television executives may arrange for an occasional documentary on women, or even an occasional series. But they retain a clear view that programmes about women have their special place and can be over-done. ('But we did a *Panorama* on women last month!')

In some newspapers, items about women are published mainly in the 'women's pages' – which robs them of their status as news, implies that they are of no import to men, and identifies them as stories of special rather than general interest. There have been debates within the women's movement about whether or not women's pages should be abolished. Without them, most newspapers would not raise feminist issues at all, and a wide range of important events would go unreported. It is broadly agreed that the best strategy is not to call for an abolition of women's pages, but to extend them, raise their status, and at the same time put pressure on editors to hire more women in the newsroom and to redefine editorial priorities. Here, as in education and other fields of employment, 'positive action' policies are urgently needed.

In December 1980, Jeremy Isaacs, new chief of television's Fourth Channel, gave the first indication of some willingness among the media's power élite to alter the standard approach. He announced in an interview with the *Guardian*'s then women's editor Liz Forgan:

We have got Panorama and World In Action on our screens already. I don't see why my weekly current affairs programme shouldn't be produced by women. I would like to get women to make such a programme which depends for its success on its ability to interest viewers, not to promote a cause, but which has the added bonus that it comes from people who are standing at a different angle to the universe from the male sex. It may therefore come up with a different set of attitudes, a different mix, a different set of priorities.[7]

Isaacs followed this up by hiring Liz Forgan as a commissioning editor for the Fourth Channel. It remains to be seen whether he and Forgan together will put such a bold idea into practice. And will the other television channels take the view that the Fourth is the proper place for zany experimentation, and carry on as before?

Clear parallels can be drawn between the intransigence of the news media and that of the education system. In both cases, men hold a monopoly of power. In both cases, men *claim* the exclusive right to define what is objective and real, defending this with quasi-liberal appeals against 'censorship'. In both cases, too, feminist analysis has developed along similar lines: beginning with calls for equal opportunity and a challenge to sexist content, it has led to an acknowledgement that the whole system needs to be unravelled and re-knit into a new shape, which allows no less than equal room for the experience and needs of women.

There will be little progress unless women themselves gain positions where they can shape the content of the media. So it is an important development that feminist groups such as

195

Women in Media and the Women's Broadcasting and Film Lobby have begun to make an impact on women's employment opportunities. There are now many more women who wield influence in the media than there were in the early 1970s, although their numbers are still relatively insignificant. They are often isolated and their rise does not necessarily reflect a spread of women's access to media skills on the ground floor.

The double standard in women's magazines

Elsewhere in the media, the ideas of the women's movement have met with an intriguing range of responses. Most magazines for teenage girls have ignored it altogether. *Jackie*, for example, continues to serve up an unvaried diet of boys-boys-boys (and how to grab them out of the clutches of treacherous female friends). A typical episode, taken from the issue of 31 January 1981, tells the story of schoolgirl Caroline, who misbehaves in a science lesson and gets detention for it: leaving school late, she meets a good-looking boy at the bus stop . . . almost loses him to Beastly Barbara . . . but triumphs in the end.

I wondered fleetingly whether there was a school rule about being kissed in school uniform. If so, Daniel and I had just broken it.

This is rich with lessons for the reader of *Jackie*. Science is alien, and opposed to the ideal of femininity; rejection of it brings the reward of a romantic enounter. A girl is not expected to be interested in academic attainment: finding a boy/man to love is the main thing, and in this quest, other females represent the enemy.

Meanwhile, some of the grown-up glossies have been performing precarious balancing acts. *Cosmopolitan*, launched in Britain in 1973, initially based its character (as did the highly successful US original) upon a corruption of the 'liberated' idea. It has peddled the image of a 'free' and 'independent' woman, whose freedom and independence are expressed almost exclusively through her (hetero)sexuality, and who toils endlessly towards this goal. *Cosmo* woman labours day and night, to conjure from each, separate part of her body, and from every nook and cranny of her psyche, enough sexual allure and energy to get her next man. For this she needs not only a steady flow of advice on how to have 'relationships', but also a formidable array of artificial aids – hair colourings and conditioners, anti-spot cleansers, bust conditioning creams, de-flaking lotions, moisturizers, hypo-allergenic skin tonics, deodorant tampons, electric muscle-toners, depilatories, rouges, vitamins, mud-packs, breath fresheners, quick-set nail repairers and cosmetic tooth-whiteners – all advertsed in *Cosmo*. Yet at the same time, *Cosmo* woman is intelligent, she goes out to work, and she is open to new ideas.[8] As the years have passed and the influence of the women's movement has spread, the features on sex, beauty, fashion, men and relationships have been mixed more and more with straightforward feminist writing. One issue in February 1981 managed to combine articles on 'Men to love and men to leave', 'Meet the most dashing, desirable Scotsmen', 'Why sex has a fantastic future' and 'Raise your body consciousness', with a guide to the feminist classics (de Beauvoir, Greer, Rowbotham, etc.), a report on discrimination against women in the medical profession, and an attack on films which glamorized violence against women:

We always knew there would be a backlash against women's progress into so-called equality, [wrote Anna Raeburn] but although it was expected I don't think many of us could have anticipated it in this insidous form and I don't think we can afford to be sanguine about it. Boycott these films...

Having built a commercial success on a corruption of feminist ideology, *Cosmo* is now trying to incorporate the real thing – and this is at least partly a result of feminists being involved editorially, in the planning and production of features for the magazine. However, the need for advertising revenue dictates that the magazine must remain contradictory, pushing images of femininity that feminism is bound to reject. *Honey* magazine has been caught in a similar dilemma.

Screen images

In television drama, attempts have been made to co-opt the 'liberated' woman and enlist her in the male cause. Women are allowed to appear strong and independent without seeming freakish, but only on certain conditions. They must be as women who want to get on in a man's world. The strongest examples – *Policewoman, Juliet Bravo, Charlie's Angels* – are all busy enforcing rather than challenging the system which oppresses women in general. As Helen Baehr has noted in her critique, 'The "Liberated Woman" in Television Drama',[9] these are strong women 'reconstructed into redeemers of the patriarchy'.

Some profound and sympathetic portrayals of women's *problems* have occasionally surfaced in slots such as BBC's Play for Today, but as Baehr has demonstrated, plays which address themselves directly to women's liberation usually descend into parody and end by reaffirming the values and conventions with which feminism takes issue.

Underlining all this is what the former newscaster Anna Ford has referred to as 'body fascism'. For a woman to make it on TV, her body and her demeanour must conform to a rigid set of standards. Men can be short, fat, ageing, bald, have misshapen noses and crooked teeth, warts, specs and straggly beards – and still spend hours in front of television cameras. A woman who is neither young, slim nor even-featured is lucky to get a bit-part as a victim, a villain or a lunatic.

New and old games for advertisers

Advertisers have gone to town on the 'liberated' theme – using it to sell everything from kitchen units to jeans and perfume. In her book *Decoding Advertisements*, Judith Williamson explains how advertisements become 'hollowed-out systems of meaning' by referring to things – and people – in a way which robs them of their own significance; this, in turn, affects the way we experience our own lives and those of others. The people we see in advertisements 'don't do half the things *we do*: they don't sweat, neither do they go to work and produce'.

Most of our lives are the 'unlived' lives of advertisements, the underside of their world picture. So this reality becomes almost literally unreal – sublimated, unconscious. As a teenager, for example, it is really possible to live almost totally in a sort of dream world of magazine stories and images, and this seems *more real than reality*.[10]

The dream world of advertisements has a stronger pull because the dream is a shared one. Even though people's real experiences are often very similar, these seem isolated, while the impact of the media and social images is a truly universal experience.

Not only can advertisements take the meaning out of 'ideas, systems and phenomena in society', but they do so all the more successfully when they are dealing with something which is hostile to advertising itself. The women's movement, says Williamson,

has provided advertisements, one of the most sexist fields of com-

198

munication there is, with a vast amount of material which actually enhances their sexist stance. There is a television ad for an aftershave 'Censored' where a woman is beating a man at chess. But then he puts on the aftershave and she is so wildly attracted to him that she leaps up, knocking over the chess board where she had him check-mated, and jumps on him like a wild animal. Now, far from the effect being to make us realize how inadequate the man is if he cannot stand being beaten at chess by a woman, her 'cool' and intelligence and obviously 'liberated' image are in fact made to devalue themselves: because the point is that *even* a cool, 'dominating' woman, an intellectual threat to a man, even she will become little more than an animal, and a captivated one, on smelling 'Censored' cologne for men. It is obviously more of an achievement to win over a 'liberated' woman than one who was submissive all along. Many ads are based on this sort of line: 'she's liberated *but* . . .'[11]

Meanwhile, the *un*liberated woman, and uninverted messages of female passivity, dependence and sexual availability, still come in very handy for the advertisers. Naked women continue to be draped over hi-fi equipment; cars are portrayed as 'mistresses' and 'seductresses'. Advertisers have their own non-statutory code, administered by the Advertising Standards Authority: ads are meant to be 'legal, decent, honest and truthful' and they are not supposed to cause 'grave or widespread offence' in the light of 'prevailing standards of decency and propriety'. Many feminists take the view that a lot of ads fall short of the mark, and have complained regularly to the ASA.

In 1980, the Authority looked into thirty-seven complaints based on allegations that ads were offensive to women. Twenty-nine were dismissed. Typical of those not upheld was an advertisement for Kawasaki motorbikes, which pictured a woman's legs and feet (in stiletto-heeled shoes) with her knickers around her ankles. The caption read: 'We'll never let you down'. The Authority 'deplored the advertiser's low level of taste' but 'considered the advertisement was unlikely to cause grave or widespread offence'.[12] Also unsuccessful was a complaint from the EOC and the TUC against an insurance advertisement depicting a scantily clad woman. The headline warned: 'Guard Your Goods . . . A Lorry Load of Goods – Like a Beautiful Girl – Will Vanish If You Don't Look After It.' The ad was intended for lorry drivers and the ASA 'did not believe that it would be offensive to those who received it'.[13] Another 'scantily dressed female' was featured in an ad for cut-price carpets, under the caption: 'My business is on the floor'. The complaint was dismissed on the ground that the ad 'had been appearing from time to time and neither the publishers nor advertisers had received any previous complaints'.[14]

By the end of 1980, the Authority was prepared to admit that 'the portrayal of women in advertising was a matter of concern'. It was a sticky corner for the ASA to be in, but the escape route soon became clear. It has commissioned a survey to find out whether the complaints it receives about sexism reflect women's attitudes throughout the country. The research is not complete at the time of writing, but according to preliminary findings, most women say they *aren't* offended by sexist ads. In that case, the ASA can relax, assured that all those complaints must have come from odd individuals, out of step with the rest of society. And the naked woman can stay on the floor.

The pornography debate
On the question of pornography, the women's movement has found itself trapped between the libertarian devil and the deep, Tory-blue sea. Few feminists are in doubt about the kinds of image they object to: it is not so much a matter of intellectual assessment, as of gut-level response. They *know* which images exploit their sex, and they know they want an end to them. But how to go about it? They don't want to be pressed into service with the Mary Whitehouse brigade, or the Festival of Light, who stand for a moral and political order which denies the very essence of feminism. Their more natural allies, perhaps, are the libertarians, with whom they share egalitarian and anti-authoritarian instincts. But the libertarians are more interested in fighting censorship – at all costs – than in tackling the problem of women's oppression; and in any case they have difficulty understanding that 'women's liberation' is not the same as that fine old sixties' notion of 'sexual liberation', for which they are still crusading (a little wearily perhaps, and with the help of dope, T-groups and *Forum* magazine). The libertarians are in favour of photographs of women's genitals (or whatever) being published provided the women don't mind being photographed and nobody is hurt in the process.

Standing aloof from the libertarians, but with one foot bravely in their camp, are the liberals. They aren't exactly in favour of pornography, but they aren't against it either, provided it is kept in its proper place. The liberals were the driving force behind the Williams Committee, which reported in 1980, with a recommendation to lift censorship of pornography, but to restrict sales to specially designated places and to ban any public display.[15] Unlike Whitehouse and the Festival of Light, they do not believe that pornography induces violence or other anti-social acts, maintaining that it is relatively insignificant compared with 'the many other problems that face our society today'.

Most feminists would welcome the removal of offensive pictures from public display but few of them are keen on creating new laws for the purpose, since that would mean extending the power of the (patriarchal) state, and relying for enforcement on the police and the courts, whose past record in protecting women's interests has inspired little confidence. It won't help, in their view, to sweep pornography under the carpet; what matters is changing attitudes. They have been concerned to show that sexuality is not a private affair, but that it is always present, the subject of public gaze, preoccupation and policing. They are not opposed to sexual material, but to the way that pornography represents power in sexual relations, and to its role in the formation of 'masculinity' and 'femininity'.

They see a link between pornography and anti-social behaviour, but they have quite a different idea from Mary Whitehouse of what kinds of behaviour are anti-social. Moreover, unlike Whitehouse, they do not see a clear distinction between 'pornography' and certain other representations of women. Isn't a pin-up in a newspaper, or a salacious report of a sex crime, as degrading to women and as likely to condone and encourage oppressive male behaviour as the technicolour detail of a hard-porn magazine?

The most popular response among feminists has been direct action – fly-posting advertisements in the underground, spray-painting hoardings, showering blue-movie screens with paint-filled eggs and marching through Soho and other 'red-light' districts to insist on their right to walk safely at night. Protests of this kind have enabled them to express their anger and assert their power, without recourse to the male-dominated forces of social control, which they deeply distrust. The Whitehouse brigade view these manifestations with no less horror than pornography itself; the liberals disapprove of their wilful disruption of public order and interference with the 'rights' of others; and the libertarians conclude that the women have lost their sense of humour.[16]

There is not yet any clear socialist position on pornography and pin-ups; most members of the (male) left line up with the liberals or the libertarians. This has occasioned some bitterness among socialist feminists, which came to a head in 1979, in a row with the miners' leader and left-wing hero Arthur Scargill. Scargill had taken it upon himself to defend the policy of his union journal *The Yorkshire Miner* to publish a pin-up picture in every issue. Having run the gauntlet of opposition from women in Yorkshire and a feminist protest at the May Day rally in Birmingham, he accepted an invitation from the trade union journals' section of the National Union of Journalists to debate the matter in London. The event drew a large crowd – mainly of feminists. What follows is of course an entirely objective account.

Journalist Anna Coote opened the debate with a closely argued and reasonable speech in which she explained that pin-up pictures encouraged a belief that women were unequal human beings and so perpetuated discrimination. Socialist comrades, she said, should not ape the capitalist press by using women's bodies to increase newspaper sales, but should be in the front line of the fight against sexism. Scargill answered none of these points, but read a prepared speech in which he pointed out that the 'girls' were never shown in the nude; that they were usually daughters of miners and were happy to be photographed, that his members liked it, and that the pictures had done wonders for the circulation of *The Yorkshire Miner*. He argued in favour of free expression and against intolerance; he extolled the charms of the female sex and voiced a fear that humourless women's libbers were trying to erode the differences between women and men. Finally, he dismissed the whole affair as a 'storm in a B cup'. To his evident surprise, he did not endear himself to his audience, who behaved in a most unladylike manner, jeering and booing, and looking very fierce and 'unattractive' in their jeans and tee-shirts and with unmade-up faces.

He and his editor, Morris Jones, hurried back to Barnsley, consoling themselves (no doubt) that the women they'd just escaped from were extreme, unrepresentative and probably not even socialist – and went on printing pin ups in *The Yorkshire Miner*. Jones was still puzzling over the matter in 1981 when we rang him to find out whether he had yet changed the policy. He told us he had not; he was glad that the debate had 'got people questioning their attitudes to sexism', but he honestly believed that a 'picture of a swim-suited miner's daughter' did no harm to the women's movement 'which incidentally

I fully support in its struggle for equal rights and opportunities at all levels – *have you got all that down?'*

By that time, most other union journals (though not all) had already kicked the pin-up habit – in line with the TUC charter, which urges them not to publish sexist material. But there has been so little real discussion on the left around the issues raised by the women's movement, that most men continue, like Jones and Scargill, to wonder privately what all the fuss is about.

Women Against Violence Against Women

Events took a dramatic – and tragic – turn in November 1980 when Leeds University student Jacqueline Hill became the thirteenth victim of the man known as the 'Yorkshire Ripper'. Women in that part of the country had been living in fear of the 'Ripper' for at least three years – and the fear escalated with each new, brutal, ritualized attack. They had been advised not to go out alone at night by the gallant detectives of the 'Ripper Squad', who let it be known that 'no woman was safe' until the man was caught. Leeds had long been the centre of much feminist activity and now there was an explosion of rage. Women were furious that yet another murder had left the police wildly guessing. They were angry that their freedom had been further curtailed, while men were still at liberty to walk the streets. They were angry at the way in which the 'Ripper' story had been turned into gruesome entertainment by the media, while rapes, assaults and murders that were regularly committed by other men received so little attention. They were angry that newsagents and booksellers were all the while doing a roaring trade in sadistic pornography, and – perhaps most sickening of all – that the latest cult in films just happened to be one which gloried in violent attacks on helpless women. As Sally Vincent wrote at the time, there was a new trick to these films, designed to overcome audience immunity to all the 'mad axemen' movies that had gone before, They were shot entirely from the angle of the axeman himself, 'thus indicating, with no trouble at all, the universality of man as Ripper' and inviting the audience to 'identify and empathize with the killer':

We see and hear the women in the film as though we were eavesdropping on them. We peep through the undergrowth to overhear their irreverent girlish chatter about men and male sexuality. We tippy-toe up behind them while they amuse themselves heartlessly upon the altar of masculine passion. And while we spy on them we learn they are naughty girls. They have no proper respect for men. They are *asking for it!* The audience is both voyeur and aggressor. . .[17]

On 27 November 1980, ten days after the death of Jacqueline Hill, 500 women attended a Sexual Violence Conference in Leeds. This brought together a number of feminist groups who had been organizing against male violence since the 'Reclaim the Night' marches of 1977 – including Women Against Rape and Feminists Against Sexual Terrorism – and they became linked in a new campaign, Women Against Violence Against Women. It marked an important stage in the development of feminist politics, in that different forms of male violence were identified as part of the same system of dominance and control. Some women in Leeds wrote this report of the conference in *Spare Rib*:

We agreed that as women gain greater independence, so men use more sexual violence to maintain their position of power over women. Sexual harassment at work undermines our confidence; rape and sexual assault keep us off the streets; sexual abuse in the family cripples our lives and teaches us our place in the world. Obscene phone calls, pornography, rape in marriage (unrecognized in law), gynaecological practice which violates women's bodies, prostitution which exploits women and shows how perverted men are – we discussed them all. [We] planned campaigns to combat male violence and asserted every woman's right to defend herself against it. . .[18]

There have continued to be disagreements among feminists about the universality of male violence. Some assert that all men are potential 'Rippers'; others see violence more as a symptom of the political relationship between women and men than as something which is inherent in all men. All would agree that women are invariably the victims and men the aggressors. At the Leeds conference, women planned action in cities throughout the country. In London, thirty feminists occupied the offices of the *Sun* newspaper to protest at its use of rape stories for titillation. In Leeds itself, a local 'Porn Group' leafleted outside a suburban 'family' newsagent stocking pornographic magazines and video cassettes, and collected more than 600 signatures from women passing by. Elsewhere, women demonstrated outside cinemas, glued up the locks of sex shop doors, smashed windows of strip clubs, daubed angry messages on walls ('MEN off the streets'), and marched to 'Reclaim the Night'. For once, the attention of the general public was focussed not on crimes against women as isolated, entertaining horrors, but on the anger of women at the systematic nature of those crimes. The political point surfaced briefly, then sank out of public view as the tide of complacency swept in again. Police told the press: 'These women are dangerous.' There were fifty arrests.

It seems that only by continuing – and probably only by escalating – direct action of this kind can women sustain a distinctly *feminist* attack on sexual terror and pornography. (What else can they do? Sit tight in deference to the liberals? Campaign 'through the proper channels' with Mary Whitehouse for new laws and more police?) Predictably, they have been vilified and punished by the press and the police for 'anti-social' behaviour, while liberals click their tongues in disapproval and blame them for whipping up a double-edged backlash, repressive on one side, misogynist on the other.

Art and literature

The clash between the women's movement and the liberal/libertarian left over 'cultural' matters is crucial. For if feminists are to cause any noticeable shift in public attitudes, they will need to win support at that point of the political spectrum. Liberal opposition has been at its most robust in the area of art and literature – and its most glamorous moment was probably when Norman Mailer took Kate Millet to task for being irreverent about D. H. Lawrence.[19]

Feminists are not generally in favour of banning books, except possibly when it comes to early reading schemes and some non-literary texts which form a compulsory part of the school syllabus. However, they have developed their own modes of literary and art criticism, which they regularly employ. And they have made it clear that they want to encourage the writing and publishing of new non-sexist books, especially for children. The liberals are not simply offended by the idea that certain kinds of books might be encouraged or discouraged (although that's bad enough in their view); what they cannot swallow is the suggestion that any work of art – any act of creative imagination – can *be sexist*. They have often responded immoderately, lobbing words like 'censorship' around in an indiscriminate fashion.

A staunch exponent of the liberal line is the writer and literary editor David Caute, who in November 1980 launched an attack on publishers' guidelines for children's books. A working party had been set up under the auspices of the Equal Opportunities

Commission to devise non-sexist guidelines for the UK, following the example of American publishing houses, notably McGraw-Hill. The guidelines would be advisory and voluntary. They would not dictate what could or could not be published, but merely suggest an additional criterion by which works could be judged. They were intended (rather like the NUJ guidelines for journalism) to break some of the old habits of a man-made tradition, and to encourage a new approach. For example, the US McGraw-Hill guidelines counsel:

NO: Pioneers moved West, taking their wives and children with them.
YES: Pioneer men and women moved West, taking their children with them.

Caute (writing in the *New Statesman*) saw the whole thing as a sinister threat. He was especially worried that the working party was 'not confining its reforming zeal to picture books for toddlers':

it will also pass broad judgement on how to evaluate works of history, fiction and poetry (including the 'classics' of literature) offered to teenagers in secondary schools.[20]

Literature is sacred, apparently; it is above this kind of analysis. Any attempt to evaluate it from a feminist perspective smacks (in Caute's view) of totalitarianism: 'What we don't need is a new generation of Young Pioneers spoon-fed in one-dimensional virtue.' What makes David Caute (and other liberals) act like jealous lovers when feminists take an interest in their favourite Muse? Are they not suffering from the same syndrome as the journalists who believe in the objectivity of their own news values, or the teachers who think they have a hot-line to the truth?

In the past, men alone have had the power to define what is 'literature' and what is 'art'. Knowing no other order, they have assumed that *their* view is *the* view; and that only from their position – at the centre of the cultural universe – can truth and beauty properly be judged. Feminists have been trying to assert a woman-centred view alongside theirs, perhaps with the hope of eventually producing a synthesis of the two. But since men believe so deeply and unconsciously in their right to occupy the central space, these efforts of women can only be perceived as an invasion, an attack on their 'freedom' to impose their meanings on the rest of the world.

From their privileged perspective – and only from there – it looks as though there is quite enough scope for everyone. Feeling themselves unjustly nudged out of place, men find it appropriate (in an 'artistic' context as well as in education and journalism) to invoke the defensive vocabulary of liberalism: 'Social engineering' ... 'threats to press freedom'... 'censorship'... 'Young Pioneers'. They will tar the women's movement with the brush of totalitarianism to quell an uprising against their own cultural empire.

Dislodging the emperor has been a necessary goal for women, of course, but it is not the final one. Ultimately, they have to imagine and create in their own, free space and on their own terms. It is one thing to rediscover and reassess the forgotten or undervalued traditions of 'women's art' – a job done well by the feminist publishers Virago, for example. It is another thing to encourage new female authorship and to fight for greater female control of the media. And it is yet another to explore the possibilities of creative expression from a position of real strength.

Aesthetic values need to be redefined. What are the differences between 'women's art' and 'feminist art'? Can, or should, a line be drawn between 'art' and 'politics'? How important is it for women to foster collective, rather than individualistic, techniques and modes of expression? Debates on these and other questions were gathering momentum within the women's movement as the 1970s drew to a close.[21]

The process of redefinition is inextricably linked with the process of changing the political and social role of women. In the visual arts, for instance, women have to find new ways of seeing and representing themselves: in the past these have always been dictated by the status of women as objects of the male gaze – and this has set up within the female a contradiction between her sense of herself as subject, and her sense of herself as object. As John Berger has observed:

A woman must continually watch herself ... From earliest childhood she has been taught and persuaded to survey herself continually. And so she comes to consider the surveyed and surveyor within her as two constituent yet always distinct elements of her identity as a woman.[22]

Women and men see themselves and each other in such profoundly different ways that women cannot reclaim themselves in art simply by appropriating and adapting artistic modes developed by men. For example, there is no male equivalent to the female nude – whether in High Art or in 'dirty' magazines.

How can female sexuality be expressed in female terms? (There is no female equivalent to the male tradition of erotic art.) How, for that matter, can *femaleness* be expressed in female terms?

In 1980 Judy Chicago's massive exhibition, *The Dinner Party*, opened in San Francisco. It consists of a triangular dinner table, with thirty-nine place settings. The table is vast, almost fifty feet along each side. Each place setting is about three and a half feet wide and consists of an embroidered runner, cutlery, a goblet and a plate, whose different designs evoke the characteristics of a famous woman. They range from pre-Christian goddesses to Sappho, Boadicea, Susan B. Anthony and Virginia Woolf. The main feature of each setting is the 'plate', which is, in fact, a painted ceramic sculpture, based on the shape of a vagina. The names of 999 other women, also well-known, are inscribed on the 'heritage floor' in the centre of the triangle. The exhibition is completed with banners designed for the entrance, documentation of the five years' work by Chicago and her team of helpers, and a display of congratulatory telegrams from feminist artists all over the world. Its goal is 'to ensure that women's achievements become a permanent part of our culture'. It is magnificent, flamboyant, confident. It has been widely acclaimed. Many women have reported that they find it profoundly moving and inspiring – breathtaking in its scale. When was there ever such a work by women, for women, celebrating femaleness? Others have criticized it. For instance, the feminist sociologist Michele Barrett has questioned the 'dictatorial zeal' with which Chicago commanded the whole operation; her satisfaction in winning respect from, rather than challenging, the established institutions of the 'art world'; her ranking of women in hierarchical order and her use of vaginal imagery.[23] By 1981, the exhibition had been packed away in crates. Is it to be denied and buried, like so many women's achievements? Or will it find a permanent place of exhibition?

Disagreements over *The Dinner Party* will no doubt continue. The exhibition and the critiques that have followed are part of a process of change which is, in turn, vital to the development of feminism as a political force.

Notes to Chapter 7

1 *Women's Report*, vol. 1(5), July/August 1973.

2 *Images of Women: Guidelines for Promoting Equality in Journalism*, from NUJ, Acorn House, 314 Grays Inn Road, London WC1.

3 *Guardian*, 24 November 1980.

4 *Guardian*, 15 December 1980.

5 Lee, N. *One Eighth of a Say, The Place of Women on BBC Radio Nottingham's Morning News Programme*, from 118 Workshop, 118 Mansfield Road, Nottingham.

6 See also Coote, A. 'The Meaning of Man-talk', *New Statesman*, 2 January 1981, followed by Page, B. 'Sense and Sensibility', *New Statesman*, 9 January 1981, and Letters, *New Statesman*, 16 January 1981. See also Spender, D. *Man-Made Language*, Routledge & Kegan Paul, 1980.

7 *Guardian*, 1 December 1980.

8 See also Coward, R. ' "Sexual Liberation" and the Family' in *m/f* 1, 1978.

9 Baehr, H. 'The "Liberated Woman" in Television Drama', in *Women's Studies International Quarterly* vol. 3(1), 1980.

10 Williamson, J. *Decoding Advertisements*, Marion Boyars, 1978, p. 170.

11 Ibid.

12 ASA Case Report 68, p. 14.

13 ASA Case Report 67, p. 8.

14 Ibid. p. 5.

15 Report of the Committee on Obscenity and Film Censorship, November 1979, Cmnd. 7772. HMSO.

16 See also Ellis, J. 'Photography/Pornography/Art/Pornography' in *Screen*, vol. 21(1), Spring 1980.

17 Vincent, S. 'Women who ask for it', *New Statesman*, 19/26 December 1980.

18 *Spare Rib* 103, February 1981.

19 Mailer, N. *Prisoner of Sex*, Little and Brown (USA), 1971.

20 Caute, D. 'No more firemen', *New Statesman*, 14 November 1980.

21 For example, see Coward, R. 'Are women's novels feminists' novels?', *Feminist Review* 5, 1980; and Barrett, M. 'Feminism and Cultural Politics'.

22 Berger, J. *Ways of Seeing*, Penguin 1972. See also Tickner, L. 'The Body Politic: Female Sexuality and Women Artists since 1970' in *Art History*, vol. 1(2), June 1978.

23 Barrett, M. 'Feminism and the Definition of Cultural Politics', in *Feminism, Culture and Politics*, ed. Rosalind Brunt and Caroline Rowan, Lawrence & Wishart, 1982.

8 Sex

As *The Dinner Party* suggests in conveying the idea of female power through the imagery of female sexuality, the relationship between power and sex lies at the heart of the struggle for women's liberation.* What distinguishes this political movement from others is that women have begun to confront the political implications of the physical and psychological aspects of human life and to challenge conventional notions about sexuality. One such notion is that sexuality belongs to a private sphere which floats free of economic and political affairs. Another is that it is simply an expression of economic relations, which will be altered as a result of economic transition.

The issue of sexuality has always loomed large in the women's liberation movement. It has been at the centre of some of the fiercest disagreements among feminists, while at the same time lending an important new dimension to feminist politics. It holds within it a fundamental challenge to patriarchy. In this chapter we try to show that what women do with their bodies, how they seek pleasure and how they meet their sexual needs, has a profound effect on the way they see themselves and are seen by others; and that this in turn affects their social and economic relations, their access to power and the way they inhabit their own personalities. We look at the ways in which feminists have challenged the conventional meanings imposed on sexuality by a patriarchal society, and at how these meanings have – in a sense – hit back at feminism, hindering its development as a united political movement. Finally, we explore the possibilities of breaking away from oppressive definitions of heterosexuality and lesbianism.

*For those readers who have turned straight to the chapter on sex, you'll find our description of *The Dinner Party* at the end of the previous chapter.

Recipe for a heterosexual woman

Feminists have had to contend with some powerful myths. One is that sex is a purely natural phenomenon and therefore apolitcal (like the multiplication of cells, perhaps, or the fall of snow in winter). Another is that the natural expression of sexuality is what we know as heterosexuality. A third is that a woman's sense of her own sexuality is natural, rather than something that has been constructed by social and economic factors. In fact, there is very little that is 'natural' about a woman's sense of her own sexuality. Consider the teenage girl, who has been taught the 'facts of life' in a school biology lesson, tracing cross-sectional diagrams of ovaries and testicles, with the penis fitting neatly into the vagina and the spermatozoa zooming up to fertilize the egg. She may add this wisdom to her personal experience of the monthly 'curse' or 'period': a time of physical discomfort and fear of being betrayed by shameful smells and stains. Her favourite magazines urge her to paint her face and shave her legs and trap her breasts in polyester lace – for these, not the natural features of her body, are the signs of 'femininity'. She must smile and speak softly, listen and flatter, dress with care and move with grace – because this, rather than her own spontaneity, will make her *desirable*. She is drilled in the protocols of physical interaction: all that kissing and cuddling and feeling and fondling leads inexorably to the Sexual Act, when the biology lesson springs triumphantly into 3-D. She learns that 'losing her virginity' is one of the most significant moments of her life. This *is* sex. How often she performs this Sexual Act, by what means and with whom, thereafter determines whether she is 'bad' or 'good', a 'tart' or a 'tease', 'easy' or 'frigid'. She is not expected to initiate the action, except with such subtlety that the other imagines it was *his* idea. He 'gives it to her'; she 'gives herself'. There is a danger, moreover, that he may force it upon her whether she likes it or not, and there are ways in which she can be deemed to be 'asking for it' that are beyond her immediate control. To guide her through the snakepit, she has the catechism of Romantic Love, which teaches that one day, if she follows the correct path, she will find the right man, to whom she can belong and so live happily ever after. The centre of her own erotic pleasure, the clitoris, remains – like the mad woman locked in the attic – an awkward half-secret.

Of course, if she isn't careful, she may find herself pregnant and pressed into motherhood and marriage before she is entirely sure that she has found true happiness with Mr Right. She may find, whether by dint of her economic dependence, or for fear of physical force, that she is obliged to remain with a man she does not especially like. If, as she performs the Sexual Act in the marital bed at more or less regular intervals, she manages to express herself freely without shame or fear and enjoy herself to the full when she herself wants to, it will be *in spite* of what she has learned, not because of it. She wasn't born to practise sexuality this way, nor did she achieve it; she had it thrust upon her.

But if the lessons of her formative years fail to bring her physical or psychic fulfilment, they achieve a lot else instead. They endow her with a sense of herself which has a profound effect on the way she leads her daily life – how she perceives and behaves towards men, women and children; her domestic arrangements; how she seeks and gains affirmation; what she dare and dare not do. As we have seen in earlier chapters, the patterns of everyday life greatly influence the kind of work we do, our economic strength or weakness and our capacity to shape our own future.

Conventional heterosexual practice – that bizarre mixture of myth and coercion – is defended more vigorously than any other precept on which our society is supposed to be founded. (Is religion more keenly observed? Is equality before the law more jealously guarded? Or freedom of expression?) A woman who becomes an engineer or a Cabinet minister may be a rare phenomenon, unwelcome to some, but she is not seen as a threat to the social fabric. A woman who has sexual relations with another woman *is* seen as such – for all the broadmindedness of our post-sixties culture. Disapproval and abuse are heaped on the female who has sex with many different people, but who will call a promiscuous male a 'loose' man or a 'tramp'? The law takes more trouble to protect children from any contact with unconventional sexuality than to shield them from violence.

Some will argue that this sort of thing is necessary to ensure the future of the race. But of course that is ridiculous. *Most* heterosexual practice is not intended for reproduction – quite the contrary. Physical love with a member of one's own sex doesn't prevent procreation, it merely postpones it on that occasion; and there is plenty of evidence that peoples whose sex lives are not predominantly heterosexual want to procreate, and do.

The modern myth of homosexuality

What is most significant about contemporary attitudes to sexuality is that we have a rigid picture of two types of people: there are heterosexual people and there are homosexual/ lesbian people. There are arguments about whether these apparently opposite conditions are inherited or produced by various influences during our formative years. But what comes across most strongly is that almost everyone is supposedly identified as one or the other. 'She *is* a lesbian ... he *is* a heterosexual...' Even people who fall between the categories are defined in these terms: 'She *is* bisexual' is taken to mean that she is neither heterosexual nor lesbian *because* she is a bit of both.

The idea of a 'homosexual person', rather than just a person who engages in physical love with a member of the same sex, is relatively recent. Lillian Faderman has shown in her book *Surpassing the Love of Men* that passionate friendship between women – whether or not it involved physical love – has in the past been accepted simply as something (many) women did, and has not always been seen as a threat to the social fabric. This is partly because the idea of women having an autonomous sex drive was, until recently, beyond the grasp of those who had power to make and enforce society's rules. (As in the case of Queen Victoria, there was a wide assumption that women didn't indulge in any such thing.) But it is also because that kind of behaviour, if it did occur, was not seen as defining the subject as a certain type of person, nor as undermining her femininity:

There were in several eras and places many instances of women who were known to engage in lesbian sex, and they did so with impunity. As long as they appeared feminine their sexual behaviour would be viewed as an activity which women indulged in when men were unavailable or as an apprenticeship or appetite whetter to heterosexual sex. But if one or both of the pair demanded masculine privileges, the illusion of lesbianism as *faute de mieux* behaviour was destroyed. At the base it was not the sexual aspect of lesbianism as much as the attempted usurpation of male prerogative by women who behaved like men that many societies appeared to find most disturbing.[1]

Platonic passions between women were no threat as long as they did not interfere with the conviction that the only possible sexual object for women was men. The idea of what homosexuality stands for has gone through a metamorphosis since the mid nineteenth century, affecting men first and women later –

as it gradually came to be recognized that women were capable of erotic pleasure and of actively seeking that pleasure.

Until 1885, the only law dealing with homosexual behaviour related to buggery – a capital offence since the early sixteenth century. (All other homosexual acts were made illegal by the 'Labouchere' Amendment to the 1885 Criminal Law Amendment Act. This tightening up of the law was consolidated by the Vagrancy Act of 1897, which outlawed homosexual soliciting.) The concern of the law was to prohibit non-reproductive sex and this was quite distinct from the twentieth-century concern with homosexuality. The first is about sinful behaviour which belongs to the panoply of sin to which we are all heir; the second is about a certain kind of person.

The idea has developed over the last hundred years that homosexuality is an 'unfortunate condition', and, as Jeffrey Weeks argues, in *The Making of the Modern Homosexual*, the 1957 Wolfenden Report represented the final acceptance of this definition, which signals a homosexual *type* – i.e. one who suffers from the condition.[2] This definition has served the purpose of regulating the distribution of homosexual behaviour. For if homosexuality is something that only 'homosexuals' do, it follows that others do not. Thus, the construction of a homosexual identity has entailed the construction of a heterosexual identity, and has served to police the behaviour of all people.

Lie back and think of England

Unfortunately for many women, conventional heterosexual practice isn't always a great deal of fun. As an erotic sensation, penetration of the vagina by the penis can leave a lot to be desired. The incidence and intensity of the female orgasm have preoccupied sex reformers and psychoanalysts throughout the twentieth century. Its low incidence or non-occurrence ('frigidity') has been identified as a major cause of sexual maladjustment and marital breakdown. Some investigators reckoned that it signalled lack of consent, others imagined it was part of the feminine condition. Generally, it has been assumed that female orgasm is something that does not occur spontaneously: it has to be *mobilized*.

All the major studies of female orgasm have recorded mammoth failure rates. In the 1930s, Dickinson and Beam reported in the first substantial analysis of marriage, *A Thousand Marriages*, that in nearly two-thirds of their cases, sex was not

satisfactory.[3] Hannah and Abraham Stone, popular sex coun-
sellors of the post-war era, said in their widely read book *A
Marriage Manual* that failure to reach orgasm was 'the most
frequent sexual complaint among women who are otherwise
entirely normal'.[4] The British sex reformer Eustace Chesser,
who wrote many popular manuals on sex and carried out his
own survey of sex and marriage in the 1950s, known as the
Chesser Report, concluded from surveys of Britain and American literature that 70 per cent of women never reached satisfaction.[5] Seymour Fisher's study, *The Female Orgasm*,
estimated in 1972 that only 39 per cent of women had orgasms
during intercourse.[6] A feminist heir to this tradition of sexual
investigation, Shere Hite, has shown in *The Hite Report* (1978)
that only 30 per cent of women have orgasms 'during intercourse without direct manual stimulation'. From this she draws
the conclusion that:

not to have orgasm from intercourse is the experience of the majority
of women ... often the ways in which women do orgasm in intercourse
have nothing to do with intercourse itself.[7]

She goes on to throw down the gauntlet to the investigators:

Even the question being asked is wrong. The question should not be:
why aren't women having orgasms from intercourse? But rather: ...
why have women found it necessary to try everything in the book,
from exercises to extensive analysis to sex therapy, to make it
happen?[8]

Alongside this steady accumulation of evidence, new concepts
of female sexuality have gradually developed. Even before the
mass surveys got under way, British feminists such as Dora
Russell, Marie Stopes and Stella Browne were asserting wom-
en's rights to sexual pleasure, free from fear of unwanted pregnancy. 'There has grown up a masculine mythology
suppressing and distorting all the facts of women's sexual and
maternal emotions', wrote Stella Browne in 1917.[9] In *Married
Love*, which took the world by storm in 1918, Marie Stopes
went so far as to assert that a man might stimulate his wife to
orgasm during pregnancy without penetrating her:

the time will come when it will be sufficient for him to be near her
and caress her for relief to take place without any physical
connection.[10]

Yet while feminists in the early part of this century campaigned for female pleasure, they saw sex essentially as part

216

of a maternal cycle. Their ideal was the sexually satisfied earth mother; their ideas were anchored more in eugenics and evolution than in eroticism. They played an important part in constructing the modern ideology of heterosexuality, popularizing in a plethora of marriage handbooks the notion that women's pleasure must be mobilized to match the man's, for successful execution of the Sexual Act.

The ideal scenario was described by Dr Helena Wright in *The Sex Factor in Marriage* (1920): the sole purpose of the clitoris was pleasure, she observed; man had the joy of arousing woman and 'creating in her an ardour equal to his own' ... at the moment of sufficient excitement the woman was ready to receive the male and the mutual climax consummating the act was completed. 'Thought is abandoned, a curious freeing of the spirit, very difficult to describe ... a pleasure of the soul.' [11] Having dished out advice on how to achieve the ideal mutual orgasm, Dr Wright was eventually prompted to revise her prescription. She worked in one of London's first family planning clinics and heard the experiences of many men and hundreds of women who visited it: they had tried the recipe and it didn't work. In 1947, in *More About the Sex Factor in Marriage*, she condemned the notion that 'women will have an answering orgasm felt in the vagina induced by the movement of the penis'. This misconception was so widespread, she said, that it amounted to a 'penis-vagina fixation', and she expressed doubt about 'the efficacy of the penis-vagina combination for producing orgasm for a woman'. [12]

Her observations were vindicated six years later when, in 1953, Alfred Kinsey published his massive study, *Sexual Behaviour in the Human Female*. [13] As a result of his findings Kinsey shocked the West and especially Freudian orthodoxy by suggesting that there was no difference between the 'infant' and the 'adult' orgasm: this was heretical because it dissolved the ideological barrier between the allegedly 'immature' clitoral orgasm and its 'mature' vaginal version. It implied that penetration of the vagina did not, after all, add a superior quality to the female climax. Freud had maintained that maturity in a woman was symbolized by the transfer of her erotic interests from the clitoris to the vagina.

Again in 1966 William H. Masters and Virginia Johnson pointed out in their substantial work, *Human Sexual Response*, [14] that 'the primary focus for sexual response in the human female's pelvis is the clitoral body'. Even though the clitoris had been recognized as a site of pleasure, they observed, it tended to be consigned to a supporting role in 'foreplay'. As soon as the woman was aroused, it was bypassed on the way to penetration, instead of being given the attention it deserved, as a source of pleasure in its own right, more exciting and excitable than the vagina.

In other fields of market research, similar data about the extent of customer dissatisfaction might have led to withdrawal of the product. But here, vested interests in continuing production have evidently been too strong. Most commonly, the conclusion has been drawn that the customer is at fault, not the goods. It women are discontented with their sex lives, the problem lies chiefly with them: it is interpreted as a failure of female physiology or psychology, not of the Sexual Act itself. The latter is apparently necessary to men and therefore *must* be necessary to women. Masters and Johnson rocked the notion of necessity, only to stabilize it by amending it. The puzzle could be solved, they claimed, by synchronizing vaginal penetration with stimulation of the clitoris by means of genital 'traction' during intercourse. Thus, the female orgasm was still to be orchestrated to coincide with the male orgasm.

Under the collective microscope

This was the state of play when the women's liberation movement began to take shape in the late 1960s. As we have seen, a key feature of the movement has been its insistence that 'the personal is political'. In the safe space of small groups, women started to share their secrets – and what emerged, among much else, was an epidemic of sexual failure. Women were bored with their husbands in bed; or their husbands were bored with them; or they only had orgasms when they masturbated; or they felt awkward and humiliated; or they hated their own bodies; or they feared they were frigid. There they were, at the height of the Permissive Era, when everybody was supposed to be having such a terrific time, and yet ... fucking was a let-down. It wasn't true of all the women. Some were evidently satisfied, but so far, this knowledge had only enhanced the others' sense of failure and fear of being 'abnormal'. In spite of *all* the evidence to the contrary, the dominant view remained that the Sexual Act should consist of penetration of the vagina by the penis, ideally culminating in mutual orgasm; any other activity, regardless of how it benefited the female, was peripheral or compensatory.

The effect of discussing the problem in consciousness-raising groups was to start to politicize it. As sex, love and monogamy were scrutinized under the collective microscope, they were seen not simply as autonomous functions of 'human nature', but as aspects of a power struggle. Women began to recognize conventional heterosexual practice as the glue which holds up the patriarchal order – by symbolizing and reinforcing male power and female dependence, by regimenting social relations and by helping to set the patterns of everyday life.

It was this perspective that Anne Koedt expressed in her paper 'The Myth of the Vaginal Orgasm', in which she drew political conclusions from existing evidence about the role of the clitoris in female sexuality, and from the suppression of that evidence.

One of the elements of male chauvinism is the refusal or inability to see women as total, separate human beings. Rather ... men have chosen to define women only in terms of how they benefit men's lives. Sexually, a woman is not seen as an individual wanting to share equally in the sexual act, any more than she was seen as a person with independent desires when she did anything else in society. Thus, it is easy for men to make up what facts are convenient about women, as society is controlled so that women have not been organized to form even a vocal opposition to the male 'experts'.[15]

Koedt suggests that 'the establishment of clitoral orgasm as fact would threaten the heterosexual *institution*', and that men are too fearful of losing their hold over women to imagine 'a future free relationship between individuals'. Male power relies heavily on the continued sexual dependency of women and this becomes more crucial as women seek greater social and economic independence. 'What we must do', Koedt insists, 'is redefine our sexuality':

We must discard the 'normal' concepts of sex and create new guide-lines which take into account mutual sexual enjoyment. While the idea of mutual enjoyment is acknowledged in marriage manuals, it is not followed to its logical conclusion. We must begin to demand that if a certain sexual position now defined as 'standard' is not mutually conducive to orgasm then it should no longer be so defined.[16]

By pursuing the 'logical conclusion' of the evidence, the women's liberation movement has begun to question the priorities

219

and protocols of heterosexuality and challenge the supremacy of the Sexual Act. Perhaps penetration isn't *the* magic moment after all. Perhaps the vagina's welcome of the penis is only one of many sexual acts – which cannot be ranked in order of importance, nor mapped out in stages, like an assault course up a mountain side. If this is so, traditional notions about sexual desire and fulfilment cease to make any sense. Women's pleasure need not be seen as dependent on men's. And if penetration does not 'complete' the sex act, then physical relations which omit it cannot be dismissed as incomplete or immature. Female sensuality and female eroticism have to be allowed their own meanings and their own horizons. They might meet and mingle pleasurably with men's, but they are neither defined nor patrolled by them.

Breaking out of the old routine

The possibilities for change and development seemed infinite in the early years of the movement. At the second national women's liberation conference in Britain, in 1971, there were workshop discussions on sexuality which ranged over far more complex territory, and were far more creative and radical than anything that had gone before. Everything was open to question: marriage, monogamy, heterosexuality, lesbianism, bodies, babies ... nothing was sacred or fixed. The movement has enabled many individuals to question old routines and alter their perspective on sex – often through encounters with other women. Love affairs raged between women in the early 1970s. Some felt it as an erotic extension of sisterhood; it was simply about love of women. For others, it seemed a delightful alternative to their exhausted efforts with men. Geraldine Park was one who found that her identity as a fragile 'English rose' was transformed when she went to the States to stay with her new female lover:

I wore jeans for the first time! I had a whole new conception of myself, my body, the way I could flirt with people – anybody I felt I could be really raunchy, experience myself as both the seducer and the seduced. It was a way out of any set text. It was crucial, that experience, learning what a woman's body is like. All I'd had before was this mystified sense of myself, vicariously presented through my knowledge of how a man responded to a woman (who might be me or a fantasy figure for all I knew). That sense of the concreteness of my physical form has remained with me...

Marion Thomas recalls the effect of reading 'The Myth of the Vaginal Orgasm':

It was my first discovery of my own sexuality. I was sleeping with men and not coming. I was allowing them to be the ones who knew about lovemaking and running the show. And I just kind of joined in. That pamphlet pointed out that you could have pleasure on your own, with another woman or with a man, and that you didn't *need* to have a man there. Soon afterwards I had my first good sexual relationship with a man, at 23. I discovered I was a very sexual person who had a great deal of pleasure. . .

Both alternated for a time between relationships with women and with men. 'Being with women', says Marion, 'I rediscovered the sensuality I knew I had. The lack of role-playing was very important – and the way sex and emotion were very bound up. I learned a lot about what it is to give as well as receive. . .'

This kind of exploration among feminists was not confined to trendy London circles. Pauline Barry remembers that in her women's group in Bradford in the early 1970s 'there were 45-year-old working-class women having lesbian experiences for the first time in their lives. Or people going out with a bloke one night and a woman the next.' It broke up some marriages, metamorphosed others, left some people frightened and hurt. But for most it has been a positive development, which has expanded awareness and pulled the rug out from under the old Me-Tarzan-You-Jane act, which once passed for 'making love'.

Feminists whose practice has remained exclusively heterosexual have learned and changed too – as a result of talking to other women, reading, experimenting alone or with lovers and (very often) fighting it out on a daily basis with their menfolk. Others, meanwhile, have continued to have sexual relations with women and not with men – because they desire women, because they have managed to find a supportive social milieu, because they don't desire men (even dislike or hate them), because they feel that only thus can they express their sexuality and their politics – and for combinations of all these reasons. Angela Lloyd recalls that when she became a lesbian in 1971 the fact that her life was anchored in a supportive group of like-minded friends was vital to her:

I loved the women-centredness of their companionship. They were all women who had left their homes and had this great struggle for freedom. They offered a personal and social life I'd never dreamed possible. I didn't make a political choice about lesbianism, but the political context of these women's lives had a great effect on me. It was very courageous to give up marriages, homes, take off with the kids, squat in women's houses, play in bands. Motherhood was such a meeting ground of feminism, yet that isn't in the histories...

Defensive and defeatist strategies

It seemed possible in the early and mid 1970s that the women's liberation movement could transform human sexual relations. However the initial questioning and exploration has not yet been developed; ideas haven't been thought through in detail. Apart from Anne Koedt's paper, little has been written about sexuality from a feminist perspective. And so the step has not yet been taken from challenging the status quo to working out an alternative approach. Early initiatives which could have led to the development of a new feminist sexual politics have been crushed between two opposing tendencies: the first is a defensive strategy which might be described as 'heterosexual chauvinism' and the second is separatism – in our view defeatist. They may not reflect the aspirations or the experience of the majority of feminists, but they nevertheless have force because they suggest ways of dealing with sexuality which are relatively straightforward, since they do not break with traditional categories. Both are shaped and defined by the values of patriarchal sex. Do you fuck with men or don't you? Should you or shouldn't you? Having first challenged the supremacy of the Sexual Act, feminists have allowed it to retain such significance that these questions have at times threatened to tear the movement apart.

At its most glamorous and flamboyant, heterosexual chauvinism appears like a revamped *femme fatale*. It is the kind of feminism men like best. It slaps their knees for being sexual slobs and chastises women for being sexual slovens. Above all, it promises the superfuck. Germaine Greer set the tone in her book *The Female Eunuch*, published in 1970. Greer shares with the libertarians of the 1960s a faith in the naturally disruptive effects of a sexualized culture, and a concern with sexual repression in society. She shares with women's liberation a concern with power in sexual relations: 'Men have commandeered all the energy and streamlined it into an aggressive conquistadorial power.' But the burden of her argument, like that of Masters and Johnson, is to protect the conventions of heterosexuality, not to change them:

If the right chain reaction could happen, women might find that the clitoris was more directly involved in intercourse and would be brought to climax by a less pompous and deliberate way than digital massage...

(The Sexual Act, we know, has not a shred of pomposity about it, and is always done by mistake.) The clitoris would be merely an object of scorn – all digits and spasms in Greer's world – if it weren't perceived as such a terrible menace:

The banishment of the fantasy of the vaginal orgasm is ultimately a service, but the substitution of the clitorial spasm for genuine gratification may turn out to be a disaster for sexuality... Masters and Johnson's conclusions have produced some unlooked for side-effects, like veritable clitoromania...

Beware the clitoris! Her notion of 'genuine gratification', which she insists must involve the vagina, runs very close to the Freudian *faux pas* about mature and immature sexuality. What Greer fails to see is the difference between the vagina as *a* place of pleasure, and *the* place; the hierarchy of sexual values remains intact.

She holds out hope of some sort, however. Women can save themselves from the worst effects of male sexual power-play if they will only 'accept part of the responsibility for their own and their partner's enjoyment':

This involves a measure of control and conscious cooperation. Part of the battle will be if they can change their attitude toward sex and embrace and stimulate the penis instead of taking it...

According to the code of heterosexual chauvinism, fucking is what all the best women do. And if one is clever, one's feminism can even increase one's sexual prowess! But this is a delicate business. One is in the parlour of the male ego and one must take care not to rumple the antimacassars or knock ash on to the rug. Germaine Greer makes it plain that however many faults men may have, they are indispensable when it comes to sex, because penetration turns it into the Real Thing. The message must be reinforced assiduously, or one risks being banished to the back-kitchen for failing to show proper respect. Even if one has dabbled with lesbianism in the past, one must dissociate oneself from it entirely.

Shortly after Greer published *The Female Eunuch*, radical feminists in Britain began to prepare their own intervention in feminist body politics, which took quite a different tack. *Thoughts on Feminism*, their paper published in 1971 for the

November national women's liberation conference in London, argues that 'as long as the Sex Act remains the norm for sexual relations, we remain the habitual givers, pawns in the male power game. And we will continue to be dominated by men ... as long as we have our closest emotional/sexual relationships with men, Women's Liberation can be no more than a hobby.' Heterosexual contact, the paper suggests, penetrates even the psyche: 'Our personality alters as we become less penetrable (vaginal) and increasingly self-contained (clitoral).' The answer is to give it up.

The mainstream of the movement baulked at the challenge. Its concern was with strategies which enabled women to survive *in* the world. This radical feminist paper amounted to revolutionary defeatism: run for cover and snipe at those who malinger on the front line.

Worse was to come. As we observed in Chapter 1, there was a struggle in the early 1970s between socialist and radical feminists, over the structure of the London women's liberation workshop – and in particular over whether men should be allowed across the threshold. The radical feminists held out for exclusion and won a tactical victory. Thereafter, the workshop became an increasingly separatist enclave, with other feminists going their own ways. It was not the radical feminists' wish to retain space free for men that was damaging, but their assertion that separatism was the correct path for *all* feminists. In the summer of 1974, the workshop newsletter published a relentless attack on heterosexual women, reprinted from a document written by New York radical lesbians. Called 'The Clit Statement', it was run as a serial over many weeks: 'Straight women think, talk, cross their legs, dress and come on like male transvestite femme drag queens', it accuses and, in a later episode, describes straight women as 'agents'.

Ironically, Germaine Greer said something similar herself – 'I'm sick of being a transvestite, I refuse to be my own female impersonator' – but in that context, the sharing of discontent about inauthentic ways of being women was directed towards a restructuring of femininity 'The Clit Statement' was an attack not only on forms of femininity, but on women themselves. As such, it contravened the founding principle of radical feminism. The New York Redstockings, who had formulated the 'pro-woman' line in 1969, issued a powerful riposte. But British radical feminists remained silent. Even in the mainstream of the movement, there was little open retaliation. Perhaps it seemed too difficult to sustain a political and personal critique of heterosexuality alongside a political and personal commitment to it.

The effect was to drive heterosexual women (a large majority among feminists as among all women) on to the defensive. They felt roughed up by the very movement in which they had sought safety. Not only did they feel that they themselves were under attack, and their idea of what women's liberation stood for was on trial, but they were also required to defend heterosexuality – in a way that left them no room for their own manoeuvres against patriarchal sexual practices. The Greer style of defence held little meaning for most of them; it lay, unwelcome, in their line of retreat.

Groups began to disaffiliate from the London workshop; women stopped taking its newsletter. Many now found that their feminism was confined to campaiging corners, or to the informal networks of their female friends. Increasingly, they felt they couldn't participate in the politics of the women's liberation movement, where the dominant question was whether one was for or against heterosexuality, rather than how to formulate strategies *within* it, or how to reform feminine psychology. Socialist feminists had developed no positive perspective of their own. There were ritual rows at one national conference after another, until the last one in Birmingham in 1978 – when the split was so bitter and painful that no one was prepared to organize another such gathering.

In the late 1970s a new grouping, 'revolutionary feminism', emerged from the radical feminist current, generating yet more explosive texts. Leeds Revolutionary Feminists confounded an already depressed movement with a paper published in 1979, 'Political Lesbianism: The Case Against Heterosexuality'.[18] This asserts that penetration is 'an act of great symbolic significance, by which the oppressor enters the body of the oppressed'. It denies that heterosexual women are the enemy (hardly reassuring at this stage), but insists that they are 'collaborators with the enemy':

Every woman who lives with or fucks a man helps to maintain the oppression of her sisters and hinders our struggle.

All feminists, the Leeds paper claims, can and should be political lesbians:

Our definition of a political lesbian is a woman-identified woman who

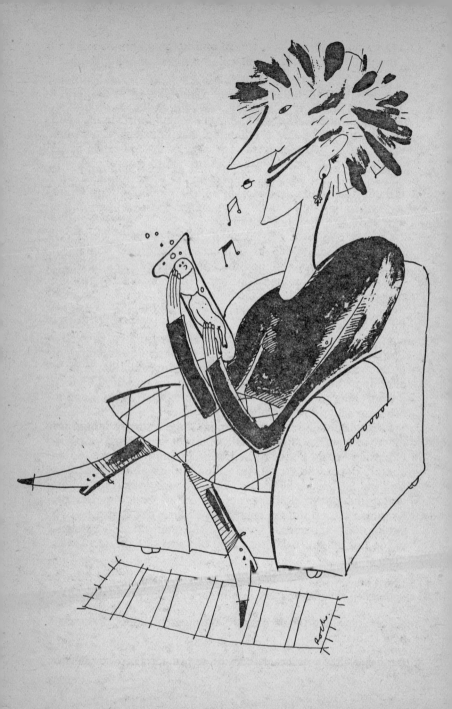

does not fuck men. It does not mean compulsory sexual activity with women.

When this was published in the movement's national newsletter, *Wires*, the challenge was taken up with more bravado than before. Lesbian and heterosexual women wrote letters, subsequently published in *Wires*,[19] which attacked the Leeds Revolutionary Feminists for denying 'the principle that every woman's experience is real and valid', and for failing to understand the nature of the feminist fight against patriarchy – for mistaking (as it were) the edifice for the glue which holds it together:

Somehow they reduce the whole structure of male supremacy to fucking. Withdrawing sexual services from men becomes the total strategy – how exactly this will bring them to their knees is not explained. Of course, it is a lot easier to make heterosexual feminists feel guilty than it is ... to confront the structures of the patriarchy which go beyond immediate personal relationships.

The critics rejected the doctrinaire approach of the Leeds group as being inimical to women's politics. 'The only point in women changing their lives is if *they* want to... We have to discover, as we go along, what it is that women want, not to try to dictate it now.' It was pointed out that the paper denied the unconscious dimension of sexuality and, not least, that it implied that lesbianism had nothing to do with eroticism:

In particular, it ignores the importance of women's sexual relations with other women whilst making the question of whether women have sexual relations with men central to the whole definition of political lesbianism.

One letter suggested that the paper was not about sexuality at all, but a political exercise in making the movement a 'closed group of cadre units'.

As before, however, the arguments about heterosexuality were defensive. They proposed no way out, no revision of the movement's aims, no redefinition of the terms of the debate. The old categories of 'gay' and 'straight' remained undisturbed and the questionable propriety of the Sexual Act continued to divide feminists.

Divide and rule

What remains to be done is to explore the experience that lesbians and heterosexuals *share* and to build on this common

227

ground a political understanding of sexuality. Undoubtedly, there are women's groups who have looked into the matter, but this approach has yet to be brought out into the open, to the forefront of feminist politics, where it needs to be. Meanwhile, there have been pressures on women to accentuate their sexual identity in traditional, polarized terms.

On one side, the political priorities of Gay Liberation have impinged strongly on the feminist approach to lesbianism. This movement, which combines male and female homosexuals (the former predominating), emerged during the same years as women's liberation. It is based on a celebration of what is still felt to be a minority and deviant identity. The lesbians who were part of it in the early 1970s tended to be women whose homosexuality pre-dated their involvement with the women's liberation movement: they came to it by a different route from those who discovered a sexual desire for women in a feminist milieu. There was considerable tension between the 'old' and 'nouveau' lesbians. 'Old' lesbians had a sense of allegiance to the homosexual community, to which they had paid their dues: in that setting, any intimation of androgyny or bisexuality threatened betrayal, because it was so often associated with not coming out – with plunging into the world of gay pleasure and never paying the price, never letting on to family, friends or employers. Their response to the 'nouveau' lesbians was to be highly suspicious of it; to any sign of bisexuality, directly unsympathetic.

As for the idea that feminism is the theory and lesbianism the practice, which began to be articulated by radical feminists in the early 1970s, some of the 'old' lesbians were unsympathetic to that too – because they were socialists, not separatists. Moreover, it was too threatening to the organizing principle of gay politics, which was about naming your gay *identity*.

Gay liberation did not leave room for the possibility of lesbianism being an alternative choice to heterosexuality (albeit an unequal one, bearing heavy risks), nor for the possibility of both being part of a spectrum in which the similarities are more significant than the differences. In that sense, it initially mirrored the way in which society marginalizes homosexual desire as being something experienced only by homosexuals.

Lesbianism in the women's liberation movement has been as much about women as about homosexuality, as it is conventionally defined. It has been more about desire than about identity as one specific *type* or another. As such, it represents

228

a challenge to the very *category* of 'homosexuality' – and a correlating challenge to the 'heterosexual' category. At the same time, however, the movement as a whole has had to cope with the queer-bashing abuse that has rained on it. 'They're just a bunch of dykes' has been a typical slur. The manifest affection between feminists – all that 'huggin' and a kissin'' – gets them labelled if nothing else does.

Before they have been able to formulate a response which holds them together, women have been forced back into their traditional corners. It is a tried-and-tested strategy for undermining rebellion: divide and rule. Trapped by the old patriarchal definitions, those who do not already identify as lesbians and who do not want their feminist politics dismissed as symptoms of deviance, have found themselves protesting that, even if some of their best friends are lesbians, *they* most definitely are *not*. When it comes to sex, the strategy works like a dream. If a woman wants to challenge the established protocols of heterosexuality, or let the cat out of the bag about the erotic imperfections of the patriarchal fuck, how is she to respond to her partner's benign murmur that maybe she doesn't like it because ... she is *really* gay? There is no confident feminist affirmation of heterosexuality to which she can refer, only the clitorophobic defence of the Greer school.

Feminists fighting for their children in custody cases have sometimes been accused of being 'unfit mothers' – a charge levelled automatically against lesbians – and have had to struggle to be recognized as 'real women', meaning unsullied by any traces of lesbianism.

Both Geraldine Park and Marion Thomas, whom we quoted earlier, have resumed a fixed heterosexual identity. It isn't because they have stopped desiring women – but because they haven't stopped desiring men, and have found the combination of this urge and the urge towards social conformity irresistible. 'I had this very strong sense of how awful it would be', Geraldine explains, 'to be looked at by somebody who had none of the libertarian notions about lesbianism being a good and healthy thing, and to be found disgusting. I felt profoundly uncomfortable being subject to other people's destructive judgements. I don't believe there is an essential womanhood – we are constructed, held in place.'

'I want to be *in* the culture, not exiled from it,' says Marion. 'I did find lesbianism terribly painful. Terribly exiled. The intolerant, harsh world is beastly to homosexuals. The fact that I could handle relationships with men again, and that with men I do feel I have social acceptance – these things have been influential. But I really affirm and insist on my right to love women.'

Alongside these women are thousands of feminists who have never desired other women and who are committed to sexual relationships with men: when their feminism is challenged, the incentive to assert a heterosexual identity and to deny any personal association with lesbianism is probably even stronger.

These are effects of what Adrienne Rich has described as 'the lie of compulsory female heterosexuality', which afflicts

not just feminist scholarship, but every profession, every reference work, every curriculum, every organzining attempt, every relationship or conversation over which it hovers. It creates, specifically, a profound falseness, hypocrisy, and hysteria in the heterosexual dialogue, for every heterosexual relationship is lived in the queasy strobelight of that lie. However we choose to identify ourselves, however we find ourselves labelled, it flickers across and distorts out lives. . .

And, as she says, it has caused '*an incalculable loss to the power of all women to change the social relations of the sexes, to liberate ourselves and each other*'.[20]

The same lie is chiefly to blame for that sense of betrayal which has made the gay liberation movement so suspicious of bisexuality. It has meant that even in the women's liberation movement, lesbians have been obliged to reaffirm and defend their homosexuality. As a result, the new feminist lesbianism has developed its identity within the sphere of gay politics – which isn't its home ground, whose priorities it doesn't share and which doesn't reflect the conditions in which it flourishes. Women who desire women but to whom the 'lesbian' label doesn't mean anything have been left in political limbo. As for bisexuality, it has been dishonourably discharged. Even when radical feminists promote the political choice of lesbianism, it is more as a feminist way of life than as an expression of erotic desire.

What women want, not what men decree

Women warned each other, at the first national conference held by lesbians in Canterbury in 1974, that lesbianism was being used as a derogatory term to divide their movement. But no counter-strategy emerged to prevent this, except a determination to defend lesbianism, which was vital, but not enough. On that same occasion it was decided that lesbianism should be a major topic at the forthcoming national women's liberation conference in Edinburgh, on the ground that it was the most misunderstood issue of the movement and that existing aims expressed heterosexual priorities.

Out of the Edinburgh conference, after much heated argument, came the movement's Sixth Demand: 'An end to discrimination against lesbians, and for women's right to determine their own sexuality.' But unfortunately, since the movement doesn't yet know what it wants to say about sexuality, the demand has tended to confuse the issue. It affirms a commitment to lesbians' civil rights but ignored their erotic interests. By combining two separate aims, it seems to associate self-determination with a specific lesbian identity, as though other less clearly-defined expressions of sexuality are not relevant.

Neither the Sixth Demand nor the politics of gay liberation – any more than the perspectives of separatism or heterosexual chauvinism – express what has been (potentially) revolutionary about the sexual atmosphere within the women's liberation movement. For here are the beginnings of a positive commitment to female eroticism, as something powerful and autonomous, which is shared by heterosexuals, lesbians and bisexuals – and which transcends all such definitions, robbing them of meaning except as barricades thrown up in defence of patriarchy. If the political significance of this could be seized, then femininity could be taken out of its strait jacket and celebrated rather than shunned. It could be positive and strong as well as sensual, desiring as well as desirable. It would not necessarily deny men, and it would certainly not rely on them. It would be what women wanted it to be, not what men decreed.

Defined by women rather than by the rules of patriarchy, sisterhood and love between women take on new meanings. Adrienne Rich, describing her concept of the 'lesbian continuum', has begun to explore what this might be:

I mean the term ... to include a range – through each woman's life and throughout history – of woman-identified experience; not simply the fact that a woman has had or consciously desired genital sexual experience with another woman. If we expand it to embrace many more forms of primary intensity between and among women, including the sharing of a rich inner life, the bonding against male tyranny, the giving and receiving of practical and political support; if we can also hear in it such associations as *marriage resistance* ... we begin to grasp breadths of female history and psychology which have lain out of reach as a consequence of limited, mostly clinical, definitions of 'lesbianism'.[21]

Every woman, Adrienne Rich observes, moves in and out of that continuum at different stages of her lifetime. It is the thread on which feminism is woven.

From this perspective, it is not useful for women to differentiate themselves from one another according to whom they most often share their beds with. It is essential, on the other hand, to challenge the institutions of heterosexuality and homosexuality and to understand the means by which women are held captive within them. In plumbing the depths of the myth and coercion, the women's liberation movement needs to defend and transform heterosexuality and defend the continuity of a specifically lesbian culture, as well as to strive for a new sexual culture which transcends both.

Notes to Chapter 8

1 Faderman, L. *Surpassing the Love of Men*, Junction Books, London 1981.

2 Weeks, J. 'Deviance, Desire and Sexual Deviance' in *The Making of the Modern Homosexual*, Hutchinson, 1981.

3 Dickinson, R. and Beam, L. *A Thousand Marriages*, Balliere Tindall & Cox, London 1932.

4 Stone, H. and A. *A Marriage Manual*, Gollancz, 1952.

5 Chesser, E. *Marriage and Freedom*, Rich & Cowan, London 1952.

6 Fisher, S. *Understanding The Female Orgasm*, Pelican, 1972.

7 Hite, S. *The Hite Report*, Hamlyn, 1978.

8 Ibid.

9 Browne, S. 'Women and Birth Control' in Eden and Cedar Paul (eds.) *Population and Birth Control: A Symposium*, New York 1917.

10 Stopes, M. *Married Love: A New Contribution to the Solution of Sex Difficulties*, Fifield, 1918.

11 Wright, H. *The Sex Factor in Marriage*, Noel Douglas, London 1930.

12 Wright, H. *More About the Sex Factor in Marriage*, Williams and Northgate, London 1947.

13 Kinsey, A. *Sexual Behaviour in the Human Female*, Indiana University Institute for Sex Research, 1953.

14 Masters, W. and Johnson, V. *Human Sexual Response*, Churchill, London 1966.

15 Koedt, A. 'The Myth of the Vaginal Orgasm' in *Notes from the Second Year*, 1970.
16 Ibid.
17 Greer, G. *The Female Eunuch*, Paladin, 1971.
18 Leeds Revolutionary Feminist Group 'Political Lesbianism: The Case Against Heterosexuality', first printed in *Wires* no. 81, reprinted in *Love Your Enemy?*, Only Women Press, 1981.
19 Reprinted in *Love Your Enemy?*, ibid.
20 Rich, A. *Compulsory Heterosexuality and Lesbian Existence*, Only Women Press, 1981.
21 Ibid.

9 *The future*

We have tried to give an account of the development of feminist politics since the late 1960s, to show how far the objectives of the women's liberation movement have been realized and how they have met resistance. We don't claim to have produced a definitive history – it is more an interim report.

In the early 1980s, the women's liberation movement is entering an exciting new phase. Feminist ideas are current, rather than strange and fantastical as they once seemed, and we understand the nature of female subordination a lot better than we did in the early 1970s.

It is beyond the scope of this book to present a detailed manifesto. We want instead to argue for a certain broad approach to feminist politics, which will help to keep up the momentum of the struggle in the 1980s and 1990s, whatever adverse conditions women may face.

The women's liberation movement has always had to assert its own meanings and resist those imposed on it by men. Although we have not been informed of the fact by television news readers or by the leader writers of Fleet Street, the women's liberation movement is one of the most important political developments of this century – a major revolution, still under way. We must keep this in mind, especially as we know that women's movements have been buried and forgotten in the past. Likewise, the scope and stature of the changes that have occured as a result of women's liberation must not be underestimated. We have described many of them in the foregoing chapters and we cannot hope to give an adequate summary here. A few pointers will have to suffice.

The idea that women and men should be treated equally – an extreme aspiration in the late 1960s – is scarcely contentious today. In September 1981, the Trades Union Congress ratified a detailed set of proposals for positive action in favour of women, in education, training, employment and within the unions themselves. A whole new library of books, papers and pamphlets has been produced by women, containing a whole new body of theory, a new perspective on contemporary society, a new sense of history. The word 'sexism', barely invented in 1970, now represents a concept which is widely acknowledged and, on the left at least, patriarchy is gaining recognition as a power system which predates and shapes capitalism. Who would have imagined in 1969 that women would stage a nationwide mass protest against male violence? Or that within a few short years there would be national networks of refuges for battered women and rape crisis centres? Or that 80,000 women and men would march to defend abortion rights? Or that trade unions would begin to organize against sexual harassment at work? Or that feminist ideas would be given regular, serious coverage in many leading women's magazines?

Women are proud of being women and being among women in a way most of us were not fifteen years ago. What all this indicates is a revolution in consciousness, which has affected women and men who have never been near a women's liberation meeting, and which presages profound social change. We are still in the early stages, but we have covered a phenomenal distance in a short space of time.

Perhaps the most important achievement of the 1970s, however, has been a new understanding of the mechanisms of male power and female subordination. We need to safeguard this knowledge and ensure that it isn't suppressed, or squandered. It must be passed on to each new generation, so that when the message comes through again – as it surely will – that women are already treated fairly ('so what's the fuss?'), or that a *real* woman's place is at home with her children, it will be met with the contempt it deserves.

In other words, women's liberation must reproduce the means of its political survival. We need an autonomous feminist movement no less now than we did in 1970. It is much larger than it was, although its identity is less distinct. It shows no sign of melting away, but there is a danger that it will if we don't actively encourage its growth and development. There is a case for stronger organizational links between women's groups and campaigns, perhaps on a regional basis, with an emphasis on being accessible to as many women as possible.

We need to explore the reasons why feminists are divided against each other. As we have tried to show, the main disagreements that have arisen in the past have been over attitudes

236

towards men and relations with them. Yet our common commitment to women is surely stronger than our differences about men. There have been divisions, too, between the 'old lags' who have been around in the movement for years and those who are new to feminism. Individuals have been deterred from seeking out other women in the movement for fear that they themselves are not 'up to the mark'. The irony is that one rarely meets a woman who – whatever her length of service in the cause – does not suspect there is someone else up the line who is 'more feminist' than she. (We speak as old lags who have often been beset by fears that others will catch us while we are either literally or metaphorically painting our toenails!) It is part of our condition as women today that none of us is genuinely liberated. It is a symptom of our subordination that we consistently underrate ourselves. It is intrinsic to our experience of feminism that we are all learning and changing all the time, and that nobody has all the right answers.

What is important is that we continue to learn and to change ourselves, and that we support each other in this. Consciousness-raising is not just a relic of the early 1970s, nor is it a finite exercise, like learning quadratic equations. It is a vital political activity, on account of its form as well as its content. It is collective and democratic. It stresses the need for every participant to work out her politics for herself, in a supportive context, rather than to receive wisdom from above. It fosters solidarity. It makes personal experience the base on which theory and strategy are built. It addresses the subconscious dimension of female subordination. Indeed, 'consciousness-raising' is the process of bringing into awareness deeper levels of female experience – by naming and affirming individual feelings and experiences and finding out how far they are common to women in general. It is a means of challenging and transforming our constructed sense of femininity. Feminism is unique as a political movement in that it sees itself both as the subject of change and the agency of change.

In the early 1970s, it was commonly felt that after a couple of years of consciousness-raising, it was time for women to move on to something more 'action-oriented', such as campaigning, or trade union work. But consciousness-raising *is* action, and women go on needing it – if not continuously then in patches over the years. We must see that the tradition is not lost. It can always be combined with other activities that are undertaken by women in small groups. This challenges a separation of political functions: 'action', belonging apparently to campaigns, 'experience' belonging to small consciousness-raising groups, and 'theory', belonging to scholastic study. Feminism needs to embrace all levels. The world cannot be apprehended from experience alone and political programmes do not emerge only from parties and power struggles.

It is in the nature of feminist politics that it is conducted on many different levels at once. We are struggling to change ourselves, to change society and to change our relation to society. We are struggling within the family, with parents, children, siblings, husbands – to transform oppressive relationships, to change patterns of behaviour, and to redistribute labour and wealth. We are fighting against cherished traditions and powerful taboos. We are struggling to assert the value of the roles we already perform, to create new ones for ourselves, and to break into those traditionally preserved for men. We are fighting to improve the material conditions of our lives, and to that end we are fighting for power within trade unions and political organizations, as well as against the vested interests of employers and international capital. As we enter into spheres of activity that are dominated by men, we find we need to transform these too, if we are to survive without becoming surrogate men. We are struggling to change the values and priorities of men alongside us, as well as the way they conduct themselves – in short, to change the world. All the while, we are fighting to assert our own interpretations of what we are doing and our own definitions of what we are, against the man-made versions, which tend to ridicule, belittle or ignore our efforts and achievements.

Because all this is going on at once, we can be sure that there is no single-slogan road to women's liberation. The 'Wages for Housework' campaign is a case in point. It has been quite useful in focussing attention on women's unpaid labour. The fact that it provides no solution to the problem of domestic inequality (let alone to the problem of female subordination) would matter less if its protagonists did not present it as though it were somehow a *key* to women's liberation. As with the call to political lesbianism, this creates a sectarian spirit within the movement ('Are you for us or against us?') which we could well do without. The same could be said of anyone who insisted that the *only* way to proceed was through the trade unions, or by entering into psychoanalysis – or of anyone who denied the value of either of these. Not surprisingly, however, the numbers who see feminism in such stark terms have declined considerably since the mid 1970s.

Generally, we perceive our struggle for liberation as an *offensive*: we are on the attack, as it were, actively seeking change. Of course, when economic conditions deteriorate and the government of the day tries to drive us back to our traditional roles, we have to defend ourselves. But there is another respect in which we are under attack, which is seldom seen as such. This is the offensive waged by men against women through the education system and the media. We cannot regard schools or colleges, the press or broadcasting simply as sources of obdurate resistance. For they are constantly fighting against us, pushing male values and male views, and driving us backwards. This happens across a vast range of activity – from history lessons in which children are taught to disregard female achievements, to Page Three of the *Sun*, where readers get their daily dose of propaganda about the nature and worth of 'femininity'. It penetrates deep into the psyche, through the system of grammar, for example, in which 'he' stands for *he or she*, and the hidden codes of advertising, which invert the meaning of women's liberation. We know it is important to transform the means of education and communication; we cannot afford to underestimate the adversity we encounter in these areas, and how it affects our efforts elsewhere.

And what about men, who have caused us so much trouble, our brothers, lovers, fathers, workmates, comrades, oppressors? There are no simple answers to this one, for sure. We shall need to fight with them and against them at the same time, often at the same moment. We must defend the right of women to live separately from men, *and* the right of women to live with men and love them. In our political struggles we need to carve out time and space for ourselves as well as to participate with men: if we don't do both we shall find ourselves marginalized or swamped by them. We need to recognize that men as individuals can be economically oppressed, socially impoverished and psychologically cramped by the system which sustains the power of men in general. There are many who are genuinely committed to change, and to ending female subordination. We can accept their excellent intentions and good will, and work with them on common ground. But we shall have to bear in mind and remind them of the subconscious ways in which they resist conceding power, and their propensity to run for cover when things get tough.

Moreover, we cannot cooperate usefully with them unless we admit there are conflicts of interest between women and men – and get men to admit it too. These conflicts must be openly confronted and explored as a matter of priority, not only in the trade unions but in any political grouping where women and men combine; only then can we begin to resolve them. A condition of participating in the mainstream of politics as feminists, and not simply as women, will be to challenge men as men, and the politics they produce as men. Otherwise, it is women, and not men, who are always seen as the problem.

Men who support women have to put their own relationship to masculinity and patriarchal power into crisis if they are really to embrace feminism. By denying that their relation to women is contradictory, they promote themselves and their interests as universal. And they overlook the fact that they, men, are a problem for women. The 'unity' that is claimed on the left is superficial. Feminists are inevitably accused of being divisive when women's interests are asserted, and particularly when they appear to challenge men's priorities. Of course, these conflicts of interest cannot be resolved overnight. The seventies have taught us something about the complexity of the task ahead and the nature of the odds against us. How much can we achieve in the next, say, twenty years if we cast our collective imagination forward and plan in the long term? We must plan well ahead.

The women's liberation movement has so far remained on the edge of institutional politics, dabbling a toe in the water, finding it cold. Most feminists have felt there are better things to do elsewhere, without getting caught up in the hostile currents of the male-dominated 'mainstream'. If we are seriously planning to transform society and liberate ourselves, we shall have to get in and swim.

This doesn't mean abandoning our own politics – but while we continue to organize separately and develop our own ideas and strategies, we must also carry the form and content of feminism into the mainstream. And we must seek to wield power ourselves – *as feminists*. That is, unless we are content to ask favours of powerful men for the rest of our days.

This is a logical extension of the feminist-based campaigns for positive action. It is beginning to happen in the Labour

Party, where there is a strong feminist drive to achieve fuller participation for women – an expression not of ruthless careerism, but of a will to transform Labour politics. It is happening, slowly, in the trade unions and in some local authorities. It goes on alongside the development of feminist activities in different areas of employment – in medicine and law, for example, in publishing, broadcasting, the civil service and education.

Grass-roots activity will always be the lifeblood of our movement, our strength, our centre, our first concern. Only thus can we maintain a capacity for self-help politics of the kind expressed by the Women's Aid movement, for consciousness-raising and for protests like the Miss World Demonstration, the National Abortion Campaign and Women Against Violence Against Women – which are not solely concerned with legal or institutional changes. Our grass roots commitment is also about enabling people to act politically on their own behalf, rather than just being conscripts or clients who are subordinate to their leaders. The problem is that the movement can always be a pressure group when we want to force those in power to make changes that we need. But that always makes us dependent on them. We must engage with power ourselves.

We have seen that the organization of social and economic life renders it very hard for women to 'make it' on men's terms. We want to change the terms, of course. And as part of that process, we shall have to make the most of the small but increasing numbers of women who are able and willing to go ahead. The women's liberation movement has a deep distrust of the mechanisms of power and the individuals who get involved in it. There is no reason to abandon that distrust: it is entirely justified. But if we know that power corrupts, and if we have evidence that women who accede to power are easily swallowed up into the corrupt fraternity, our response need not be to spurn all new aspirants as mere 'opportunists'. Nor should we be content to send up a few, isolated hopefuls, like distress signals in the night – light the blue touch paper and retire. We can support these women and inform them; we can develop a sense of accountability to feminism. We can try to encourage sufficient numbers of women, so that individuals are not isolated, but can function as feminist groups within the mechanisms of power, accountable to the women's liberation movement and sustained by it.

When it comes to formulating policy, it is not enough simply to *add on* a shopping list of feminist demands to objectives which already exist on the left. We need a new starting point, a new set of critera, a new order of priorities. Patriarchal politics – whether on the left, centre or right – has a distorted perspective. Its analyses of what is wrong and how things work in society, as well as its objectives, begin from and are focussed upon one relatively limited area of life: production. As women, we assert a different approach to politics, which has a double axis: reproduction and production. This embraces domestic work as well as paid work, and relations within the family and community as well as relations between labour and capital.

Our starting point for an 'Alternative Strategy' – with which the left hopes to counter the policies of the Labour right and the Conservative government – would be different from that which has so far been proposed. The male left begins with the objective of regenerating industry and creating 'full employment'. It takes men's and women's relation to each other as given, and proposes no change. It de-sexualizes politics, and in so doing denies any political room for feminists. It is blind to the existence of children and domestic work and thus has nothing to suggest about transforming men's relation to children and child care. And it characterizes the left's objectives in purely economic terms, so that the politics of sexuality and culture are beyond its pale.

Set in the light of female experience, the aim of 'full employment' takes on a different meaning. Most women are already over-employed, working a 12- to 16-hour day. The real problem for them is what work they do and how much they get paid for it – if they get paid at all.

A feminist approach to developing strategy might begin by asking a different question: not 'How do we create full employment?' but 'How shall we care for and support our children?' (We mean this not in the sense of private domestic choices, but of our collective responsibility towards the next generation.) Much turns on the question, in particular the redistribution of labour and wealth within the family. It does not eclipse the aim of redistributing wealth between labour and capital; but in our view it is the appropriate context in which that aim should be set.

Beginning with the question of child care, we are convinced that it is to the benefit of children, no less than of parents, if children are looked after by men and women equally. Young children grow up with a limited picture of the respective characters and capacities of males and females; this is one of the

242

ways in which sex stereotypes become rooted in people's minds. While men continue to segregate themselves from children, they are cut off from a range of experience which would broaden their understanding and change their political priorities (and which they might even enjoy). We would argue, too, that children benefit from the company of other children and adults, outside their immediate family, and that collective child care is a positive advantage, not just a means of compensating for the absence of wage-earning mothers. If there is anything wrong with nurseries and day-care centres today, it is that they are under-resourced and poorly organized. We have described in an earlier chapter (p. 38) the efforts of feminists to establish nurseries along democratic, non-sexist lines.

A feminist strategy might thus combine generous resourcing for child-care facilities outside the home, both for under-fives and for school-age children outside school hours, with a commitment to reorganize paid employment so that parents of both sexes can spend equal time with their children. (Even if care facilities were ideal there should be no need for children to spend between thirty-five and forty hours a week in them: we are suggesting a combination of community-based and parental care.)

The arrangement of time spent in paid employment is a crucial factor if we are to change the current pattern of male absenteeism from child care and other domestic responsibilities. It would be necessary, in our view, to reduce working hours substantially, aiming for a *maximum* thirty-hour week, with firm restrictions on overtime. This could put an end to the present distinction between 'part-time' and 'full-time' workers, which acts so much to women's disadvantage (the statutory dividing line is thirty hours). It would help to create new jobs at a time when even the official figures show unemployment nearing the three million mark. And it would begin – *only* begin – to create the conditions in which men and women could participate equally in domestic work as well as paid employment. As we have seen, male absenteeism from domestic work has been one of the main causes of women's continuing low pay and powerlessness in the labour market.

If a new government were to embark on a public spending programme aimed at reducing unemployment, is it possible that all new jobs in the public sector could be limited to thirty hours? This would mean that more people could have jobs. It could be combined with a system of incentives and/or sanctions to reduce hours in the private sector, perhaps beginning in areas where the work-load is contracting – and it should be seen not as an emergency stop-gap, but as a positive alternative to redundancy, a means of encouraging a permanent change in the pattern of working time. (The labour movement has made little headway towards even a thirty-five-hour week: it has never promoted it as a means of democratizing domestic life.)

These proposals obviously raise vital questions about pay. How can living standards be maintained and improved if working hours are reduced? We reject the conventional response of the male left that any proposal for change which threatens the wage is automatically unacceptable. We believe this springs from a fixed idea about the nature of family support – which is that each family has one main source of income, provided by a male employee breadwinner. As we have already shown, the 'family wage' approach perpetuates female dependency and male control. It discriminates against large families, since the individual wage does not vary according to the number of children the wage earner has to support. And it is no help to the families of the unemployed. Moreover, it is based on a concept of the family as a harmonious economic unit, which takes no account of conflicting interests within the family – especially those between women and men.

We need to restructure family income. We can begin to do this by fighting for genuine equality between male and female workers, so that women are able to contribute as much as men. We have described earlier the developing campaign for positive action in favour of women. This approach is necessary in education, training and employment, as well as within trade unions. It need not entail discrimination against men at the point of entry to employment, but if it is to be successful it *must* break down the infrastructure of male privilege, and ensure that women have real equality of access to skill, to the means of organization and to all levels of employment. The reorganization of working time and the provision of child-care facilities are an essential part of positive action. It will also be necessary to amend and strengthen the Equal Pay and Sex Discrimination Acts especially to facilitate complaints against indirect discrimination and to provide statutory backing for positive action programmes.

At the same time, we need an effective strategy against low pay. This will have to include an overhaul of the Wages Council system, and the introduction of a statutory minimum wage. The

244

latter has been strongly resisted in the past, on the ground that it interferes with trade union bargaining, and will tie wages down to the minimum. Against this, it must be said that free collective bargaining has done nothing to solve the problem of low pay; that there are still four and a half million workers with earnings below the poverty line; and that the gap between the lowest level of earnings and average earnings is no narrower today than it was a hundred years ago.

Positive action and the fight against low pay are two important elements in the strategy to restructure family income. We suggest, however, that it is not in the best interests of children to depend on their parents' wages as their primary means of support. This works to the disadvantage of children whose parents are out of work, and of those who have only one parent, or more than one or two siblings. We need to increase child benefit substantially – until it is commensurate with the real cost of supporting a child. This principle is already accepted in relation to one group of people who do not earn wages – pensioners. If it were extended to children it would ensure greater equality between families as well as independent security for children, and it would help to break the economic control which men exercise within the family.

In addition to a realistic level of child benefit, we need to ensure proper support for adults who have care of dependants, whether sick or elderly relatives or small children. This can partly be met by extending the period of paid parental leave and making it available to the mother or the father, depending on who stays at home when the child is not at a nursery. But we also need to make provision for those not covered by parental leave – and there are continuing debates among feminists about the precise form this should take. One suggestion is that there should be a taxable benefit, available to adults who are responsible for looking after dependants, regardless of whether the recipient is in waged work, and regardless of the recipient's marital status. If possible, the benefit should not serve as an incentive to keep women out of paid work (a 'stay-at-home' allowance), nor should it be subject to any means-test or 'cohabitation rule'.

We have dealt so far with the purely financial aspects of family support. Clearly, the services and facilities provided by the state are of considerable importance too. A feminist strategy would place a strong priority on extending the 'social wage' – by providing better housing, transport, health care, welfare and social security, as well as introducing new services, such as community restaurants and washing facilities, to ease the burden of domestic work. Since women are still the main 'consumers' of these state services, the emphasis is bound to be – rightly – on quality and availability, rather than primarily on jobs (which has tended to be the main concern of trade union based campaigns against cuts in public services).

Just as incomes need to be restructured in order to minimize the economic dependence of individuals within the family, so state provisions must be reorganized in order that they are not conditional upon membership of a traditional family unit. People who live singly, or with a lover of the same sex, or with groups of friends, must be free to do so without suffering social or financial disadvantage. As we have seen, the welfare state is based on an assumption of female dependence, and its rules and regulations reinforce patriarchal control. A feminist strategy would seek to transform the principles on which the welfare state is founded.

A strategy which is informed by female experience and based on feminist priorities looks to the state as much as to the employer to maintain and improve living standards. (For many people, of course, the employer is the state.) But we cannot rely on the state as a benefactor, any more than we can rely on employers. We shall have to struggle to win what we need, and no doubt we shall have to fight to preserve what we have gained. It is therefore essential that trade unions extend the scope of collective bargaining to local and national government, in order to win improvements in the social wage – and that they invest no less energy in this than in bargaining with employers about pay and conditions at work.

When we have worked out the best way of caring for our children and the most effective means of supporting them; when we have resolved to redistribute labour and wealth within the family; and when we have decided how to restructure paid employment and reorganize state services, then we can move on to the question of how to pay for what we need. First, there could be some redistribution among working people. For instance, it has been pointed out that by abolishing the married man's tax allowance, an extra £4 a week could be added to child benefit without making any extra claim on the exchequer. Secondly, there could be a major redistribution of resources between different areas of public spending. Billions of pounds could be redirected to housing, welfare services and child care if the government would ditch many of its expensive policies such as subsidy of the Common Agricultural Policy and its heavy commitment to 'defence' spending.

Last but not least, there must of course be a redistribution from employers to workers – by taxing profits, for example, and by restricting the export of capital; by taking into public ownership banks and other key concerns; by introducing a statutory minimum wage; and by winning through collective bargaining (backed up by legislation if necessary) a substantial reduction in working hours without a commensurate loss in the value of earnings. We do not expect any of this to happen overnight! We have already stressed the importance of long-term planning.

The biggest obstacle, in our view, is not finding the necessary resources, but persuading men to relinquish their privileges. Chiefly, this means giving up their privilege to absent themselves from unpaid work and monopolize jobs that are skilled and higher-paid. If women are to share domestic labour equally with men, then men will have to increase their time spent on unpaid work. If women are to increase the level of their earnings to the point where they match men's, then men's earnings will inevitably decline in relation to women's. If women are to occupy skilled, higher-paid jobs in equal numbers with men, there are bound to be fewer of these jobs available to men. Jean Gardiner and Sheila Smith summed up the problem in their article on 'Feminism and the Alternative Economic Strategy':

Whilst positive action merely aims to provide women with the positive support and encouragement that will enable them to have equal access with men to employment and training, it does mean a challenge to preferential treatment for men. One of the problems in winning acceptance of these changes is that because of the subtle and often indirect ways in which sex discrimination has operated in the past, many men do not yet recognize the relative advantages they have enjoyed. The priority that has been given to men's access to jobs and to men's pay has been seen as natural rather than preferential... Mass acceptance of positive action will therefore be hard to achieve and will depend on a major ideological campaign to raise men's awareness. (*Marxism Today*, October 1981.)

As we suggested earlier, male privilege is not simply defended – it is actively promoted through the values inherent in the education system and the mass media. A strategy which seeks to end it must also make it a priority to challenge and transform these values.

Finally, we need to ensure the full participation of women as well as men in the implementation of policy. At a community level, women must be able to exercise democratic control over child care and other shared facilities. In the workplace, women must be closely involved in setting up and monitoring positive action programmes. When resources are allocated nationally and locally, women must participate at all levels of the decision-making process.

The channels of democracy in our society – unions, political parties, local councils, Parliament – have been constructed by men, for men. They are not designed to facilitate female participation, and they by-pass important areas of women's lives. They must be forced to change and here, too, men will have to relinquish privilege – the privilege of supreme power. We have grown accustomed to the idea that we are living in a democracy. But we women are still fighting for the franchise. We remain passive in the great blot called 'consensus', which each of the major political parties claims to command. As feminists we are concerned with disturbing consensus, not with helping to administer it. We will not be the silent majority.

Index

abortion 21, 24, 37, 38, 42, 92,
137–8, 146, 147, 164, 165, 236
Abortion Act 36, 42–3, 147, 156
Abse, Leo 99
ACAS (Advisory, Conciliation
and Arbitration Service)
115–16, 117
ACE (Advisory Centre for
Education) 180
Acts of Parliament
Abortion Act 36, 42–3, 147, 156
Criminal Law Amendment
Act 215
Divorce Reform Act 99
Domestic Violence Act 42
Employment Act 95
Employment Protection Act 95,
106
Equal Pay Act 48, 59, 61, 106,
107–10, 113, 114, 115, 116, 117,
123, 124, 132, 139, 140, 144,
149, 150
Sex Discrimination Act
21, 48, 103, 106, 110, 111–23,
124, 132, 133, 139, 140, 174
Sexual Offences (Amendment)
Act 43
Social Security (Pensions)
Act 106
Vagrancy Act 215
ACTT (Association of
Cinematographers, Television
and Allied Technicians) 145,
147
Adamson, Sir Campbell 99
advertising 96, 189, 197, 198–200,
239
agricultural workers,
19th-century 57–8
Aims for Women at Work 145
Alexander, Sally 21
Allen, Lord 150
Anthony, Susan B. 208

Anti University 17
Anti-Discrimination Bill 37
see also Sex Discrimination Act
APEX (Association of
Professional, Executive,
Clerical and Computer
Staff) 71, 144, 162, 167
arts, visual 207–8
ASA (Advertising Standards
Authority) 199–200
Ashdowne-Sharpe, Patricia 129
Astell, Mary 9
ASTMS (Association of Scientific,
Technical and Managerial
Staffs) 147, 162, 163–4, 167
AUEW (Associated Union of
Engineering Workers) 161

Baehr, Helen 197
Bank of America 131
Barker, Jane and Downing,
Hazel 73
Barnes, Mary 25
Barrett, Michele 208
Barry, Pauline 221
battered women 40–42, 236
Battersby, Audrey 16
beauty contests 11, 23–4
de Beauvoir, Simone 28, 45, 197
Benefits 93
Bennett, Theresa 120
Benyon, William 147
Berger, John 207
BIFU (Banking, Insurance and
Finance Union) 147, 167
Bird, Emma 71
bisexuality 214, 220–22, 228, 230,
231
see also homosexuality,
lesbianism
Black Consciousness 29
Bondfield, Margaret 136
bra burning 10–12, 192

Bradford Council 71, 73
breadwinner, concept of
    male 36, 50, 57–62, 155, 166
Breakthrough 48
Breughel, Irene 75
Bristol Women's Liberation 10,
    18, 26
British Paper Box Federation 108
British Standards Institute 71
Broadhurst, Henry 154
Browne, Stella 216
buggery 215
Burnham Committee 126, 131
'Burning Bra' 10–12
'Burning Pillar-Box' 10
Butler, Joyce 104
Byrne, Eileen 178, 179

Callaghan, James 83, 85–6, 87,
    151
Campaign for Labour Party
    Democracy 137
capitalism, as patriarchy 22,
    32–3, 53–69
Capstick, Sheila 119
Carmichael, Stokely 13
Castle, Barbara 18, 190
Castle, Ms 125
Catholic Church 42
Caute, David 205
censorship
    of pornography 200–203, 204
    of sexist materials 179, 180,
    195, 205–7
Central Arbitration
    Committee 109, 110, 144
Central Electricity Generating
    Board 71
Charlton, Valerie 15, 38
Charter for the Under-Fives 85,
    146
Charter for Women at Work
    (TUC) 149
Chartered Institute of Public
    Finance and Accounting 91
Chesser, Eustace 216
Chesser Report 216

Chicago, Judy 208
child benefit 62, 97–8, 101, 245,
    246
child care 24, 36, 38–40, 50, 64,
    83, 87, 89, 95, 100, 101, 126,
    133, 146, 152, 157, 162, 242–3,
    244, 248
Children's Community Centre,
    Camden 39, 40
Chisholm, Judith 191
Chiswick Women's Aid 40–41
Church of England Children's
    Society 87
civil disobedience 10–12, 23–4
Civil and Public Services
    Association 160
Civil Rights movement 29
Civil Service 112–13
'Class Struggle and the
    Working-Class Family' 58
Clegg Commission 61, 151–2
Clegg, Professor Hugh 151–2
clerical work, women in 51, 56,
    71–4, 77
Clit Statement, The 224
clitoris, as centre of female
    sexual pleasure 18–19, 212,
    217–18, 223
Club and Institute Union 119
Colville, Lord 105
Communism 28, 31, 38
community, as alternative to
    welfare state 81–93
Confederation of British
    Industry 65, 99, 115, 127, 128
consciousness-raising 14,
    157–60, 162, 218–19, 237
contraception 12, 21, 24, 37
Co-ord 42
Coote, Anna 120, 202
Corrie, John 147, 148
Cosmopolitan 196–7
CPAG (Child Poverty Action
    Group) 97
craft courses 121–2, 174
CRE (Commission for Racial
    Equality) 125

Criminal Law Amendment Act
215

Daily Express 191
Daily Mirror 189, 191, 193
Daily Star 191, 192
Dale, R. R. 171, 173
day care facilities *see* child care
Decoding Advertisements 198–9
Delmar, Rosalind 16
demonstrations 10–12, 18, 23–5,
42, 43
Denning, Lord 99, 120
Department of Employment 49,
51, 68, 107
Department of the Environment
94
Dialectic of Sex, The 27–8
Dickinson, R. and Beam, L. 215
Dinner Party, The 208, 211
discrimination
direct 111
indirect 106, 111, 112–13, 114
divorce 98, 99
Divorce Reform Act 99
Dobereiner, Peter 191
Domestic Violence Act 42
Durrant, Patricia 113
Dweck, Carol 173

education 105, 106, 171–85, 191,
195, 239
cuts in LEA spending 83, 89,
180–81
discrimination in 121–2, 124,
125–6
girls and science subjects 171,
174, 175, 177, 178–9, 182–3, 184
national feminist
conference 173
teachers' attitudes 175–7
sexist materials 174–5, 180, 181,
205
Educational Review 171
EEC (European Economic
Community) 109
EETPU (Electrical, Electronic,

Telecommunications and
Plumbing Union) 145
elderly, care of 81, 84, 85–7,
89–93
Electrolux 125
El Vino 119–20
Employment Act 95
Employment Protection Act 95,
106
Enough! 10
equal opportunity
employers 133–4
Equal Opportunities
Commission 40, 48, 65, 66, 67,
71, 76, 105, 106, 110, 114, 117,
120, 122, 123–9, 131, 132, 133,
135, 145, 159, 181, 182, 183,
199, 205–6
equal pay 18, 24, 38, 48, 59, 61,
67–9, 85, 107–10, 149–52, 155,
166
Equal Pay Act 48, 59, 61, 69, 106,
107–10, 113, 114, 115, 116, 117,
123, 124, 132, 139, 144, 149, 150
Equal Pay and Opportunity
Campaign 128
Equal Pay and Opportunities
Project (LSE) 108, 113, 117
*Equality for Women within
Trade Unions* 162
Equality Working Party, NUJ 190
ERICCA (Equal Rights in Clubs
Campaign for Action) 119
European Court of Justice 109,
114, 124
Evans Brothers 174

Faderman, Lilian 214
Fairbairns, Zoe 93
family
as alternative to welfare
state 81–93
divorce 98, 99
see also child care
family allowances 36, 37
Family Forum 97

'family wage' 50, 58–62, 96, 97, 146, 155, 156, 244

Family Wage, The 58

fatherhood 63, 83

Fawcett, Millicent 105

Fawcett Society 105

Female Eunuch, The 20, 222–3

Female Orgasm, The 216

Feminine Mystique, The 13, 17

'Feminism and the Alternative Economic Strategy' 247

Feminists Against Sexual Terrorism 204

Festival of Light 200, 201

Finniston Report 177

Firestone, Shulamith 27–9

Fisher, Seymour 216

Ford, Anna 198

Ford motor factory strikes 18

Forgan, Liz 195

Forum 200

Fourth Channel, TV 195

Freeman, Jo 36

Friedan, Betty 13

Fromer, Nan 25

Fryer, Bob, Fairclough, Andy and Manson, Tom 161

Galbraith, Hazel 34

Gallagher Ltd 144

Gardiner, Jean and Smith, Sheila 247

gay liberation 228, 231

General Household Survey, 1978 61

General Motors 131

General Problems of Low Pay 59

Gill, Tess 120

Girls into Science and Technology 182–3, 184

Glasgow 10

GMWU (General and Municipal Workers Union) 145, 152, 158, 162, 163, 167

Gorer, Geoffrey 98

Gray, J. A. 171, 173

Gray, Sheila 119–20

Greer, Germaine 20, 197, 222–3, 224, 225

Gregory, Jeanne 115, 116

Grossman, Rachel 70

Grunwick Ltd 155

Guardian 72, 138, 191, 192, 194, 195

Hakim, Catherine 49, 51

Halifax Building Society 71

Hall, Catherine 15, 25

Halpin, Kevin 150

Hamilton, Willie 104, 105

Happy Families 99

Harrison, Betty 38

Harrison, Marjorie 163

Hart, Jean 34

Healey, Denis 83, 151

health service 59, 83, 84–93

health work 56–7

Heath, Edward 36, 37, 104, 106

Hemel Hempstead 37

heterosexuality 19, 31, 212–13, 215, 217, 219–30

Hill, Jacqueline 203, 204

hire purchase, sex discrimination in 118

Hite Report, The 216

Hite, Shere 216

Hobbs, May 37, 105

Hoeey, Kate 138

home economics courses 121–2, 174

homeworkers 65, 66, 75, 150

homosexuality 214–15

   see also lesbianism

Honey 197

Hospital 57

hours of work 63, 156

   see also part-time workers

housework 13, 15, 17, 25, 81

housing 94

Housing Needs and Action 94

Howe, Lady Elspeth 127

Howe, Pat 103

Howe, Sir Geoffrey 83, 97–8

Hubbard, Ruth 178

Human Sexual Response 217
Humphries, Jane 58

ICI (Imperial Chemical
    Industries Ltd) 133–4
Images of Women 190
Imperial Tobacco Ltd 144
Inmos 70
Inner London Education
    Authority 183
International Women's Year 106,
    107
Isaacs, Jeremy 195
Islington Green comprehensive
    school 176
isolation
    of mothers 13, 15, 16, 85, 94, 98
    of women in Parliament 135–7
*I want to work but what about
    the kids?* 126

Jackie 196
Jacklin, Carol 173
Jeffreys, Sheila 30
Jenkin, Patrick 84, 85, 86, 87, 89,
    97
Jenkins, Jeanette 114
Jenkins, Roy 114
*Jeremiah v. Ministry of
    Defence* 120
job evaluation
    guidelines 110
    schemes 109
Jones, Morris 202–3
'Joreen' *see* Freeman, Jo
journalism 189–97
    women in 191, 194–6

Kaldor, Mary 138–9
Kellner, Peter 156
Kelly, Alison 173, 181–2, 183
Kingsway Children's Centre 39
Kinsey, Alfred 217
Koedt, Anne 18–19, 20, 25, 219,
    222

Lacey, Robert 189

Ladybird Books 174
Lancaster, Terence 190
Land, Hilary 58
'latchkey kids' 84, 89
Lawrence, D. H. 205
Lazonick, William 54
Learning to Lose 174–5, 184–5
Leeds 30, 43, 203, 204, 225, 226
Leeds Revolutionary Feminist
    Group 30–31, 225–6
legal aid 116–17, 123
lesbian national conference,
    1974 230
lesbianism 26, 31, 211, 213,
    214–32
Lester, Anthony 114
' "Liberated Woman" in
    Television Drama, The' 197
Life 42–3
literature, feminist analyses
    of 205–7
Liverpool 24
Lloyd, Angela 221
Lloyd, Selwyn 105
local authority spending 88–93,
    95–6, 180–81
Lockwood, Baroness Betty 127
London Trades Council 38
'Longest Revolution, The' 17
LSE (London School of
    Economics) 108, 113, 117

Maccoby, Eleanor 173
McArthur, Mary 154
McGraw-Hill 206
Maden, Margaret 176
magazines 197
Mailer, Norman 205
*Making of the Modern
    Homosexual, The* 215
Malos, Ellen 18, 22, 46
Man Alive 87
Manchester 29, 34, 43, 103, 107
manifesto of women's liberation
    (Redstockings) 14–15, 27, 30
manual work, women's 45, 48,
    51, 59, 145

Maoism 21, 34, 35
Market and Opinion Research
   International 75, 153, 156, 157
Marriage Manual, A 216
Married Love 216
married man's tax allowance 96–
   7, 245
Marsland, Terry 147, 148
Marxism 17, 31, 32
Marxism Today 247
'masculinity' 29, 174, 178, 201
Masters, W. H. and Johnson,
   Virginia 217–18, 222, 223
maternity leave 37, 38, 86, 95,
   106, 152, 164
media, the 45, 189–208
   attitudes to women 189–92
   hostility to feminism 24
   magazines 196–8
   newspapers 189–96, 204
   non-appearance of
      women 192–3
   non-participation of women 194
   radio 194
   television 194
micro-technology 69–74
Millet, Kate 205
Miss America Pageant 11
Miss World competition 23, 241
Missing Half, The 171, 181, 183
Mitchell, Juliet 17, 45
*More About the Sex Factor in
   Marriage* 217
Morning Star 119, 150
mortgage agreements, sex
   discrimination in 118–19
motherhood 15, 16, 37, 38–40, 63,
   83, 85
Mothers in Action 37
Murray, Len 148, 149–50, 151
*Myth of the Vaginal Orgasm,
   The* 18, 25, 219, 221

'Naked Ape' 191
NALGO (National Association of
   Local and Government

Officers) 145, 147, 152, 153,
   167
Nandy, Dipak 114
Nasse, Mrs 111
National Abortion Campaign
   42–3, 147–8, 241
National Board for Prices and
   Incomes 59
National Child Care
   Campaign 40
National Children's Centre 85
National Conference of Labour
   Women
   1978 85
   1981 137
National Day of Action for the
   Low Paid 151
National Federation for Women
   Workers 154
National Insurance, married
   women's contribution 74
   guidelines for promoting
      equality 190–191, 206
National Union of Tailors and
   Garment Workers 167
National Union of Teachers 66,
   68, 167
National Women's Coordinating
   Committee 23, 24, 35
National Women's Liberation
   Conference
   1970, Oxford 20–23
   1971, Skegness 26, 34, 35, 220,
      224
   1972, Manchester 29, 34
   1974, Edinburgh 231
   1975, Manchester 103, 107
   1978, Birmingham 225
NCCL (National Council for Civil
   Liberties) 37, 128, 129, 132
*Nood for Revolutionary
   Feminism, The* 30
Negotiating for Equality 145
New Architecture Movement
   Feminist Group 94
Newcastle 43
New Earnings Survey, 1978 68

New Left Review 17
New Statesman 206
newspapers 189–96, 204
New York Radical Feminists 14
Night Cleaners Campaign 37,
    105
Nightingale, Florence 56–7
NJACWER (National Joint Action
    Campaign for Women's Equal
    Rights) 18, 21
non-discrimination notice 123–4,
    125
NOW (National Organization for
    Women) 13
NUGW (National Union of
    General Workers) 154, 161
NUJ (National Union of
    Journalists) 147, 160, 194, 202
NUPE (National Union of Public
    Employees) 145, 151, 152, 161,
    162, 164
nurseries *see* child care

orgasm, female 18–19, 215–20,
    223–4
'orgasm, vaginal' 18, 19, 25,
    215–20, 223
Owen, Jenny 162
Oxford 20–23

Pankhurst, Christabel 9
Panorama 195, 196
Park, Geraldine 220, 229
Parliament, women in 135–9
part-time workers 65–6, 66–7, 74,
    75, 113–14, 150, 243
Patterson, Marie 148
pay for women 18, 24, 48, 50,
    57–69, 78, 107–10, 149–52, 155,
    156, 157, 164, 166–7
  average comparative
    earnings 67
  see also equal pay
Peckham Rye women's
    group 16, 34
Penguin Books 174
pensions 36, 86, 106

Perks, Judge 121, 123
Phillips, Ann and Taylor,
    Barbara 55
Phillips, Mr Justice 125
pill, the 12
pillar-box, burning of 10
Pizzey, Erin 40–41
playgroups 85
  see also child care
police 210, 203, 205
Policy Studies Institute report 95
'Political Lesbianism: The Case
    Against Heterosexuality' 225
pornography 200–203, 204
positive action 104, 126, 129–35,
    137, 145, 146–52, 160–67, 181–4
Price, Belinda 112
Price, Colette 30
private clubs, sex discrimination
    in 119
prostitution 204
Provident Financial Group 71

Quinn, June 118

radical feminism 14–16, 26–31,
    32, 33, 45, 100, 223–5, 228
radio 194
Radio Nottingham 193
Raeburn, Anna 197
Rank Xerox 134
rape 43–5, 204
Rape Crisis Centres 43, 236
Reclaim the Night 43, 204
Redstockings 15, 27, 29–30, 224
refuges for women 40–42
Revolutionary Students'
    Federation 16
Rice, Gay 119
Rich, Adrienne 230, 231–2
Rickford, Frankie 119
Rights for Women Unit,
    NCCL 37, 128
Rights for Working Parents 145
Robarts, Sadie 132
Rochdale 37
ROW (Rights of Women) 128

Rowbotham, Sheila 12, 17, 197
Ruskin conference 20–23
Russell, Dora 179, 185, 216
Ruttle, Judge 119

Sainsbury food chain 133
Sarachild, Kathie 30
Scargill, Arthur 202, 203
schools *see* education
school meals 89, 92, 93
Science Research Council 111
science subjects 171, 173, 178,
     182–3, 184
Scott, Marion 175
Seear, Baroness Nancy 104, 105
Seebohm Report 87
segregation at work 51–2
service industries, women in 51
'Sex and Skill' 55–6
Sex Discrimination Act 21, 48,
     103, 107, 110, 111–23, 124, 131,
     132, 133, 139, 174
  applications in education 121–3
  difficulties of enforcing 115–18
  early stages (Bills) 103, 104–6
  examples of cases 118–21
  weaknesses of 113–15, 117
  see also Equal Opportunities
     Commission
Sex Factor in Marriage, The 217
sex-typing 173, 175, 176, 182
*Sexual Behaviour in the Human
     Female* 217
Sexual Offences (Amendment)
     Act 43
Sexual Violence Conference 204
sexuality 18–20, 30–31, 211–32
Sheba 45
'She Can Do It' 45
Short, Renée 105
Shrew 23, 172–3
silicon chip 69–74
Six Point Group 105
SNCC (Student Non-Violent
     Coordinating Committee) 13
Social Security (Pensions)
     Act 106

socialist feminism 27, 28, 31–3,
     45, 143, 202, 224, 225, 228
Soho, London 43
Southampton 37
Southeast Asia Chronicle 70
Spare Rib 30, 43, 45, 189, 204
spatial skills 171, 174
Spender, Dale 175–6, 184–5
SPUC (Society for the Protection
     of the Unborn Child) 36, 42–3
Stacey, Nicholas 92
Stageman, Jane 159–60
Standing Commission on Pay
     Comparability (Clegg
     Commission) 151
Stephen, Jessie 10
Stone, Hannah and Abraham 216
Stopes, Marie 216
Strachey, Ray 58
Study Commission on the
     Family 99
suffragettes 10–11, 12, 21
Sun 192, 204, 239
Sunday Times 108, 129, 153, 189,
     192, 194
supplementary benefits 58, 61,
     96, 107
Surpassing the Love of Men 214

TASS (Technical, Administrative
     and Supervisory Section,
     AUEW) 144, 161, 162
Tamarick Tree, The 179
Tameside, Manchester 125
tax allowance, married
     man's 96–7, 246
teachers 66, 172, 175–85
  proportions of male and
     female 183
  see also education
teaching materials 174, 180, 181,
     205
television 194, 195, 197–8
  women in 198
TGWU (Transport and General
     Workers Union) 37, 152, 162,
     164, 167

Thames Television 132–3, 134
Thatcher, Margaret 62, 83, 87,
    88, 91, 95, 135, 152, 180, 190,
    192
  as Education Secretary 105
Things I Can Do 174
Thomas, Marion 221, 229–30
Thoughts on Feminism 223
Thousand Marriages, A 215
Times, The 114
Titmuss, Richard 98
trade unions 10, 16, 18, 21, 31,
    37–8, 43, 46, 66, 68, 89, 91, 104,
    108, 110, 117, 121, 131, 132,
    133, 143–67, 194, 202–3, 236,
    238, 241, 244
  action on behalf of women
    144–8
  'family wage' philosophy 58,
    61–2, 155–6, 244
  female membership 37, 76, 143,
    152, 167
  hostility to women 118, 125,
    154, 163–4
  micro-technology dilemma
    69–71
  position of women 152–60,
    163–7
  positive action 132, 146–7,
    160–63
  representative at tribunals 117
  unwillingness to negotiate for
    women 110, 144, 149–52
  women strikers 18
  women's exclusion 53, 54, 55,
    153
  see also individual unions
Trades Newspaper 58
Treaty of Rome 109
tribunals
  Employment Appeal 112, 114,
    125, 145
  industrial 110, 111–12, 115–18,
    124, 125, 139, 140, 145
Trotskyism 21, 35
TUC (Trades Union
  Congress) 18, 37, 38, 39, 40,
    43, 59, 69–70, 85, 115, 127, 128,
    129, 132, 133, 144, 145–67, 199,
    203, 235
  Women's Advisory
    Committee 146, 148
  Women's Conference, 1975 147,
    1977 160, 1978 147, 1980 146,
    1981 146
Tudor Britain 174
Turner, Pat 163
*Tyranny of Structurelessness,
    The* 36

UCATT (Union of Construction,
    Allied Trades and
    Technicians) 145
under-achievement
  of boys 184
  of girls 171, 177, 181–4
  of West Indian and Asian
    children 177
unemployment 50, 74–6, 78, 79,
    92–3, 243
  effect of micro-technology
    on 69–74
United States, affirmative action
    in 130–31, 133, 146
USDAW (Union of Shop,
    Distributive and Allied
    Workers) 21, 150, 167

'vaginal orgasm' 18, 19, 25, 29,
    215–20, 223
Vagrancy Act 215
Vallance, Elizabeth 135–6, 137–8
Victoria, Queen 214
Vincent, Sally 203
violence
  domestic 40–42, 236
  male 40–45, 203–5, 236
Virago 45, 207

Watchell v. Watchell 99
Watford 37, 103
Waddington, Sue 110
wage bargaining 54, 62, 117
Wages Councils 67, 244

Wages for Housework 238
Warwick University 161
Weeks, Jeffrey 215
welfare state, the 83–93, 246
Where? 180
White, James 147
Whitehouse, Mary 200, 201, 205
Whitfield, Helen 121–2, 123
Whyte, Judith 182
wife-battering 40–42, 236
Williams Committee 200–201
Williams, Jan 16
Williams, Raymond 177
Williams, Shirley 179, 192
Williamson, Judith 198–9
Wilson, Harold 86, 135
Wires 45, 227
Wise, Audrey 21
Wolfenden Report 215
Wollstonecraft, Mary 9
Woman's Own 63, 83
Women Against Rape 204
Women Against Violence
   Against Women 43–4, 204, 241
Women in the House 135
Women in Education 172
Women in Manual Trades 45
Women in Media 45, 190, 196
Women Only Press 45
Women's Abortion and
   Contraception Campaign 37
Women's Action Committee,
   Campaign for Labour Party
   Democracy 137
Women's Aid Federation 40–42,
   43, 95, 241
Women's Broadcasting and Film
   Lobby 196
*Women's Liberation and the
   New Politics* 17
women's liberation movement
   demands 24, 26, 96, 231
women's liberation, United
   States 13–15

women's liberation
   workshop 35
women's magazines 197
Women's Press 45
Women's Report 37, 41, 105, 189,
   191
Women's Research and
   Resources Centre 45
Women's Rights Unit, NCCL 37,
   128
Women's Rights Working Party,
   Lewisham 96
Women's Social and Political
   Union 10
women's suffrage movement
   10–11, 12
Woolf, Virginia 208
work, women in 12, 13, 48–52,
   76, 77
   clerical 51, 56, 71–4
   contract cleaning 59
   health 56–7, 59
   homeworkers 65, 66
   local authority 61
   manual 45, 48, 51, 145
   micro-technology 69–74
   part-time 65–6, 66–7
   production industries 51, 54–6
   service industries 51
   skilled occupations 48, 50–57,
      109, 150, 153
   teaching 66
   see also hours of work, pay for
      women, tables pages 77–9
working life 63, 64
Working Women's Charter 38,
   145
Workplace Nurseries 145
Wright, Helena 217

York 43
Yorkshire Miner, The 202
'Yorkshire Ripper' 203–4
Younger, George 90